PROGRESSIVE EDUCATION FOR THE 1990S
Transforming Practice

PROGRESSIVE EDUCATION FOR THE 1990s
Transforming Practice

EDITED BY
Kathe Jervis and Carol Montag

FOREWORD BY
Joseph Featherstone

Teachers College, Columbia University
New York and London

Published by Teachers College Press, 1234 Amsterdam Avenue, New York, N.Y. 10027

Library of Congress Cataloging-in-Publication Data

Progressive education for the 1990s: transforming practice / edited
    by Kathe Jervis and Carol Montag; foreword by Joseph Featherstone.
        p.   cm.
    Includes bibliographical references (p.) and index.
    ISBN 0-8077-3133-1. —ISBN 0-8077-3132-3. (pbk.)
        1. Progressive education—United States. 2. Progressive
    education—United States—History. 3. Education—United States—
    Experimental methods. 4. High school—United States. I. Jervis,
    Kathe. II. Montag, Carol.
    LB1027.3.P76 1991
    371' .04—dc20   91–24967

Printed on acid-free paper
Manufactured in the United States of America
98 97 96 95 94 93 92 91   8 7 6 5 4 3 2 1

To Lillian Weber

CONTENTS

FOREWORD

There's a great paradox in the history of progressive education. On the one hand, it has been an educational movement committed to escaping the past—to being "progressive" in the sense of creating something as fresh and new as childhood itself. To look forward was to escape the dead hand of the past. (The very term "progressive" has a whiff of automatic progress in it.) On the other hand, progressive education in the last fifty years has often seemed stuck in its own past, its eyes firmly fixed on increasingly ancient glories. John Holt, our wonderful village atheist who died not so long ago, used to mock us all, saying, "A conservative is someone who worships a dead radical." A recent Japanese visitor to the United States noted that classrooms in the traditional shrines of educational progressivism didn't seem as lively as those in public schools, which often have no consciousness of being "progressive," but are clearly mining progressive veins. Maybe the perils of ancestor worship are particularly clear to Japanese eyes.

At the same time, to pile paradox on paradox, the progressive education movement has remained largely ignorant of its real history, which is a story of failure as well as success—above all, like our own efforts today, a story of struggle. Not knowing this history, we are unable to build realistically on the strengths and weaknesses of the past. This is part of the reason why it's hard for us to develop a tradition we can build on in a cumulative way, why we keep resurrecting progressive education from the grave instead of getting on with the vital work.

This odd relationship to the past may be typically American. We tend to revere the past. Many (though fewer) of us still cling to a belief in an automatic escalator called "progress." Yet, because we are unable to see how history is both like and yet unlike the present, we don't really understand the past, and so we end up living in what I call the United States of Amnesia.

It helps to hear stories about our common struggle. The quality of struggle—of failure, even of tragedy—is missing from the traditional stories of this movement, which tend, in the U.S. fashion, to be success stories. Figures like John Dewey get celebrated for the time-bound answers they came to, rather than for the perennial questions they asked, the struggles they lived, or the magnificent failures they embody. The difference I'm groping for is the difference between erecting a monument to the biblical Jacob—or giving him an honorary degree—and imitating him: wrestling all night in the dark with the angel.[1]

My preference is for having it out with the angel, all night long. For what do progressives wrestle? Not answers, I would argue, but certain themes. We wrestle with common dilemmas that come out of the effort to give educational shape to certain enduring commitments. The most basic of the commitments are political. There is first of all a rock-bottom commitment to democracy—in politics and education, as a way of shared life—which opens a whole Pandora's box of questions. How do you make a school an embryonic democracy in a society increasingly divided by race and social class? How do you help students find their own voice, work together, take responsibility for their own learning, and all the rest? Not by the mainstream methods of teaching Montaigne derided long ago as "thundering in children's ears." Not by "freeing" children from all adult authority, in some parody of 1960s education. (Progressive education's sentimentality on this score may be one of its most serious errors.) How, then? By a constant wrestling in the night, a dialectical struggle between the claims of the child and the curriculum, adult authority and youthful energy, mediated through the school as a certain kind of community committed to discourse and dialogue—committed to the struggle. So, although it gets submerged and lost from time to time, let's remember that democracy is the grand theme of this tradition, our deepest commitment, and that it is riddled with paradox and a history of magnificent failure. You've all heard some version of this saying: Like Christianity, like progressive education, democracy has never really been tried. If we take the challenge on as we should, let's do it in the proper spirit—Jacob's spirit. The truths that emerge here will be dialectical and double-barreled, and most of them will take more than one sentence to utter; they will take hard, sweaty wrestling in the night—the struggle that wears us out and renews us.

The challenge is similar for the other grand themes and dilemmas of progressive education: making live experience count for more in learning, making schools and classrooms into communities of learning, helping children learn how to make and remake knowledge, creating a culture commensurate with the dream of democracy, developing schools that can embrace cultural difference instead of smothering it, struggling for peace.

We will work to better purpose if we know more about the movement's past. Perhaps we can recapture a realistic version for today of one of our tradition's most appealing themes: the depth of aspiration for public education. A while ago I was walking in the Brooklyn Botanical Garden. I was bowled over by the obvious cultural ambitions of the people who put it all together. They

---

[1] I am indebted to Paula Lawrence Wehmiller for the use of the image, "wrestling with the angels," the title of her annual presentations to the NAIS Institutional Leaders Workshop and The Friends Council on Education.

really did believe you could create something first-rate and democratic that would be more beautiful than anything most kings and aristocrats could walk in—a garden for everybody. Their ambitious version of the democratic dream reminded me of the story about Big Bill Haywood, the famous old Wobbly leader. Reporters asked him why he smoked 25 cent cigars (expensive for that time). He said, "Boys, nothing's too good for the masses."

That's a side of the old progressive tradition we need to reclaim in the face of the stunted expectations for public institutions in a conservative era. We need to become more ambitious for public schools that would help everybody's children take part in making culture—the best that has been thought and said and sung and painted. Do away with the minimalism of current expectations for our schools, and the combination of miserliness and bastard pragmatism that is turning them into dreary environments for teachers and children. A public vision of thoughtful progressivism, rooted in rich examples of good practice, will almost certainly receive a more respectful hearing now in public education than at most times during the last decade. If we don't have such a vision, who does? If progressive education is to become vital again, and not just a museum-piece, we need to reach back in time to understand the past, and not just celebrate it. We also need to reach out to others. My Japanese friend was right: there's wonderful stuff happening in schools, even as the hearts of our cities are dying. Many of the teachers practicing it do not know much about progressive tradition (though many trace roots to the educational ferment of the 1960s). Progressives need to reach out for educational, intellectual, and political coalitions and alliances, or the movement won't become significant. We need voices able to link progressive values in education to progressive values in politics, to clean off the stained and abused word "democracy," and make it as fresh and new again in the streets of Detroit as it is in Prague.

Who can say whether such talk will lead to real change? In the United States of Amnesia we have learned to be wary of the awful sweep of the reform pendulum. Talk can be cheap. Still, the reigning slogans matter. They limit or liberate teachers in important ways. Talk matters—especially for an educational tradition that sees good conversation as the goal and standard for a sound education. In high schools all over the country, it is surely of interest that teachers, students, and parents feel encouraged to talk about such issues as community, alienation, boredom, the lack of deep understanding and involvement, and authentic assessment.

The good work described in this volume builds on a set of traditions that is somewhat patchy at the high school level. A long and rich history of work with children under twelve has left progressives rightly confident that they have a lot to say about different promising approaches to teaching young children. This is less true of the work with high school and university students. I found this out as a high school principal, when I felt myself more in the role of explorer than I expected to be. There are many splendid high school examples to ponder— the Eight Year Study schools, and so on. In some private schools, a paradoxical blend of privilege, dissenting traditions, and commitments to certain fundamental values like community and democracy have nourished varieties of good progressive practice over the years in the teeth of the mounting pressure to get Ignatz into Yale. There is the fascinating experience of public alternative high schools and the many schools-within-schools whose history over the last 20 years or so remains to be chronicled. And there is the work of many good isolated teachers doing variations on progressive themes. Still, there is a tentativeness about work at high school and college levels, a tentativeness that this volume reflects at the same time that it offers promising paths.

Today it looks more clear than it has for a long time that the underlying question is democracy: whether we can educate everybody's children so they are able to enact and make culture—to master the complex meanings that go into acts of understanding, sympathy, and citizenship. This is the oldest and most important question about mass education, and it remains unanswered. What kind of aspirations can we have for our citizens? Can we educate most people to grow to something like their full height, politically and culturally speaking? Or are most destined to be low bushes with here and there a mighty oak tree? Some of us dream of a forest of oaks.

Would there ever be agreement that this sort of demanding democratic cultural vision should guide our practice and our efforts at reform? Of course there would—and should—be debates about the kind of culture that gets made, and all the rest. What does making science actually mean? How do nonartists participate in art? How much do you have to know in a given field before you start making complex meaning, or does that question miss out on the intricate process by which people need to start out complex, rich, and deep from the very start? (Doing culture might be more like learning to ride a bicycle—you have to try to do it—really do it—before you know you are doing it.) What is our relationship today to the cultural past? Whose past? What does educating everybody's children imply for the education of my child? Whose version of culture do we teach? The literary canon is rightly a profound question, more important than an exchange between irritated professors. Indeed, being able to put forth and defend a position on today's versions of a literary canon might be one test of a decent education. How could we begin a process of educating our teachers, old and new, for such a challenge? The list of questions shows what Dewey kept insisting, that real democratic education will have to be an experiment.

I'm not saying we should forget about the many bones of contention between democratic and anti-democratic points of view about education in the United States. The root educational issue is the difference between democratic and hierarchical views of education, life, politics, and culture. Some disagreements are fundamental, and go far beyond the schools. But if we could agree that our goal—unprecedented in world history—is to offer a democratic version of a liberal education to everybody's child from preschool on, that would be a signal intellectual advance; the ensuing problems, awesome as they would be, would be merely practical.

I wrote that last phrase for effect, of course. The merely practical task—unprecedented in human history—of offering everybody's child an ambitious education has revolutionary implications, and not only for education. It is the big question so often abandoned and dodged—today's progressive challenge, yesterday's, almost certainly tomorrow's, too. It is what many of the writers in this book are grappling with in their separate essays. They don't offer answers, but promising questions that point us all toward some initial steps. In our current state of educational confusion, that's a good deal.

A progressive tradition tied to a revival of democracy will find ways to honor not only familiar icons like Dewey, but also figures out of our other democratic traditions like W.E.B. DuBois. In his great American classic *The Souls of Black Folk* (1969), DuBois painted the indelible picture of himself as a teacher going out to teach culture to the poor, and having his own idea of culture transformed in the process. The result was an American classic that, if we only listened, could help guide us to a new democratic progressivism today.

Intellectually, certain basic ideas and approaches linked to progressive education are already becoming fashionable in many university and foundation circles. One straw in a rising wind is the "Curriculum Congress," held in the fall of 1990 by the Educational Commission of the States and CHART, an ambitious collection of Rockefeller-supported curriculum projects. A variety of mainstream groups—everyone prominent in curriculum development participated—reviewed recent projects in the humanities. They issued a draft manifesto which included among other progressive-sounding statements the following (emphasis theirs): *Higher expectations and standards for all students, not just the college bound;...more heterogenous grouping of students and less ability tracking;...more responsiveness to the diverse needs of an increasingly diverse student body;...more active learning.* This is news.

One quote keeps ringing in my mind as I think about the struggle and the qualities we need to build something sustained and lasting. It is from a dead radical whose ideas come alive again from time to time—John Dewey. Summing up his own career, he wrote, "Forty years spent in the wilderness is not a bad fate—unless of course one mistakes the wilderness for the promised land" (Dewey, 1930, p. 20).

REFERENCES

Dewey, J. (1930). "Absolutism to Experimentalism." From *Contemporary American Philosophy*, Volume II, edited by George Adams. New York: MacMillan Company.

DuBois, W.E.B. (1969). *The Souls of Black Folk.* Reprinted from the 1902 original. New York: New American Library.

Joseph Featherstone
Michigan State University

ACKNOWLEDGMENTS

We gratefully acknowledge the support of Mary Jane Yurchak, former director of The Laboratory Schools of the University of Chicago, and Donald Monroe, Superintendent of the Winnetka (IL) Public Schools, for convening the Sixth Progressive Education Conference in Chicago in 1989. We give a special thanks to Carl Falstrom, who typed (and retyped) the manuscript.

PROGRESSIVE EDUCATION FOR THE 1990s
Transforming Practice

INTRODUCTION

CLASS VALUES

CAROL MONTAG

> They open their textbooks and see once again the familiar and impenetrable formulas and diagrams and terms that have stumped them for years. There is no excitement here. *No* excitement. Regardless of what the teacher says, this is not a new challenge. There is, rather, embarrassment and frustration and, not surprisingly, some anger in being reminded once again of long-standing inadequacies. (Rose, 1989, p. 31)

This is a description of high school students who, nearing the end of their formal schooling, have been imprisoned by their education, rather than being liberated by it. These students have had no one to make connections between their lives and the curriculum, no one to take the time to find their strengths, no one to care about them as developing young people preparing for life outside of school. In his book, *Lives On the Boundary*, Mike Rose (1989) writes of the disappointment and disillusionment facing many of our children. For them, school is one time slot after another, determined by a series of bells. They are rewarded for regurgitating what someone else thinks. How did they arrive at this dreary point? The contributors to this book know that there is an alternative to what Mike Rose describes. You will find a different educational vision here—one that strives for inclusion and honors diversity, as Patricia Carini suggests in the title of her essay. Not all the contributors agree on how to reach the goals, but as you read each essay, you will hear new voices that continue conversations that began over one hundred years ago.

Underlying every article is the political issue of class values. This is a deliberate play on words. Progressively oriented teachers struggle each day to create classrooms that support their values by providing challenging, yet safe and unthreatening environments in which children of diverse backgrounds can come together to pursue their personal interests. But teachers are undermined by the class conflict outside of schools. We live in a wider world where mak-

1

ing money has become an obsession, and where greed, lying, and cheating have become social norms. Washington is the source of the worst values of all. Politicians ask educators to exchange money for higher test scores in science and math as part of an arrangement to ensure the nation's place as number one in the world. The bargain is not in the interests of children. The message to educators is clear, but the goal Washington has defined is unattainable. Politicians don't know or care about how children think or learn.

The inequity of class in another sense is not just economic but social. Historically influential figures—among them Francis Parker, John Dewey, and Carleton Washburne—founded progressive institutions, some in urban centers. Their schools were, for the most part, rich, white, and upper middle class. These progressive schools had the best resources and were able to practice the best of progressive education as they knew it, unaware of the race and class issues that educators face head-on in today's schools. These student populations were far from diverse. They were as homogeneous in their culture and as respected by politicians as are the Japanese schools of today. Washington praises that monoculturalism still, failing to recognize the multicultures in our schools—schools filled with differences. It is just those differences the progressive educator thrives on, praises, and respects. As Patricia Carini explains in her essay, "I mean to position the issue of differences concretely, to make it handleable and not merely abstract: differences and conflict, far from being avoidable, are the very material of life." Opportunity for all children will require that politicians share at least some of the values of progressive educators and show a willingness to enter into a collaboration with classroom teachers and their principals.

The starting point needs to be in the classroom with the belief that children who are different are the fabric of this country. Politicians will need to place the highest value on urban, public education, wanting the most for the majority of the American children who inhabit these settings. And it will require that children and teachers be thought of as belonging to the same social and economic class as other groups of professionals. Educators who work with children must be considered as acceptable and valuable as lawyers, doctors, or people in business, just as they are in other countries. The educators' yield is children,whose success is the active threat to Washington. This country needs to listen and act upon the pointed message of Deborah Meier, founder of the Central Park East Secondary School: "Just give them what you have always offered those who have the money to buy the best, which is mostly a matter of respect." Children cannot cross the boundary Mike Rose speaks of without powerful advocates who will fight against standardized testing. These tests unfairly categorize individuals and create ability tracking, a narrow, class-bound way to think about children. Social realities require both politicians and educators to confront class issues. The children are the victims of class, in and out of schools.

The authors in this collection envision an education without tracking and testing. They see that progressive education begins with the strengths of children, the celebration of difference, and a curriculum with many points of entry. Teachers describe what they choose to do in their classrooms based on the firm conviction that they can assess children's needs far better than the author of a textbook or an administrative caveat. Progressive educators believe, along with Vito Perrone, that "what we know most about children and young people is that they are always learning. That is their nature. As they touch the earth, observe the culture that surrounds them, listen to stories, and speak, they are gaining a personal relationship with the world."

One thread of this book is that those early progressive values Perrone speaks of are still valid for high school classrooms. It has long been a misconception that progressive education is appropriate only for very young children, that it is not academically rigorous enough for middle and high school. How curious that in so many schools the relaxed and happy classrooms of the kindergarten through the fifth grade are acceptable, but thereafter, life gets mean, hard, and boring. Passivity becomes the accepted mode of behavior and children are no longer children, but objects, cut off from their own choices and active involvement with their teachers. They are no longer developing persons in a humane environment; they are the convenient fit in a predetermined classroom curriculum and schedule. No longer is there a shared journey of young people and their teachers, or a meaningful interaction between them. The collaboration becomes a one-sided effort, handed down from on high.

Sadly, the progressive Eight Year Study high schools described in Kathy Irwin's piece have joined the competitive prep school world. These high schools look very much alike as they fill up their students with Advanced Placement courses, the purpose of which is to pass an exam with a score of "Five." Trying to forget the pain and stress of it all, these students just go on to the next test. Gone from many older progressive independent schools are the woodshops that gave adolescents (and much younger children) an opportunity to combine academic rigor with the broadening experiences of "figuring out" how an engine works, and how to put together a wooden object from scratch. These students are looking very much like wooden objects themselves these days as they sit lifeless in their classes for hours on end as their teachers decide what is right for them to learn.

Progressive values have also eroded in the elementary schools. The younger siblings of these competitive high school students are bombarded daily by the textbook manufacturers' versions of progressive education. In the past few years the market has been glutted by materials that appeal especially to "pseudoprogressive " schools. These curriculum materials have the right sound to them: "whole language," "literature-based reading," "every day mathematics," "process writing," "invented spelling." There is a seed of progressive intent in these programs, but they have become formal systems in the hands of remedial clinicians in schools searching for instant mastery of skills.

There is no title *How To Do Progressive Education* on the shelves of book stores or in school catalogues. Progressive education is more complex than lesson plans. There are no progressive education materials or prepackaged methods to find out how children think or learn. The commercial publishers who attempt to tap into progressive values have missed the point: there is no easy way to uncover children's own educational agenda. There is no commercially produced program that will open doors for children who are different or who don't learn according to a standardized testing schedule. An emergent curriculum, authored by the children themselves, grows out of their strengths and their interests. It is valuable because the children have constructed it as carefully as a block tower and have given it meaning. There can be nothing more powerful than this kind of teaching and learning.

Schools need examples of good progressive practice: teachers who eschew basal readers, use books written by the children themselves, and trade books from the library to teach reading. They know that children learn best when they are involved in the things that interest them. Teachers who engage in inquiry with young children have complete respect for children's ideas and thoughts. Schools need teachers to whom it would never occur that children aren't sophisticated enough to ask good questions. These teachers use real coins to teach about money, and make books with children that are cloth-covered, often stitched by hand, and filled with original writings, poetry, and illustrations. They don't need manufactured jargon to name what they do with children. They don't need specialists to force slick texts and materials on them. Nor do they need standardized tests to determine the curriculum or measure the "progress" of children.

High school teachers would do well to visit such early childhood classrooms. Mary Mathias, a teacher in Winnipeg, found that the high school valued her elementary school experience. In her essay "Educating Against All Odds," she writes about the transition she made from first grade teacher to high school teacher. Deborah Meier, who purposely looked for teachers with early childhood experience writes, "Kindergarten teachers know that learning must be personalized, just because kids are idiosyncratic. It is, alas, the last time children are given independence, encouraged to make choices, and allowed to move about on their own steam. The older they get, the less we take into account the importance of their own interests."

Good progressive education means building on an understanding of children's thinking. It is a process that takes time, care, and the commitment to careful observation. Nowhere is this more clearly described than in the story of Jason and Matt, whose teacher Kay Hibl engaged in meticulous observation and documentation to illustrate how diverse two children's thinking can be about the same situation. Before introducing any curriculum, the progressive educator understands that the foundation for learning is rooted in the children's thinking and an understanding of how different that can be. Again Patricia Carini explains: "Like preference and aversion to which they are related, intuitions of difference and likeness color our thoughts, lend vividness to perception, permeate our relationships with others, and, in general, serve an orienting function in our lives, both individually and collectively."

The contributors to this volume are evenly mixed between men and women. We have gathered together diverse ethnic voices. Among them are an African-American high school teacher writing about blacks in predominately white schools, and a Latina parent writing about her dream for her children and why she founded a new school which was not based on tracking by ability. Two thirds of the authors work in public settings, belying the stereotype that often associates progressive education with elite private schools. Some authors are unpublished classroom teachers, now ready to share their experiences with others, and some are well-known academicians. All but two contributions began as presentations at the 1989 University of Chicago/Winnetka Public Schools Progressive Education Conference. Lillian Weber, founder of the Workshop Center at City College of New York, was unable to attend, but she sent her personal reading list. Marvin Lazerson's *Democracy, Progressivism, and the Comprehensive High School* was given at the 1986 Bank Street/Teachers College Conference.

Conferences celebrating progressive education began in 1975 when Lillian Weber brought together educators to explore the early history of the progressive movement. A collection of essays, *The Roots of Open Education In America* (Dropkin and Tobier, 1976), grew out of than conference. Since then, *Reunion, Reaffirmation, and Resurgence* (Jervis, 1983) and *Education for Democracy* (Jervis and Tobier, 1987)—proceedings of national progressive education conferences—have contributed to a growing literature, much of which is authored by classroom teachers, that documents recent progressive thought and practice. In her introduction to *Roots*, Lillian Weber, to whom this book is dedicated, reminds us of the meaning of progressive education:

> The ideas...after all, are about person, about difference, about continuity, about human striving to make both sense of the world and an impact upon it, about potentiality and the conditions of life that nurture or suppress the flowering of potentiality, about the conditions that allow the recognition and emergence of ideas, and about the professional, theoretical, and institutional context of schooling. Inherent...is a broad acceptance for all persons as active learners, capable of intelligent active efforts to survive. (Dropkin and Tobier, 1976, p. 5)

Progressive Education for the 1990s: Transforming Practice offers an opportunity to further the progressive mission—for the children.

REFERENCES

Dropkin, R., and Tobier, A., Eds. (1976). *The Roots of Open Education in America.* New York: City College Workshop Center.

Jervis, K., Ed. (1983). *Reunion, Reaffirmation, and Resurgence.* Miquon, PA: The Miquon School.

Jervis, K., and Tobier, A., Eds. (1988). *Education for Democracy.* Weston, MA: The Cambridge School of Weston.

Rose, M. (1989). *Lives on the Boundary: The Struggles and Achievements of America's Underprivileged.* New York: Free Press.

Part 1

Progressive Values and Historical Reflections

1

LARGE PURPOSES

VITO PERRONE

Progressivism as a social, political, and educational movement had its contemporary beginnings at the turn of the century as America was undergoing enormous change. Our cities were undergoing rapid growth, economic conditions were in a state of transformation, and immigration was at extremely high levels. Correspondingly, housing did not keep pace with the demand, leaving many in deplorable, generally unhealthy conditions; poverty levels were high; environmental conditions in neighborhoods and workplaces were particularly undesirable; and the diversity of languages and cultures caused far more dismay than celebration.

While enrolling increasingly larger numbers, though remaining far from anything approaching democratic universalism, the schools were struggling—not just with the numbers of students and their diversity but in relation to purposes. In many respects, conditions today are more similar than different. Our current circumstances look a lot like those in 1900 in regard to societal and schooling challenges, which is just one of many reasons to reestablish historical perspective.

Progressivism in education was guided historically by a belief that schools needed social power and at their best were rooted in cultural understandings, ethical commitments, and an ongoing struggle for democracy—in other words, large purposes that transcended mere materialism. Many schools with progressive traditions have turned their backs on that history, avoiding the use of the word *progressive* in the same way as many of our politicians avoid the term *liberal*. But schools with powerful progressive traditions have an important legacy which involves keeping alive such thought. To lose a focus on democracy—for example, not to be closely connected in our practice to the world, its problems, and its promise—is to lose the moral base of our work.

A version of this article appears in Perrone, V. (1991). *A Letter to Teachers: Reflections on Schools and the Art of Teaching*. San Francisco: Jossey-Bass.

In this period of time when the schools have become a matter of enormous public concern, several different entry points to my topic are possible. While I will, in fact, make several entries, the guiding theme will be *large purposes,* which is my way of returning to a more basic set of educational scaffolds and a perspective ordered by a progressive stance toward education. It is, of course, out of large purposes that we are more genuinely able to speak about the schools, teaching, and learning. Other starting points keep us absorbed by fads and searches for some fabled *one best system.*

At its best, whether we think of the present or the future, education is first and foremost a moral and intellectual endeavor, always beginning with children and young people and their intentions and needs, always rooted in powerful purposes—an endeavor concerned with the forest rather than the trees. By and large, in most schools we tend to be more attentive to technical than to moral and intellectual directions, more attentive to the isolated pieces, to the trees and not the forest. Education at its best is not sufficiently the preoccupation. In this regard we aren't close enough to what I recall of Emily Dickinson's lovely and thought-provoking lines, "I dwell in possibilities, and...not wishing to miss the dawn, I open every door...."

What we know most about children and young people is that they are always learning. That is their nature. As they touch the earth, observe the culture that surrounds them, and listen to stories and speak, they are gaining a personal relationship with the world, gaining what Jean Piaget calls a balance between changing the world and changing themselves.

If we kept such a view about children constantly before us, we wouldn't be so quick to assume clinical approaches to education, full of so many labels that imply deficits in children. Not to begin with children's natural strengths and energy is to limit the possibilities, to assume for too many children an education with too little power. Do we fit the child to the school or make the school fit the child? It might be interesting to engage that question fully again and see where we are. I believe the school as an institution has come almost everywhere to overshadow the child.

In this regard, we are called increasingly in the schools to see our world through a lens of economic competitiveness, the latest of the public imperatives. Today, the focus is on Japan and West Germany, with Korea, Taiwan, China, Singapore, and Brazil, among others, close at hand. We need educational settings that challenge young people intellectually and morally, that provide those skills and understandings that are generative of ongoing learning in the schools and in the world. We must want for our children and young people the best education we can imagine. But placing so much stress on economic competitiveness—stronger math and science programs to win the war of technology, for example—is distracting even as it is distressingly accepted by schools of all kinds, including those of progressive persuasion. It is a formulation that too often prevents us from seeing the world as fully connected and its people as having mutual needs. Growth everywhere is a matter for celebration. And celebration easily becomes too instrumental. The zero sum formulations associated with competition—gains in Japan meaning necessary losses in the United States—are also self-defeating. Representing the world in these terms masks the inequities that currently exist and the imperatives to work actively toward their redress. This view has a moral dimension which needs to be addressed. Is hunger in Africa acceptable? Is the burden of debt carried by Brazil, Peru, Mexico, Nigeria, and Poland their just due? Is that where competitiveness leads? It has that potential.

To speak of economic competitiveness in relation to the world also has an impact at the level of the school and classroom. Must our goal in the schools also be rooted in competition, or can cooperation be a principal objective? What are some of the ways to think about this? Shall we, for example, track or not track? Provide challenge for some and little for others? Place limits on the possibilities for some and open the world to others? Perpetuate inequities or work toward their eradication? Clutter our discourse with labels which pit students against each other by race, class, perceptions of intelligence, or gift? Shall we accept the message of test scores or go beyond them? How many of us have seriously challenged the various ways schools separate students? Do we speak about the inequities in the world and not attend to those which exist in our schools? And, as you know, the inequities tend to be large and growing larger.

What if we spent time on this question: *What do we most want our students to come to understand as a result of their schooling?*

Reading and writing might be a quick response to the question, but is it enough? What if students learn to read and write but don't like to and don't want to? What if they don't read the newspapers and magazines, or can't find beauty in a poem or love story? What if they don't see Romeo and Juliet in their lives? What if they don't listen to a broad range of music, notice the trees and the sunset, look at the stars, or go as adults to artistic events? What if they don't have a vision of themselves as thoughtful mothers and fathers, and aren't prepared for the responsibility of parenthood? Will these students be optimistic about the world and their place in it, and participate in politics and community life? Will they be able to locate the Union of South Africa but never understand the pain of apartheid? Will they know about the loneliness of many of our elderly while remaining indifferent to them? Will they be aware of the hunger in this world while still wasting collectively tons of food each year?

I often ask, are our children being provided a basis for active participation in the life of their communities? Are they learning the meaning of social responsibility, of citizenship in the broadest sense? When we aren't clear about such questions, not keeping them in mind or making them a part of our ongoing discourse, we tend to fill our schools with contradictions which over time can foster cynicism and limited support—hardly the basis for making them the centers for inquiry, authority, and change that they need to be. I'll offer two vignettes.

At a recent Peace Studies Symposium at the University of North Dakota, Brian Petkau, a Canadian teacher, presented *A Prairie Puzzle* (1982), a powerful personal statement about the presence of nuclear missiles across the North Dakota landscape and about what these weapons represent in terms of danger to human life. Several young North Dakota students who were in the audience expressed considerable anger about "how little they knew." They asked why they hadn't learned more about the missile fields, as well as the kinds of weapons that existed and their mechanisms and costs. They stressed the need to know of their potential as targets. In not making the nuclear arms in North Dakota, in the country, or in the world, a matter of serious study in the schools these students attended, what kinds of values were being expressed? Were students being prepared for active citizenship?

The second vignette, from *New Voices: Immigrant Students in U.S. Public Schools* (1988), is a more positive entry into citizenship. At an elementary school in Revere, Massachusetts, the principal of an all-white, fully English-speaking school, upon learning several years ago that close to two hundred Cambodian children would be attending the school in the fall, started a process aimed at inclusion and social learning of a large sort. The principal and teachers made a decision that it was critical for everyone in the school—children, teachers, custodians, secretaries, lunch workers—to know who these Cambodian children were, where they had come from, and why they were coming to Revere. "Getting Ready for the Cambodian Children" became the full curriculum for several months, the basis for all studies. The train of normal coverage was stopped. It was a real curriculum, and as a result it was vital. Those in the school community learned how to speak to the Cambodian children, and also gained considerable knowledge about their cultural patterns and their suffering. As part of their preparation, they learned about prejudice and the harm that prejudice brings to people who are different. They also learned how prejudice disrupts communities—whether schools, neighborhoods, or cities. Their learning had meaning, and it made a visible difference. It grew out of social values, commitments, and a willingness to make decisions related to such values and commitments. Unfortunately, it was an unusual response. It ought to be the usual. In progressive settings, what is true in the world should be the curriculum virtually all of the time.

The foregoing vignettes and their import border on the political as well as the moral. While I know that there are many pressures to keep such values out of the curriculum, to stay close to the technical, the schools would do better to address such issues more directly.

Robert Bellah and his associates, in their popular *Habits of the Heart* (1985), suggest in this regard that adults are having increasing difficulty explaining their ethical commitments to their children. But children and young people need to know that their parents and teachers have important values. Those beliefs and values come through in many ways. What kinds of values do we present as educators, and how do we express our deep concern for the students and the society? How do we act out our citizenship and show our love for learning? Do we display an ongoing inquisitiveness about the world by wanting to know how it works and why it works in those ways? Do we ask powerful, critical questions and seek alternative explanations? Do we ask often about events being examined, and what they mean? And why should it matter? And do we engage each other in conversations about them?

Friedrich Froebel (1887), a theoretical and practical giant in the early childhood field, used the garden metaphor extensively in his writing about children, drawing on the concepts of unfolding, blooming, and flowering. His metaphor is worth reflecting more upon.

Experiences do, as Froebel suggested, build on each other; the more powerful they are, the larger their potential for being fully educative, fully generative. While each stage of life, each experience, is important in its own right, each is also integrally connected to what precedes and follows it. Such an understanding should cause us to ask about the continuities between the experience and content of preschools and the primary grades, the primary and intermediate grades, the intermediate grades and the middle/junior high schools, and middle schools and high schools, and the importance of returning at each level of schooling to earlier themes. Is it possible, for example, to go to Chicago's Field Museum of Natural History or the Smithsonian too many times? To reread particular books too many times? To revisit Martin Luther King's or Dorothy Day's life too many times? I hear, though, that primary children everywhere are told: "You don't want to read that book again," or "You will learn about that when you get to the fifth grade." Such refrains are replayed all along the schooling track. That, by the way, is one of the means by which difficult questions are set aside and not attended to. Progressive settings shouldn't deny tough questions.

Further, such understandings about continuities should help us understand what we lose or close off, when we consider curriculum narrowly and in terms of isolated, disconnected studies. Separating learning, as we tend to do, typically leads to less understanding, not more. Alfred North Whitehead (1959) wrote in this regard, "In separation all meaning evaporates" (p. 59). Can we possibly maintain intensity with six or seven separate, generally unrelated, nonthematic subject matters covered in a day, especially when we feel we must get through everything so quickly? We often lament the poor quality of children's work, but rarely work long enough at anything to assure it is of high quality.

Returning to the question of large purposes, we would do well to call for the development of "active inquirers." If we saw this as a major goal, much that exists in the school—the workbooks and textbooks, the predetermined curriculum, the reductionism, the teaching to tests—would begin to fade. Those in the schools would be free to make living in the world a larger part of the curriculum.

By taking this formulation seriously, we would be more attentive to students' inclinations and what they value—what they truly care about. To do otherwise, Patricia Carini (1986) suggests, is "to rest content with the appearance of knowledge and forfeit all pretense of educating responsible thinkers, capable of forming opinions and taking actions" (p. 22).

It is out of this personal intention and personal knowledge, not those small pieces of disconnected knowledge, that bridges to extended learning are constructed. An education that builds bridges, makes fuller learning more more possible, and expands a child or young person's potential for independence is, in today's terms, an "empowering education." That is a goal worth striving for. It is also an education that is possible.

To pursue such thoughts leads inevitably back to the issue of breadth and depth. May Sarton, in *I Knew a Phoenix* (1959), an example I never tire of using, gives us an interesting glimpse of what Whitehead meant in relation to depth and intensity. She suggests that her sedentary adult life may well stem from a school environment in Cambridge, Massachusetts, in the 1920s where she traveled for months along the dusty roads of Athens, climbed for weeks in the Himalayas, and painted the great landscapes of this world. She used up so much of her energy, her whole being, that she had to sit and rest in adulthood. This is obviously an overstatement, but wouldn't it be wonderful if all our students had such intense remembrances of their schooling?

Another way to conceptualize the continuities and bridges which keep learning possibilities open, is to consider the cultivation of imagination. Imagination is in essence a perspective, "a way of seeing connections and meanings beyond the routine and commonplace" (Lazerson et al., 1985, p. 70). It is the kind of direction that Alice Seletsky (1988) writes about when she discusses her teaching. Such a perspective demands a curriculum that truly challenges young people and that is laden with questions and multiple possibilities for entry and active learning. It suggests, as well, time to observe, sit, think, and rework ideas.

When considering imagination, we are also called upon to think again about questions of certainty and uncertainty with regard to knowledge and the content of the classroom. Joseph Featherstone (1988) suggests that the metaphor of Mark Twain's *Life on the Mississippi*, with the shifting river needing to be understood with a high degree of tentativeness, might be helpful. There is a virtue in keeping ideas alive, with their complexity fully in view.

In this regard, Tolstoi (1967) noted on the basis of his work with peasant children that "to the teacher, the simplest and most general appears the easiest, whereas for a pupil only the complex and the living appears easy—only that which demands interpretation and provokes thought is easy" (p. 289). Like Featherstone in his understanding of Mart Twain's education, Tolstoi didn't view ambiguity and uncertainty as something to remedy, but as the soil for deep learning. We would do well to keep such a perspective in mind. The simple and the certain is not the road to democracy in our contemporary age. The simple and the certain also don't provide a basis for optimism.

In relation to this concern about optimism, Paul Fussell in *The Great War and Modern Memory* (1975) suggests that World War I permanently ended what was becoming at the time a pervasive sense of optimism. The enlarged social, political, and economic optimism that was beginning to emerge before the Great War needs reconstruction. There is a need for new understandings that the world, however defined, is not static, that change is possible and that it demands a personal and collective investment. An education of consequence ought to encourage such understandings.

Eleanor Duckworth, author of *The Having of Wonderful Ideas* (1987), provides us with yet another way to think about purposes. She equates the essence of intellectual development with the "having of wonderful ideas," which she defines as those occasions when a student, on his or her own, comes to understand a relationship or how something works. Duckworth reminds us: "There is no difference between wonderful ideas which many people have already had and wonderful ideas which nobody has happened on before...in each case, it is a matter of making new connections between things already mastered" (p. 231). I like that formulation very much.

A school committed to supporting "the having of wonderful ideas" is establishing the goal of getting all young people as close as possible to their upper limits of learning potentialities. As it is, most don't come very close to that upper limit. The expectations aren't high enough, the environments for learning are too sparse, the questions asked are too small, and the resources are too limited. Inevitably, powerful purposes have been absent.

In thinking about the schools in general, as well as our own schools—those in which we live much of our lives or to which we are most committed—we need always to reach back to guiding purposes, to our richest, most powerful, most generative conceptions of education, and work toward them. These largest purposes need to be fully a part of our common language. They are the basis for an education of meaning in progressive terms.

REFERENCES

Bellah, R., et al. (1985). *Habits of the Heart: Individualism and Commitment in American Life.* Berkeley, CA: University of California Press.

Carini, P. (1986). Education, Values, and the Child's Impulse to Value. Unpublished manuscript.

Duckworth, E. (1987). *The Having of Wonderful Ideas.* New York: Teachers College Press.

Featherstone, J. (1988). "A Note on Liberal Learning." *Colloquy,* Volume 2. pp 2–7.

First, J. M. (1988). *New Voices: Immigrant Students in U.S. Public Schools.* Boston: National Coalition of Advocates for Students.

Froebel, F. (1887). *The Education of Man.* New York and London: D. Appleton and Company.

Fussell, P. (1975). *The Great War and Modern Memory.* New York: Oxford University Press.

Lazerson, M., et al. (1985). *An Education of Value.* New York: Cambridge University Press.

Petkau, B. (1982). *A Prairie Puzzle.* Altoona, Manitoba: Elim Bible Institute.

Sarton, M. (1959). *I Knew a Phoenix.* New York: W.W. Norton and Company.

Seletsky, A. (1988). "My Name is Alice." From *Teaching Social Studies: Portraits from the Classroom.* Edited by V. Rogers, A. D. Roberts, and T. P. Weinland. Bulletin #82. Washington, DC: National Council for the Social Studies.

Tolstoi, L. (1967). *Tolstoi on Education.* Chicago: University of Chicago Press.

Whitehead, A. N. (1959). *The Aims of Education.* New York: Macmillan.

2

HONORING DIVERSITY/ STRIVING FOR INCLUSION

PATRICIA CARINI

This essay is continuous with certain of the themes I explored in "Another Way of Looking" (Carini, 1988). In that essay I told several stories, each of which, for me, illuminated some aspect of standards and values—including their intimate kinship.

One of the stories was a retelling of threads drawn from the fabric of Rolvaag's (1927) novel, *Giants in the Earth*, a love story woven of three strands: the story of the love affair between Per Hansa and Beret as they struggled to make the journey from Norway to a new home in Dakota Territory, Beret's love for her old home in Norway, and Per Hansa's ever-intensifying love affair with the New World. Like all love stories, this one presents the characters, as well as the readers, with such urgent life questions as seeking after and fashioning one's own self; being compelled by and seeking to be with another; striving for security and connectedness; being enticed by adventure, wider horizons, and expanded possibilities—and all the passions associated with those quests.

Amidst so much strong feeling, conflicts arise. In the story, Beret's longing for her familiar homeland and Per Hansa's sense of forward advance and challenge in settling the new land emblemize those conflicts. Each is driven by a strong sense of worth and value; each is a bearer of standards. For Beret, there is the importance of religion, education, and decency—above all, that her family should not sink into an animal existence. For Per Hansa, there is the importance of independence, self-sufficiency, and overcoming obstacles—above all, that his family should not give in or be defeated.

We are all familiar in our own lives with these kinds of intensities and divergences. Like Per Hansa, we have known the inner-dividedness of wanting two things at the same time—the passionate conviction that we must and can have them both. Faced with another, close and dear, whose preferences run at times contrariwise to our own, we are familiar with the politics of persuasion and appropriation. We know that strongly held values do not always sort themselves easily into categories of higher and lower, of better and worse, but instead strive and compete within us on equal terms. Surely, the love of home and security is not in any absolute way construable as inferior to the love of adventure. Nor can we with authority dismiss Beret's standards of decency, cleanliness, courtesy, and order in favor of Per Hansa's standards of inventiveness, success, and mastery. Neither can we assign a preferred status to a longing for the known and familiar home, or to a striving toward an ideal home realizable only in the future.

I reintroduce this story here for the *value-ground* it stakes out for grappling with the emotional intensity of differences—whether we encounter those differences in our personal lives, our schools, the larger society, or on a global scale. Through this story, I also mean to position the issue of differences concretely, to make it handleable and not merely abstract: differences and conflict, far from being avoidable, are the very material of life.

The second story I told in the earlier paper concerned a 10-year-old boy I called Morris. I told it originally as a story about the power and force of personal values and standards, and the public dimension of these seemingly private preferences. It is also a story about difference and variation occurring on three planes simultaneously. It is with the purpose of exploring these latter features that I will retell it here.

Morris (a pseudonym) was a child who stood out in several respects as out of the ordinary, or "different." Both physically and in speech, he was unusually ponderous and deliberate. His humor was droll and dry, often pivoting on word play, and not always easily grasped by his peers. As a thinker, he tended to come at an idea from the deep or underside rather than from the surface or head-on. Although at the age of 10 he was an avid reader with well-developed literary preferences and standards, he was a relatively late reader, achieving neither independence nor fluency until well into his eighth year. In general, his perspective was unconventional.

Without minimizing this kind of difference, or how it figures in the dynamics of a classroom, it is Morris's interpretation of a run-of-the-mill test category that I wish to emphasize. The category was antonyms, and the examples offered for the children's edification were "night/day" and "black/white." Familiar with Morris's slow pace, I wasn't surprised when he didn't promptly set to work on the test. I was determined to get him started and went over to urge him on. In response, Morris shook his head: "I can't do them. These (that is, night/day; black/white) are just different sides of the same things—they aren't opposites."

There is undeniable power and "rightness" to Morris's observation. It is unqualifiedly a big idea, reflecting sensitivities and intuitions with respect to the wholeness of language, experience, and the world itself. It is also undeniable that those ideas contradict the standard set by the test—a standard which emphasizes conventions of definition and reduces language into measurable units.

Linking this story back to the love story of Per Hansa, Beret, and the New World, Morris's standards and those set by the test point to different valuations of language and the world. Those valuations may be broad and vague, but as Morris's response illustrates, they are not by virtue of that lacking in potency and consequences. At age 10, Morris's feelings for words were intense. He was adamant. I, at least, could not persuade him to go against his own aesthetic—and past a certain point, would not do so. Choices have to be made. Not all differences are reconcilable.

Angling this story in another direction, Morris also draws our attention to the close kinship binding difference and likeness—a kinship that is especially evident on the margins of experience. As Morris implied, night is distinguishable from day, but they are also like to each other, both perceptibly and by reference to a larger, more encompassing cycle of time. Within that cycle there are border phases—dawn and dusk—in which night and day are visibly mingled. At high noon and midnight, light and dark stand counterpoised, but only to begin once again the slide toward the middle that will return them to each other's embrace. At any point in this dance of time, we may choose to emphasize the differences or the similarities between them, but just as dark invokes light, night invokes day. Or, to employ the image of the color wheel that for me emblemizes Morris's perception, they tend to flow into each other. By placing them in motion, by restoring night and day to the process of time, and black and white to the spectrum of colors, Morris created a larger context, opened boundaries, and shifted the emphasis from fixed opposition to distinguishable difference and distinguishable likeness.

The third and last story I am going to tell explores the attraction of opposites and the transformative power of difference. It is a personal recollection and relates an ordinary set of childhood circumstances. I grew up among a close-knit band of five cousins. Our ages spanned a mere four years, and for the most part, age didn't figure in an important way in our play and adventures. Our attachment and allegiance to each other was unwavering. Although we had other friends, we were for each other an assumed and unspoken home base. If one of us ran amuck of the many grown-ups who exercised parental authority over our lives, outrage was felt by all. As one organism we fought a neighboring family of children who were sometimes our cohorts, but who at other times we found unwelcome intruders on our special play domain—the inlet and banks of a river on which three of our houses and that of our grandparents bordered.

Although closely knit as a unit, as figures within it we moved freely, changing partners as points of common interest drew us together. Often these miniature configurations were complementary; sometimes they were exclusionary. Like the wavy circle we formed as a group, these relationships were fluid.

My special attraction to my slightly older cousin was her porcelain blonde beauty, and the sweetness and generosity of her nature. My hair was also fair, but of the dishwater blonde variety. My volatile temper was the plague of my childhood life. We were different. I felt our difference. I found her quite wondrous. I also envied her. Not infrequently, I was unkind, condescending, and over-bearing to her, making her the victim of my outbursts and strong will.

Still, we were close and often fancied ourselves sisters. Much of our play together, in contrast to the large-scale outdoor activities we cousins undertook as a unit (fort and dam building, fishing, skating), was woven from fairytales, movie and radio romances, the construction of miniature worlds, the making of dolls from flowers, and endless conversation. For one intense period of time that was especially satisfying for me, we played out and elaborated on the tale of two sisters, Snow White and Rose Red. The story was one I had read and told my cousin. Unlike many fairy tales, in this one both sisters were virtuous and beautiful. They were also very different from each other. As I recall the story, and certainly as I saw it then, their differences corresponded with my perceptions of the differences between my cousin and me. One was good and kind; the other more intense and adventurous. In the story, the contrast was symbolized by Snow White's delicate fairness and Rose Red's vivid darkness.

It was this contrast that caught my imagination. Accentuating the slight difference in our coloring, I promptly cast myself as Rose Red and my cousin as Snow White. As often happens in children's play, the original story was rather quickly abandoned, as we wove from the appealing strand of a contrast in physical appearance, a story and a metaphor about ourselves, which re-created us. To borrow Morris's phrase, we became "two sides of the same thing."

It was as if the story and play we enacted from it made a space in which her lightness and my "darkness," my intensity and her gaiety, her playfulness and my bookishness, my will and her kindliness became a shared territory (Himley, in press) in which we were coparticipants. We each had a part to play. We each had our own voices. In the space of our acknowledged differences, we explored with zest who each of us was. We talked about our favorite colors, flowers, dogs, movie stars (and the contrasts in our preferences). We imagined future lives in which our very different talents flourished. We commiserated over our very different shortcomings. We had falling outs and made them up on the strength of the understandable clash of our natures. As we traveled into adolescence together, we increasingly drew on each other's strengths to contend with problems encountered with our school work and in our social lives. Standing apart in our differences, we were drawn together. Looking at the world through her eyes, my sense of possibilities was altered and expanded. I think that something like that may also have happened for her. We were changed by each other's presence.

I have told these stories to call attention to our perception of likeness and difference as value experiences. Like preference and aversion to which they are related, intuitions of difference and likeness color our thoughts, lend vividness to perception, permeate our relationships with others, and in general, serve an orienting function in our lives, both individually and collectively.

In this respect, I would take note that any of us may, under particular circumstances, or more characteristically, tend to emphasize one over the other. Returning for a moment to Per Hansa and Beret, the drama played out in their story is understandable in terms of just such emphases. A preference for difference, a yearning after diversity of experience, tends to incline us, as it did Per Hansa, toward adventure, challenge and expansion of horizons. When instead a high value is given to likeness, then like Beret, we lean more toward home and the connectedness of experience. *Their partnership was created from the interplay of such differences*: Beret was Per Hansa's center of gravity, his holding point; he was her arrow into the unknown. Our experience of life—its satisfactions and zest, its complexities and ambiguities, its contradictions and torn edges—arise from just such interanimations. So long as the boundary between likeness and difference remain open, the experience of the one tends to strengthen our perceptions of the other. Drawing once more on Morris's observation, the experience of differences and likenesses may itself be understood as "two sides of the same thing"—sometimes counter-poised, but except at a high cost, never altogether separable from each other or sharply dichotomous.

However, as history on the broad scale and reflection on the smaller scale of our own lives calls to our attention, the experience of likenesses and differences is subject to polarization as well as interplay. Had I pursued the story of Per Hansa and Beret to its tragic conclusion, I could have described such as polarization, ending in her madness and his death. I could also have expanded on the recurrent wars my cousins and I waged on that family of neighboring children with whom we at other times played. The occasioning circumstances for these wars sprang from the high value we and our families placed on animal life and their habit of decapitating turtles and snakes and incinerating bugs. These weren't minor skirmishes, but battles conducted from our side in the name of all that is right and good. By our lights, we were justified in killing our neighbors if they killed the animals that lived in and around "our" river. They were the barbaric hordes; we were the defenders of civilization.

However, it is on the broader plane of society, including schools, that I have chosen to position the discussion of the extreme polarization of likeness and difference. I am going to focus mainly on the consequences of that disengagement.

As the story I just told of our childhood wars with our neighbors suggests, an emphasis on differences unrelieved by the saving grace of some perceived similarity pushes us past the tensions and discomforts of contradiction and the clash of our values with those of others to the denial of their existence, or right to exist. From that far distance, the other person's experience and values appear on our horizon as altogether alien and unrelated to us.

In this configuration of our social existence, the world divides neatly and cleanly into "them" and "us." The antithesis is as simple, uncomplicated, and abstract as that opposition Morris challenged by insisting that similarity be permitted to play its qualifying role. Describing "gross dichotomizing" as a "persisting habit of modern times," Paul Fussell (1977, p. 75) attributes this sundering of social existence in the west to the prolonged trench warfare of the Great War, in which:

> "We" are all here on this side; the "enemy" is over there. "We" are individuals with names and personal identities; "he" is a mere collective entity. We are visible; he is invisible. We are normal; he is grotesque; our appurtenances are natural; his bizarre. He is not as good as we are. (p. 76)

Carrying it a step further, Fussell quotes a soldier who writes of the enemy territory as "peopled by men whose way of thinking was totally and absolutely distinct from our own" (p. 77).

Adding to this description, I would observe that when we position ourselves in severe opposition to others, there tends to be a collapsing inward within our own ranks toward common values and virtues. In extreme cases of beleaguerment, those on both sides of such a dividing line may turn on members of their own groups who, expressing a view not altogether in harmony with the common sentiments, are then perceived to be deviants. As we know from bitter experience, the treatment of comrades perceived to be at odds with the prevailing code may be as violent as that inflicted on the enemy.

Fussell's metaphor is trench warfare but the description is, I believe, translatable without serious distortion to all forms of prejudice—racial, national, ethnic, religious, class, or gender. In all these instances, the "others" are rendered abstract and collective. They are often literally deprived of their names. Although "we" have friends, children, and family and live in the hope of their well-being, "they" are either dumb and emotionless, or animalistic and brutal in their passions. A moment's reflection on the characterization and treatment of African slaves in the United States offers a ready example.

These others may be perceived to represent so serious a threat to our way of life, our values, and our genes that they must be eliminated or at least isolated so that the threat of contamination and impurity is removed. When we are fixed on dichotomy, we tend toward the stark highlighting of difference and its annihilation.

Before I move on to examine the other side of the equation, I wish to note that the idea that there are persons who are of a different kind than we, *configured according to some altogether other pattern*, has enjoyed empirical and scientific support. In the current discourse, proponents of biological determinism offer a prime example. Their doctrine holds that society reflects biology because such observable differences between human groups as race, class, and gender are *genetically determined and fixed*.

These ideas are precisely correspondent with the dichotomous thinking just described. When claims are made that because such differences have been measured and verified statistically they have achieved the status of unquestionable fact, that connection needs to be borne firmly in mind. Facts do not exist in a political and social vacuum. In order to be understandable, they have to be evaluated in exactly those contexts. Questions have to be raised with respect to their value status. For example, the social commentator Christopher Jencks (1987) asks if it is reasonable to think that "traits," genetic or otherwise, can be isolated from other influences. Can we, for example, extricate a person's actions from the influence of treatments received at the hands of institutions and other persons, and ascribe them simply to genetics and a particular group membership? Questions like these are useful reminders that whatever the justification, empirical or otherwise, how we *think* about others is not without very real consequences in very real lives.

Next to this picture, let me place a sketch of the equally distorted image of similarity that emerges when it is separated from the qualifying influence of difference. If the imagery associated with dichotomous oppositions has to do with *knives* and *severing*, the correspondent imagery associated with the press of likeness toward sameness has to do with *ingestion* and *assimilation*. Just as the Great War may emblemize gross dichotomizing, Western dominance of other nations and peoples may stand in modern times as the metaphor for the gobbling up and homogenization of cultures and individual experience.

I would like to draw out two versions of the assimilatory process. In the most blatant version, those exercising controlling power ruthlessly suppress and root out the differences among the subjugated that would threaten assimilation. Language, emblems, customs, and stories of the people are as much as possible forcibly dismantled. The means of this suppression may be violent and brutal. Quite typically the subjects of such attention are either dragged by the hair or bullied into the orbit and sphere of influence of the dominating group, or are undermined and dislocated to a degree that renders them helpless and submissive.

In the other versions (and often the two are mixed) there is the assumption that the group to be assimilated will be "bettered" by attachment to so superior and powerful an ethos as that represented by the controlling group. Or, in slight contradistinction to that posture they are conceived to occupy a lower or less developed position along a progressive path that culminates in the mature and more evolved perspective represented by the dominant world view. In both cases, the likely attitude toward the "inferior" group or individual is to "help" them, to assume an unasked for responsibility for them, and to engender a relationship of dependency. The standard it tends to set is one of purity. The attitude is redemptive (Clifford, 1988).[1]

Whatever its justification—political, economic, or conversion to higher order beliefs—when persons individually are absorbed into the orbit of others or whole peoples and nations are translated into the categories of experience and the vocabulary of an exterior world view, there is a flattening out of the range of human experience. The color and texture of the human landscape is reduced.

In the intellectual background of such domineering and assimilatory attitudes, there is often a detectable outline of universalism. If others exist mostly as a projection of our own image, albeit blurred, imperfect, or not fully evolved, then there is nearly always close at hand the idea of a perfect form and a static reality to which it bears a transparent correspondence. For example, the idea of language as universal in its form, structure, and the categories of experience to which it refers bears within it a correspondent notion: that in spite of the observably rich variation among tongues, any language is *altogether translatable into any other language* since all languages signify essentially the same meanings and relate to an identical reality. Or, to phrase it another way, language construed according to a universal form resolves and absorbs the observable differences among languages.

In keeping with the universalist slant, those bent on assimilation tend to establish a hierarchical and fixed relationship among persons along the single axis of the categories of experience and the standards upheld by their own world view. If Native Americans construe time in ways other than the linear conceptualizations preferred in Western culture, those constructions tend to be overlooked or simply dismissed as imperfect with respect to the exterior standard. The judgment may be patronizing, attributing to the people as a whole a "child-like" mentality or accompanied by the severe and stereotypical attitudes reflected in the phrase, "Indian time." The Native American interpretation of reality, with its *own* individual and collective variations, and changing and evolving perspectives that are neither identical with those of their own past nor synonymous with some version of Western reality, fall altogether outside the scope of an attitude fastened on similarity.

Noticeable in this posture is the tendency noted by James Clifford (1988) in *The Predicament of Culture* to treat an entire culture as homogeneous: to speak of the Navajo mentality or the way Trobrianders think. When the controlling group is at close quarters with the subjugated, outnumbered and at a distance from their home ports, the burden of being standard bearers for civilization may incline them toward ritualization of their own customs and foster rigid conformity with respect to that standard. Again, just as gross dichotomizing may tend toward the elimination of diversity on both sides of the dividing line, assimilatory attitudes may tend toward restriction within the ranks of the dominant group as well as the suppression of diversity among the subjugated.

Whether we fasten on difference to the exclusion of similarity or on similarity to the exclusion of difference, these perspectives serve the same turn and the same purpose: the *annihilation of difference* on the one hand, and its *suppression* on the other. It is not surprising then, that the same person, or groups of persons, may tend toward both extremes, or according to circumstances, ricochet between them. As Fussell (1977) says in a slightly different context, once we are appropriated by a dichotomizing attitude, we are caught in "a binary deadlock" (p. 77).

There is in these extreme circumstances—and I believe this to be of the utmost importance—*loss of ground*: ground on which to stand apart sufficiently for us to see each other as distinguishable and ground on which to stand close enough for us to recognize each other as human. There is no room for differing, no room for intimacy, no room for contradiction, no room for negotiation, no room for the pursuit of divergent paths or of parallel ones. *The middle ground is lost. The center does not hold.*

Both of these single-pointed valuations of the world accord a negative valence to difference. When, and by whatever means, differences among us are reduced, we are deprived in that degree of the power of those differences to expand our horizons. Boundaries close and there is an inward turning. Homogeneity and dissociation alike lessen the value intensity of the world. Interest, novelty, change, and adventure are exchanged for control, certainty, conformity, stability and order.

Where sameness rules with an iron hand, the vision of what humanness can be is narrowed. In protest against that narrowness, those afire with strong passion speak with the beauty of tragic loss. Art often flowers in the ruins of human degradation, but the arena for the productive assertiveness and expression of the many shrinks. There are other reactions: rebellions, subversion, underground activities, resistance movements, terrorist tactics, revolution, civil war. Things get stirred up. Inroads are made. In the most oppressive circumstances, people continue to speak the tongue that is their own and to assert cherished values. The resilience of people is remarkable. The tragedy and loss entailed is commensurately great.

The negative attitudes towards difference and the habit of gross dichotomizing reflected in the polarization of differences and likenesses have, of course, not gone unchallenged by other forces in Western society. In the United States, democratic ideals of equality of opportunity, freedom of expression, and civil liberty, however imperfectly practiced, are powerful examples of those counterforces, as are the philosophical and ethnographic conceptualizations of cultural plurality. There are other examples. Some of them, like an appropriately complex understanding of group and individual rights, are woven into the fabric of what we call the progressive tradition in education.

Still, the influence of those extreme attitudes is strongly felt and the consequences are findable everywhere in society: in the plight of the homeless, in attitudes towards those afflicted by AIDS, in the prejudicial treatment of minorities, in the promotion of English as a national language (to name just a few). The schools and education are no exception.

In the schools, attitudes, policies, and practices that work against diversification—a positive valuing of difference and an inclusive classroom setting—

are strong, habitual, and entrenched. For example, in the interests of homogeneity, schools in the United States have a long tradition of relying on a graded system which segregates children according to birth year. It is not the only tradition, but it is a strong one. Thinking about learning and curriculum has tended to be similarly restrictive, emphasizing small units of information presented and tested incrementally and according to a linear progression. Neither the graded system, the linear conceptualization of curriculum and learning, nor the associated testing system has proved easily alterable.

In this decade, as the pressure for homogeneity increased, schools tended to become more exclusionary. Narrowed definitions of "normalcy" and school readiness are mirrored in more restrictive admissions policies, increased retention of children in kindergarten and primary grades, and the placement of ever-increasing numbers of children at ever-earlier ages in special classes.

Although responsive to external pressures, quite generally these practices have been justified as being in the best interests of the child who will be saved from future failures. Or, in another version of that justification, slower children will be given the "gift of time" and quicker ones will be permitted to advance without impediment.[2] For older youngsters, curriculum tends to be bound to textbooks, to offer little diversity of point of view, and to aim at uniformity or a thin literacy with respect to received knowledge—often with very little attention given to the cultural limitations of that knowledge. The emphasis tends to be on direct instruction addressed to discrete skills or small, isolated bits of information. Overall, the view of learners and of the purposes of education has tended to be myopic, preoccupied with short-term results and correctness as it is measurable by external means. The usual justification for these practices is the need to maintain standards. It only thinly disguises, if it disguises at all, that children and young people are being asked to shoulder the burden for prevalent societal fears of decline and loss of political and economic power.

In line with these attitudes, the differences ascribable to individuals or to race, ethnicity, class, or gender, have tended to be scrutinized, accentuated, and accorded a negative valence. In the eagerness to search out *all* the children "at risk," any individual differences with respect to those ways of speaking, learning, and thinking approved by the school culture have been treated as weaknesses. Attention to diagnosis and treatment has tended to supplant attention to the teaching–learning relationship.

In a paradoxical and cruel twist, the more differences have been teased out for negative treatment, the greater has been the emphasis on uniformity— in curriculum, in teaching practice, in school ethos, and in evaluation. While the announced purpose of these strivings for uniformity are equality of educational opportunity, in actuality, an ever-increasing volume of children, a disproportionate number of whom are male, poor, or from disenfranchised populations (or all three), are educationally disenfranchised.

Recently, there have also been isolated, but welcome signs of a widening of the educational discourse. I would note the striking upsurge of interest in values associated with progressive education. I observe a renewed attention to reading and writing as part of a larger language context and to the child's own activity as a speaker and maker of meaning as integral to that process. Both early childhood educators and those associated with middle schools have recently issued guidelines—credos actually—that are responsive to the diverse experiences, interests, and needs of youngsters.

There are other changes I feel in the air which are less concrete, and at first glance less immediately connected to education. I have, for example, felt encouraged by what I sense as a change in our feelings for knowing, knowledge, and the standards by which knowledge is evaluated. Especially heartening among the changes I sense is a gradual broadening and diversification of the scientific perspective. Probably that broadening is most fully expressed through ecological conceptualizations like those of Lewis Thomas. I find it expressed as well in the works of physicists like David Bohm and in the genetic studies of Barbara McClintock. In general, the change seems to me to be emblemized in greater attention to complex wholes and context, increased respect for description, and recognition that scientific knowledge is achievable not only by strict adherence to prescribed methods but also through other ways of looking and knowing.

Even more encouraging to me is what I perceive as an increased diversity among those laying claim to knowledge and to the making of it. More voices are being heard and more differences among them are detectable. It was from the feminist literature that the phrase "ways of knowing" caught my ear, just as earlier I was drawn to the image of "different voices." I find this immensely exciting. I expect the discourse on knowledge and knowing to roughen, grow less harmonious and more muscular and colorful as it stretches to include divergent viewpoints: not only the perspectives of women and a cluster of scientific free thinkers, but speakers from previously disenfranchised populations in our own country and from social orders not consonant with those of the West.

These changes seem to me to be important, but compared to the waves of political, national, social, and religious diversification occurring on a global scale, they are *ripples*. Recently, listening to the sociologist Elise Boulding (1989), I was reminded that within virtually every nation, populations culturally and historically connected through beliefs and values are *in*sistent and *per*sistent in their claims for identity and in their refusal to continue to be translated into the terms of the host country. In this country, I will note the claims of Native Americans for tribal identity. There are strong separatist movements in Spain, Yugoslavia, Canada, the Soviet Union, and India, to name a few.

At the same time, we are witnessing relatively large-scale migrations of national groups—in Germany, the influx of Turks; in this country, the South-east Asians. Although not always welcomed, a broader range of voices and tongues *is* being heard. As these voices lay claim to rights not consonant with the interests of the established social order, conflict arises.

On a yet broader scale, there is a breaking up of the Western world view as the single and superior vision of humanity and civilization. In its place there will be pluralized views of who and what we are, of the purposes worthy of pursuit, and of the social orders best able to sustain and safeguard those purposes. When we say, "We hold these truths to be self-evident," it is going to be necessary to specify quite carefully who "we" are—while at the same time, giving voice to those ideals and striving for their realization. Among habits of mind that in the current circumstances seem no longer serviceable or affordable are the ones to which I have been calling attention in this essay: thinking in terms of simple dichotomies and the counter-tendency to universalize categories of experience that, although important, are nevertheless local and contingent. Similarly, ideal views of the world as unified and harmonious will need to give way to visions founded on the rich diversity and variation of human experience, and on a reality conceived as plural and interpretable and *not* as singular and factual. Where we have been accustomed to value "wholes" that are relatively smooth and inwardly coherent, we will need to give equal weight and value to "parts," and to "wholes" that are rougher—configured and characterized not by coherence but by disjunction and juxtaposition.

None of this is easy to think about. There will be losses. We are faced with great complexity. As Octavio Paz (1987) remarks in an essay bearing closely on this topic, "The understanding of others is a contradictory ideal; it asks that we change without changing, that we be other without *ceasing to be ourselves*" (pp. 28–29; emphasis in original).

A very few things seem plain to me. For the schools, honoring diversity in these terms will require changes that go far beyond structural adjustments, tinkering with school organization, and as the occasion demands, making concessions on isolated issues to particular constituencies. It will mean not only permitting others to speak but struggling to learn to hear them within their own value contexts.

In ideal terms—and I don't discount those terms—honoring diversity holds out great promise for education. For example, *diversity of purposes* occasions the opportunity for the fullest, least impeded pursuit of strong interests by the largest numbers of persons. As we know from our own lives and from our work with children, when strong interests are vigorously pursued, those interests tend to extend us past the boundaries of our immediate personal concerns. Through their expressions, personal interests, preferences, and values acquire a public dimension. In this respect, strong interests have a spreading effect. There is interplay of interests. There is room for the flowering of wide opportunities: for personal contribution, for achievement of personal worth, for collective benefit. Where persons—adults or youngsters—are deeply and actively engaged with practice, *with the making of works*, and the *making of knowledge*, standards arise that are reflective of those commitments and not external to them. When and where difference is honored and abounds, the most generous views of our common humanity prevail.

In actuality, there are also contradictions to this picture. It seems to me altogether likely that honoring diversity will prove costly and inefficient. When we place a high value on diversity, there can be no promise of certainty with respect to specific outcomes. When human striving in its multifarious forms is fostered, the generation of abundant energy and activity can be expected. The directions and forms that the expression of that energy and activity will take is less clear and certainly not predictable. As well as expansion of interests and stellar achievements, there will almost surely be excesses and shortcomings. At times, disarray and messiness will prevail over clarity and order. Judgments previously referred to, and stated or unstated assumptions and principles may often need to be deferred in the interests of a continuing reappraisal of the assumptions and principles themselves. In these respects, and others, I am persuaded that *very close attention to context* and *particulars* will be required.

In actuality, where differences are allowed, conflicts arise. The closer the quarters, or the more intensely different perspectives converge on the same territory of interest, the sharper those clashes are likely to be. Not all of these conflicts will be reconcilable. Making room for differences; making opportunities for areas of agreement to be recognized; making room for agreement and difference to exist side by side; working out reasonably reliable processes for hearing divergent viewpoints without subsuming them; finding the occasions that expand the perspectives from which we can see each other, requires quantities of that most valuable of all modern commodities: *time*—time expended not in the expectation of achieving lasting solutions but in the knowledge that striving for inclusion is a demanding and ongoing commitment. Such an expenditure of time can only be made if we have a firm conviction of the importance of what we are undertaking to accomplish.

From the start I have taken our present circumstances to be anything but clear. If it is that we are living partly in a world that was, and partly in a world that is heralding its own arrival, but has not quite pulled into the station, then our footing must be at times uneven and unsure; marked perhaps by steps both forward and backward. Past postures, past ways of thinking, and previous solutions won't always seem satisfactory in these circumstances. Much of the time, these habits of mind may be the only ones available to us. Almost certainly we are going to be struggling, and struggling recurrently, with competing values.

In that same vein, ideas and vocabulary that in past circumstances were not only agreeable but serviceable and apt, may with some abruptness, ring hollow in our ears or sound rather quaint. I know for myself that words like "pattern," "whole," "coherence," and "continuity" on which I have relied in my interpretations of children and schools, feel to me of late in need of careful and thorough reexamination. The need for that inspection and rethinking is not because they are "wrong," or in the expectation that I will simply drop them or substitute others, but from the strongly felt necessity to understand and expand their meanings in what I experience to be a changed value-context.

Similarly, my ear for hearing children, in which I have had a confidence that I think is not altogether misplaced, feels to me now in need of reeducation. The aim of that reattunement is not to gain greater facility in understanding others more easily and better, but to discipline myself not to understand *too* easily and to leave more space for the voices and value-contexts of others.

In general, it does not seem to me a time in which the conditions are right for certainty or for charting definitive courses of action and thought—at least not in the expectation that we will reach the destinations for which we set sail. It does feel like an adventuresome time that demands boldness. For some time now, we will have to feel our way and stand prepared to make unexpected changes of course. What may be most required of us is to forego decisiveness and binding judgments in favor of an *evaluating* posture: a willingness to rethink and weigh conflicting ideas and actions not in the expectation of the resolution of differences, but in the hope of broadening the opportunities for people to be visible to each other.

To conclude: speaking of polarization, I used the figure of lost ground. In the earlier stories, I spoke of space being made, and referred to those spaces as shared territories. Partly, I told the stories to make space among us. Telling them, I hoped they would prompt your own memories, evoking in your minds other stories, both correspondent with mine and divergent from them. I told them, too, to suggest that *lives* and *stories of lives* are a way of making knowledge among us about our human predicaments.

For me, storytelling and stories emblemize human "works" of all kinds. Like dancing, music, drama, games, drawing, building, play, and making things in general, storytelling is a *spanning* activity. It is relatively unrestricted with respect to age and status. In telling stories, we meet not on an assumed ground of understanding but on the equal footing of being makers, mutually engaged and mutually engageable. We are joined in a conversational space. We meet as authors who, although culturally entangled, are more than collective entities or cultural products. We meet as agents in our own destinies, as transformers of our own experience. Storytelling and stories, and more generally, works and the making of works, may be only imperfectly inclusive, but they have an expanding effect. They stretch us. Through them our boundaries are opened. We are in urgent need of such spanning activities. They need to be central to what we do in school at all levels. In our times, children need to have the space to dance with others. In our times, children need to have the room to differ.

NOTES

[1] I am indebted to James Clifford for his 1988 discussion of these ideas. See especially the Introduction, "The Pure Products Go Crazy," and Part III, "Collections."

[2] I am indebted to Margaret Himley (in press) for this phrase and for ongoing discussions of its implications associated with her manuscript, *Shared Territory: Understanding Children's Writing as Works*.

REFERENCES

Boulding, E. (1989, April). *Maintaining Individual Personhood While Relating to a Diverse World*. Unpublished address delivered at an educational forum, "Educating for Value in a Democracy," sponsored by Friends Select School, Philadelphia.

Carini, P. F. (1988). "Another Way of Looking." From *Education for Democracy*, Edited by K. Jervis and A. Tobier. Weston, MA: The Cambridge School.

Clifford, J. (1988). *The Predicament of Culture, Twentieth Century Ethnography, Literature, and Art*. Cambridge, MA: Harvard University Press.

Fussell, P. (1977). *The Great War and Modern Memory*. New York: Oxford University Press.

Himley, M. (in press). *Shared Territory: Understanding Children's Writing as Works*. New York: Oxford University Press.

Jencks, C. (1987). "Genes and Crime." In *New York Review of Books*, February 12, pp. 33–41.

Paz, O. (1987). *Convergences*. New York: Harcourt, Brace, and Jovanovich.

Rolvaag, O. E. (1927). *Giants in the Earth*. New York: Harper and Row.

3

Urban Conversations
MARIANA GASTÓN
BRUCE KANZE
DONALD MURPHY

A PARENT'S RESPONSE TO TRACKING
MARIANA GASTÓN

Until my first child was five years old, I was unaware how pervasive tracking was in the public schools. My obliviousness amazes me now, but this was my first child. I had never felt the tracking issue so deeply until it involved my own flesh and blood. When my son was ready for kindergarten, I was committed to public school because I wanted him to be with other black and Latino children. District #15, where I live, requires its children to attend the school within their designated zone. Nothing in my zone was acceptable to my family, so I looked for ways to get our child into another school, even one where we didn't belong.

My husband and I decided that we did not want our child in a gifted program. We felt that the public school system uses gifted programs to hold the children who would otherwise go to a private school. Usually the race and class composition of gifted programs is reflective of predominantly white and middle-class families with only a few black and Latino children. These programs often teach children that they are better than anyone else; this attitude may breed arrogance, and, certainly, the pressure placed on the children can lead to anxiety.

Making a decision about a school turned out to be difficult. During this period, we debated our decision with many friends who had children going into the public schools. My friends were willing to live with the arrogance in order to give their kids what they thought was quality education. Our friends kept reminding us that these gifted programs have a lot of enrichment—advantages such as computers, other tangibles, and the best teachers. Teachers of the gifted are rewarded by being given less stressful teaching situations and more support. This, in turn, motivates them to attend workshops and addi-

32

tional training, which enables them to be better teachers. My impression is that lower track teachers experience greater stress and burn out, and have less energy to invest in further training. Regular programs and regular teachers were seen as not so good by parents.

I thought long and hard about this decision. I was not going to risk my first child's education for my perceptions of society's problems. I could see the truth in my friends' position that they wanted their children to have a good education; I did not want to place my child in a program where he would receive anything less.

I also needed an afterschool program. The closest school with a good reputation and an afterschool program was one that my child could even walk to, but it was not in my zone. This school was guarded by the PTA. I naively asked one of these parents about the possibility of sending my son there. She bristled and gave me a long speech about how overcrowded the school was and how phony addresses would be discovered. I was not going to get into a major confrontation with aggressive middle-class parents; I just wanted an education for my child.

Parents of children in my son's daycare told me about a small neighborhood school 20 blocks away where addresses were not so carefully checked. I learned who was the "best" teacher there and I decided to go with this choice.

When I walked into the first parent meeting for this teacher's class and saw that most of the parents were white, I knew that this disproportion must mean some kind of differentiation. In a casual New York way, I asked, "Can you give me the ethnic composition of the class?" The principal jumped out of her chair and in an agitated manner said, "We're not answering those kinds of questions here." That answer took me aback, and confirmed my instincts. This was a group self-selected by economics, race, and class. Children were in this group based not on test scores, but on what parents looked like, how parents talked, and what parents asked for. In a school with a minority working class and poor population, a kindergarten composed disproportionately of children from white professional families *is* tracked. This tracking by race and class is even more pernicious than tracking by test scores. But there I was with no other choices.

I was impressed with the teacher and happy that my child was in her class. I wanted my child with other Latino and black children in an integrated classroom, but there were no other options for him at that school. I did nothing to change his situation because he had friends and he was learning, even though there were no blocks, no clay, no easels, no dramatic play (the tracking in New York City, after all, is also about achievement in the old traditional way with pencil and paper). For the next three years, my child was with the same children who had been in his kindergarten. The one other Puerto Rican child in the class was his friend. I knew something had to be done to change the situation.

For three years some of the school parents attempted to influence what was happening in the classrooms. We met with the superintendent and the principal, and arranged meetings between the school board member in charge of the school and the principal. We successfully wrote a proposal to bring new state funds into the school for creative arts in *all* classrooms. Parents interviewed and hired the person to direct this program, specifying that these extra resources could not be manipulated by the principal for sole use by the primarily white upper track. The principal welcomed our efforts for the publicity it generated and the entire population of the school benefited. We received books and staff training. Someone even presented a workshop about teaching with blocks right in the school. But the teachers and the principal were basically immovable about spreading the school's resources around. Tracking by race and class was still the issue.

A group of us began to meet in each other's homes. We wanted a school that people could be proud of, and where parents could have a voice. We wanted a school that would be committed to all the children, not just the high achievers who were grouped together. We hoped that the school could serve as an example of a viable public school in New York City. This group of parents began to establish contacts with other alternative schools so we could learn from them.

We began to think about founding another school. About 15 or so parents drafted an educational statement: the school would be multicultural, with mixed-ability groups and no tracking. We had to demonstrate to the school board that this project interested families in the neighborhoods throughout District #15. I directed the effort to inform and recruit parents in minority neighborhoods. I knew that if we didn't make a special effort, these minority parents would never know about us. We leafleted and showed videos in people's homes of Central Park East. If the proposed school did not explicitly reach out to minority parents, it would be an exclusive school.

The school board approved funds for us to do a financial feasibility study that would determine if the school could be established without becoming a financial burden to the city. We were getting closer to founding a school. More middle-class white parents became interested, and I vividly remember the meeting on establishing guidelines for multicultural representation in our school. We started thinking in percentages: one-third black, one-third Latino, and one-third white. How could we guarantee that mix and make it happen? Minority parents were clearly not as involved as white middle-class parents. Some people felt we were too close to project approval to let this opportunity slip by simply because we had an overrepresentation of white parents. At the time, some of us were unaware of the importance of insisting on a guaranteed process for assuring a heterogeneous school population in terms of race and class. But we did insist. Some of us took the stand that we would not open the school until it reflected the ethnic population of New York City.

We wanted to prove that good progressive education works with a regular public school population. If we opened with primarily white middle-class students, we would not be making the point that this school could lead the way for public education in Brooklyn. We won that point by increasing recruitment efforts in minority neighborhoods and developing a policy requiring the school population to reflect the ethnic composition of the district. Though we had originally aimed for 60 percent Latino, 20 percent black, and 20 percent white, we reached a compromise of one-third black, one-third Latino, and one-third white. We designed a lottery weighted for ethnicity, gender, and neighborhood, which we found to be associated with socioeconomic status. It was very risky—my child was one of the last children accepted and, thanks to the sibling preference policy, he pulled in his brother. I was nervous, but we were trying to be as fair as possible so that people wouldn't feel that we were just working for ourselves.

The school has been open for four years and we are still struggling with the same issues. The ratios are the same: one-third black, one-third Latino, and one-third white. White parents apply in great numbers, but in order to maintain our diverse population, we continue to recruit minority parents *intensely.* If alternative schools do not reach out to parents who don't know about them, these small schools will remain the province of white middle-class families, and these schools will be tracked forever.

CULTURAL KNOWLEDGE

Bruce Kanze

Curriculum is a powerful tool for creating awareness and understanding across racial and cultural lines in a classroom. I've been teaching for 20 years in the New York City Public School system, the first 11 of those years in a segregated school in an integrated neighborhood on the West Side of Manhattan. The juxtaposition of a segregated school, within a diverse neighborhood in which parents who could exercise a choice placed their children somewhere else, created a negative image in the minds and hearts of the students. For the last nine years, I've taught fifth and sixth graders at Central Park East, an integrated school within the segregated community of East Harlem. Here, too, the existence of our school within a community that is flavored with Latin culture has profoundly affected what goes on inside the classroom.

In our school, the curriculum is the classroom. As progressive teachers, we make deliberate choices about what we want to present to children. We teach by extending children's understanding through questioning, but only after we listen to the children's own questions and comments. Our teaching does not routinely precede experience, but grows out of close work with children through ongoing observation of their needs and interests. Our understanding guides our choices of new experiences and our knowledge about each child makes it possible for students to do the best work they can. We are concerned about each child's development in a broad sense; when curriculum is confined within narrow academic limits, you don't see the whole child.

I am a white teacher. The experience I am about to relate demonstrated for me how deeply racist attitudes affect the thinking of children of all races, and how powerful the classroom can be in helping children bring their feelings out and learn from each other. When these feelings are brought into the open through specific experiences, they can be dealt with consciously in a safe environment, and become part of the curriculum.

Last year, I took my class on a trip to visit pen pals in a wealthy suburban community. We were somewhat bowled over during our three days there by the resources at the school and the homes in which our pen pals lived. When we got back to East Harlem, we offered our pen pals reciprocity, inviting them to stay with us in New York City. We didn't expect them to say, "Yes, we would like to visit East Harlem," but we did want them to come. When I got a phone call from the teacher saying they would visit for one day, I asked the class what they would like to do with their pen pals. The suggestions were "Let's go downtown," and "We'll show them Broadway and Lower Manhattan." I told the class that we wouldn't have enough time to go that far and suggested instead that we take a walking tour of East Harlem. To a person, the children were floored by this suggestion. "Why would you want to show them East Harlem? All they would see is run down buildings in a slum."

I asked the kids, "What does El Barrio mean?" Many of them had lived in El Barrio most of their lives, and most had received their entire education here. Most of the kids said El Barrio means "slum." It doesn't—it means "community" or "neighborhood," and it can also mean "a place where Puerto Rican culture is maintained." I had to ask myself what this prevailing attitude said about our school and the values we were unconsciously passing on to the children. I began to consider developing a curriculum that would help to reverse this overwhelmingly negative attitude. What could we do as a class?

The following school year, we began a study of the culture and language of East Harlem. This is a community in which many of the street signs are in Spanish and business is conducted in Spanish. We began to research the famous people of Harlem and found out that a lot of the important people were parents of the children in our class or people who worked in the school. We interviewed these people and learned about their literature, their music, their foods, as well as their memories of life in the community and the forces affecting them. When we wanted information about changes in the neighborhood over the past 50 years, or about reasons why people migrate from one place to another, we asked members of the children's families to come in and tell us about their personal experiences. They told us the stories they remembered their parents telling them when they were young. Once, when I read a traditional Puerto Rican folktale to the class, a girl went home and tape-recorded her grandmother's version of the same story. The grandmother had remembered hearing it at home when she was young. The story was told in Spanish and the young girl labored at translating it into English and making a book to share with the class. Often, when visitors who spoke Spanish came to our school, the children became the proud translators. All of us learned the names of Latino foods and cooked them whenever we could. We developed our own Latino cookbook. We searched out the museums in our neighborhood: some of them were formal museums; others were old buildings that contained years of memories. We dealt with our community as a valued laboratory for learning about the lives of the people around us and, in the process, the children's lives became more important. When the children had collected stories and developed strong feelings about what they had learned—so different from what they had known and thought originally about East Harlem—we created a museum about the community and invited every student in the school. At the sixth grade graduation, the students put together an exhibit of their favorite photographs of East Harlem.

Another part of our study involved an ongoing program that we started with a nearby senior citizens' center. Our children went there to learn sewing, cooking, woodworking, knitting, and tailoring from senior citizens who live near our school. The children learned to make "Negritas," which are black dolls from the Caribbean. They learned from, talked to, and became fast friends with the seniors. They shared the seniors' stories with classmates back at school. Friendships became so close that we all celebrated Three Kings Day (the traditional Puerto Rican celebration of Christmas) together with a big feast. The seniors dressed up as the three kings and told us stories about their holidays as children. They exchanged gifts with the children on St. Valentine's Day and were invited to our graduation ceremony.

What was the message we were giving to children through this study? First, there was a real immediacy to studying the children's own community. Everything that they had ever seen took on a new meaning and importance. When the children saw that the school valued the learning that goes on at home, they also saw that they were learning all the time. At least as important was the fact that by studying a predominantly poor Puerto Rican neighborhood, we were challenging many of the racial and cultural stereotypes that are so pervasive, even among children of color. The ultimate benefit was that children of many cultural backgrounds learned to value and accept one another. Cultural acceptance can and should be a direct part of children's knowledge. I remember a Puerto Rican student talking tentatively about his father's music; his father loved salsa (a lively, saucy type of Latin music) and had a large collection of tapes. The student asked if I would like him to bring in some tapes, and I said I thought it was a good idea, if his father didn't mind. Well, the music came in, and salsa became the music of our parties. The boy who brought in the music understood just how wonderful all of us felt his music was, and he felt proud.

The current political climate is so full of conflict and competition. There are some who feel that emphasizing one culture or group of related cultures diminishes other cultures. I feel the opposite. The in-depth study of the Latino culture shows how diverse and rich a culture is and gives starting points for others to say, "Wow, we have stories like that, too," or "We cook something similar," or "Our families had a rough time, too." Every child can begin to ask family members questions (that is, in fact, what happened in our class) whether the child is white, African–American, Native American, Latino, or a member of one of the many other cultures that exist within a public school.

TRANSFORMING SCHOOLS, TRANSFORMING TEACHERS
Donald Murphy

There is no simple solution to restructuring urban schools. The efforts are complex and may not work. Trying to transform schools within the existing structure is a contradictory process. Not only are we talking about changing structure, but about changing people. It is also problematic to attempt to bring people together to begin a new school. I hope the partial lessons gleaned from my experience can help other teachers anticipate contradictions they will confront in restructuring their already existing schools.

In retrospect, I can see that starting a new school requires teachers who share a common philosophy. When we are isolated in our classrooms, working within a school administered from the top down, we don't have to deal with the issues of how to choose books and how to organize our classrooms. Nobody questions us. But when we talk about starting new schools within old schools, all these issues come to the fore.

By all standard measurements P.S. 189 was an excellent school. Located in the economically disadvantaged Crown Heights neighborhood of Brooklyn, it had been ranked number one in the district for the last 10 years on the city-wide tests. But the teachers and the principal didn't see that as excellence. The principal would say, "Our kids may be good test takers, but they aren't critical thinkers; they aren't engaged in their own learning." The teachers agreed. Beneath the surface of a good school the signs of decreased teacher morale and burnout from the practice of test taking, rote learning, and worksheet education were beginning to show. Teacher frustrations were voiced more and more regularly: "What kind of students are we creating? What is the purpose of education?" Finally, we needed a meeting to discuss this.

The educators who later came to comprise the Center for Cooperative Learning began to meet in the spring of 1987. At the first meeting, over 30 staff members, out of a total of 70, asked questions like, "How can we excite students to become active learners?" and "How can we invigorate teachers to want to teach and stimulate their own desire to learn?" We agreed to continue meeting on Fridays after school. As I recall, no one wanted to chair the meetings, so we just sat and waited for the principal to arrive. The group became smaller as each week passed. We spent the rest of the spring working on a thematic approach to curriculum and on goals for our students. By the end of July, we had completed an integrated curriculum on Human Rights and a preliminary consensus of our objectives. We wanted to encourage students to:

- become critical thinkers
- work independently
- create a democratic classroom
- view themselves as the subjects of history
- value diversity of thought
- learn through personal curiosity
- use reading and writing as tools of learning.

What began as a group born of frustration became a fairly stable core of about 15 to 17 teachers in the fall of 1987. We read and discussed articles on education, receiving credit from Fordham University through staff development funding. As fall turned to winter, the principal began to pull back from the group. The meetings became somewhat disorganized, the agenda often unclear, and the discussions of reading materials less systematic and penetrating. By spring we had yet to find a mechanism to overcome these problems and the meetings continued in a disorderly fashion.

In February, as a turnabout, the principal sent a memo to the staff suggesting, that we were "ready to begin making plans to create a small school within our larger one," and enlisted assistance from a professor who attended several meetings that spring. As a long-term agenda item, I had proposed that we run our own school within a school. Almost accidentally, people agreed. Two of our group members were named co-directors. As the year came to an end, we all agreed that in the next year we would, in fact, become a teacher-run "school within a school." Looking back, I realized that we lacked a clear idea of the far-reaching implications of our decision. We also did not understand the myriad of pedagogical, organizational, and administrative tasks that we would be called upon to shoulder. We did not anticipate, despite our consensus statement, how the lack of a common vision or philosophy of education would stand in our way.

Because we had no experience in developing and running a teacher-led school, Susan Harmon, a consultant to alternative schools, and I wrote a three year grant for technical assistance over that summer. This $75,000 grant sent morale skyrocketing.

We came back in the fall faced with the operation of our school. We had 15 teachers and 360 students, 99 percent black and Hispanic. We had classes in French, Spanish, Creole, and English. For a lot of teachers it was really frightening. Many teachers continued running to the principal to get approval for this, that, and the other idea. As the year progressed, we had sharp disagreements with each other. The tension increased because we found that people were in the group for different reasons. Some didn't believe in the idea of a teacher-run school after all. Others didn't bargain for teacher empowerment because it meant assuming administrative responsibilities which violated the spirit of the union contract—for those teachers, it meant setting back the struggle to turn the work over to administrators. Another contentious issue was peer review. When we were talking about teacher evaluation, some teachers said, "No, we don't want the principal to evaluate us. We'll do that." Some members felt peer review was divisive and that evaluation was the prerogative of the principal. Others felt that peer review was the professional way of physicians, attorneys, and accountants. We also argued strenuously about report cards and how to evaluate student learning.

Our first year was characterized by a strenuous effort to forge a community of learners—both teachers and students—with a common vision and sense of purpose. Throughout the year we continually developed and refined methods of handling interpersonal contradictions. Fifteen teachers, with their own styles and approaches, were thrown together for the first time in a situation that had gone beyond discussion. People cried, argued fiercely, and walked out of meetings. Both coordinators offered to resign on more than one occasion. But during the process of that struggle we began to realize what it meant to run our own school.

There has been no radical or drastic overhaul of classroom practice, but some teachers started alternative methods of assessment and others focused on the integration of various disciplines. A number of teachers rejected basal readers and implemented a whole-language approach to literacy. Mainly, teachers raised questions without any clear resolution. Authority was granted to teachers who had no experience with administrative power. Sometimes they were uneasy and insecure. Teachers in this school are still struggling with the same issues.

Many reform efforts in New York have been initiated by parents and progressive educators with some political vision and pedagogical methodology. Unlike some alternative schools, our project did not start with a collective philosophy or a clear idea of what a school should look like. Teachers began with the concern that students were good test takers, but not creative or critical thinkers. The frustration and refusal to leave well enough alone, and our desire to help students flower intellectually motivated us to seek change. The teachers at P.S. 189 typify the majority of teachers in the New York City system. If schools are going to be restructured with current staff members, the contradictions we faced will have to be resolved.

4

DEMOCRACY, PROGRESSIVISM, AND THE COMPREHENSIVE HIGH SCHOOL

MARVIN LAZERSON

For most of the twentieth century, Americans were fairly satisfied with their high schools. Although there had been criticism, the local high school was a source of some pride for the majority of communities. Until the last decade, most Americans viewed the comprehensive public high school as both a democratic and a progressive institution.

"Democratic" and "progressive" had quite distinctive meanings, however. A democratic high school referred to a secondary school that was widely available and that offered a wide range of curricular and extracurricular choices. Almost anyone who desired secondary education could have it. The public high school was also democratic because it expressed the values and desires of local communities. It was in this sense populist, an institution with which members of the community could identify. The progressive nature of secondary education flowed from these notions of democracy. For large numbers of people, such an education was practical, and offered diversity based upon students' needs, desires, and capabilities.

Even those most optimistic about the American high school understood that there were many ways in which secondary education was neither democratic nor progressive. Select high schools existed that were unavailable to most youths. Some school curricula were so tightly structured and limited as to preclude a diversity of course offerings and options. Some secondary schools were not a source of pride and identity in their local communities. Adults and students regularly complained about the lack of practicality in school courses, and the limited adjustments to students' needs and desires. But these criticisms did not reflect the dominant attitudes toward public secondary schooling. The practice and ideology of secondary education between 1900 and the 1970s called for schools with open enrollment, communal values, a varied curriculum, and an extensive extracurriculum. That was the kind of secondary educational institution Americans wanted, and that is what they got.

This discussion raises two questions. The first has to do with how Americans came to identify secondary education as democratic and progressive in the ways I have described. The second focuses on why this kind of democratic and progressive secondary schooling has become so controversial in the last decade. Let me start with the first question by sketching out how partial notions of democracy and progressivism came together in the first half of this century to create the comprehensive high school.[1]

Between 1900 and 1940, the high school went from being a relatively minor institution that probably enrolled less than 10 percent of the 14- to 18-year-old population to one that enrolled more than two thirds of that age group. The process whereby more youths came to stay in school for longer and longer periods of time was complicated. Young people were both pushed out of the labor market and attracted into schools. Technology eliminated traditional youth jobs and created new jobs for adults. In the 1930s, the virtual disappearance of a youth labor market accelerated the trend toward staying in school. Rising surplus income prior to this time allowed families to keep their adolescent children in school. Child labor and compulsory attendance laws made it more difficult for employers to hire young people and gave secondary education a legitimacy it had not previously had. The economic desirability of college attendance increased, enhancing the high school's holding power. In a powerful way, the high school became home for a new culture—the adolescent peer group—bringing youth together for an array of social activities. By the end of the 1930s, the secondary school had become the centerpiece of an increasingly powerful culture and an educational ladder that extended from early childhood through higher education. The high school was the central institution in defining equality of educational opportunity and the place for young people to be.

This was a significant change from the nineteenth century, when most high schools were small and unstandardized. The gamut of institutions then labeled high schools included a grade or two tacked on to elementary schools, private and quasipublic academies, the preparatory departments of colleges, short-term normal schools for training local teachers, as well as four-year public high schools. In the last quarter of the century, it became clear that school districts were entitled to use tax resources for secondary education. To a great extent, high schools did not provoke much interest among Americans; few youths attended, even fewer graduated. Going to secondary school was not a requirement for jobs, nor was it necessary to graduate from one to enter college. In 1880, less than 3 percent of the country's 17-year-olds were high school graduates. Most youths left school between ages 12 and 13. Secondary education was not on their agenda.

This all changed during the first half of the twentieth century. The nature of the changes were reflected in and propelled by that extraordinary document on secondary education, the report of the Commission on the Reorganization of Secondary Education published in 1918. Commonly referred to as the "Cardinal Principles of Secondary Education," the report's message was that mass secondary education would become a reality only if it was based upon the practical results of attending school. The usefulness of any high school activity should be evaluated. The measuring rod was the activity's contribution to the seven cardinal principles: health, command of fundamental processes (basic literacy and numeracy), worthy home membership, vocation, citizenship, worthy use of leisure, and ethical character.

The Cardinal Principles gave legitimacy to the dramatic changes high schools were then undergoing: secondary schooling was to be defined by practical results, by its contributions to society and the individual. Of these contributions, none was considered more central than training for occupations. In the first three decades of the century, the vocational education movement achieved enormous popularity. It represented a shift from earlier traditions of schooling focused on work habits and skills like ciphering and penmanship that would be useful to occupational success to a much more systematic preparation of youth directly for occupations. Secondary education in the nineteenth century had always been justified as opening avenues to occupations—commercial pursuits for boys and teaching for girls—but had never been so explicitly or so comprehensively identified with job training.

Vocational education's popularity as a reform movement drew upon more than its appeal to job training. Like other reforms affecting secondary schooling, it was also viewed as a way to curb a host of social and economic ills, from countering a shortage of skilled labor and reducing labor strife to eliminating high school dropouts and opening avenues of upward mobility, thus enhancing equality of educational opportunity. The vocational movement, which reached its formal high point in 1917 with the passage of the Smith–Hughes Act providing federal funds for vocational training, had the effect of making vocational courses a basic feature of the high school curriculum. After 1920, debate virtually ceased about whether vocational preparation was a valid purpose of schooling and instead shifted to questions about the effectiveness of vocational programs. But beyond enrollments in specifically defined vocational courses, which were never as attractive to boys as the reformers hoped, lay a much more fundamental shift—schooling had come to be defined in terms of its ability to pay off. As George Counts (1926) reported in his study of the high school curriculum: "Those who administer the high schools...admit that the great motive back of high school attendance is the belief on the part of both pupil and parent that the high school is a means of giving access to preferred occupations and favored social positions" (p. 131).

The vocationalization of secondary schooling that occurred in the decades after the turn of the century was only part of a series of major shifts in the high school, including the rapid proliferation of courses within the curriculum, the tremendous growth of the extracurriculum, and the incorporation of secondary schooling into an integrated educational ladder reaching through a variety of post-secondary institutions. What was involved and how these changes became defined as democratic and progressive can be best understood by looking at one particular high school—that described by Robert and Helen Lynd (1929) in *Middletown*—the Muncie, Indiana, high school of the early 1920s.

Robert Lynd's search for a community that would exemplify social solidarity took him to Muncie, a small-sized city of around 35,000 inhabitants that he viewed as representative of contemporary American life and small enough to study. At a time when the population of many large American cities was more than 50 percent foreign-born, Lynd chose a community in which 92 percent were native-born white, 2 percent were foreign-born, and 6 percent were black. Even here, Lynd did not find social solidarity; the city was divided between the working class and business class, and not necessarily typical of American society. But Lynd did find a comprehensive high school that had many of the most important attributes then coming to dominate American secondary education. He viewed this high school through the lenses of courses he had taken at Teachers College from such progressive educators as William Kilpatrick and John Dewey just prior to undertaking the Middletown study (Fox, 1983).

When the Lynds (1929) addressed education in Middletown, they concentrated their attention on the high school, for that was where the most extraordinary changes had occurred. While Middletown's population had increased by three and one half times between 1890 and 1920, high school enrollment had grown eleven times greater, and the number of graduates had increased nineteenfold. At least 75 percent, and probably more than 80 percent, of the city's 14- to 15-year-olds were enrolled by the mid-1920s. The 14 high school graduates in 1890 amounted to one of every 810 persons in the city; in 1924, the 236 graduates equalled one of every 161 persons, and over a third of the graduates continued on to college or normal school. "So general is the drive towards education in Middletown today," the Lynds reported, "that, instead of explaining why those who continue in high school or even go on to college do so, as would have been appropriate a generation ago, it is simpler today to ask why those who do not continue their education fail to do so" (p. 184). (The Lynds' answer was financial necessity and "the formal, remote nature of much school work" [p. 185].)

The high school curriculum had also changed. From 1889 to 1990, a student chose between two four-year programs of study, the Latin and the English program, with the primary difference between them being whether one took Latin or not. The total number of courses offered that year was twenty. From 1923 to 1924, a student chose from one of 12 different programs of study: General, College Preparatory, Music, Art, Shorthand, Bookkeeping, Applied Electricity, Mechanical Drafting, Printing, Machine Shop, Manual Arts, and Home Economics. The number of courses offered that year was 102.

The expansion of the curriculum was matched by changes within subjects. English, the subject that consumed the most student hours, was no longer compulsory for students over all four years as it had been earlier. Instead, it was required for the first two years; then, depending upon one's course of study, English might be required, but was likely to take the form of commercial English (as was the case for seven of the 12 courses of study). As to the subject matter in English, the Lynds (1929) describe it as "ordeals from which teachers and pupils alike would apparently gladly escape" (p. 193), quoting one English teacher as follows: "Thank goodness, we've finished Chaucer's *Prologue!* I am thankful and the children are, too. They think of it almost as if it were in a foreign language, and they *hate* it" (p. 193).

The most dramatic curriculum change, what the Lynds called "the most pronounced region of movement" (p. 194), occurred with the proliferation of vocational preparation courses. These had become the "darling of Middletown's eyes" (p. 195), save for a small number of teachers and students who complained, much like today's critics, that the vocational orientation was diminishing the high school's role as a college preparatory school by lowering academic standards. "A generation ago," the Lynds reported, "a solitary optional senior course in bookkeeping was the thin entering wedge of the trend that today controls eight of the twelve courses [of study] of the high school" (p. 194). The centrality of vocational training to secondary education was articulated by the president of Middletown's school board: "For a long time all boys were trained to be President. Then for a while we trained them all to be professional men. Now we are training boys to get jobs" (p. 194). Had he been inclined to acknowledge their existence, he would have added that with the growth of enrollments in stenography, typing, bookkeeping, and home economics, preparation for jobs in the household and outside of it was also the expectation of schooling for girls.

The creation of the extracurriculum paralleled the curriculum changes. High schools had always supplemented the formal curriculum with activities such as debating, drama, literacy clubs, and from the 1890s on some boys' sports. But by the 1920s, the extracurriculum had become so formidable as to be referred to by the Lynds (1929) as "school life." "Today," they wrote, "the school is becoming not a place to which children go from their homes for a few hours daily but a place from which they go home to eat and sleep" (p. 211).

Athletics, clubs, sororities and fraternities, dances and parties—these were the things students liked best about going to school. These activities were also of primary importance to Middletown's citizenry. The high school's boys' athletic program in particular held the community's attention. In 1890 there were no high school athletic teams; in the mid-1920s, the basketball season produced a frenzy of excitement within and outside the school. Indeed, the basketball team was the centerpiece of civic loyalty. As the Lynds (1929) wrote: "Today more civic loyalty centers around basket-ball than around any other one thing. No distinctions divide the crowds which pack the school gymnasium for home games and which in every kind of machine crowd the roads for out-of-town games. North Side and South Side, Catholic and Kluxer, banker and machinist—the one shout is, 'Eat 'em, beat 'em, Bearcats!'" (p. 485). Much of Middletown's community identified with and took pride in these and the other extracurricular activities that engaged their youth.

Middletown's high school was similar to other comprehensive secondary schools around the United States. The patterns there were becoming more embedded in the structure of secondary education as the century progressed. Trends fundamental to the American notion of a democratic educational institution included: school life's greater inclusiveness, the curriculum's greater immediacy (for example, civics and personal development courses were becoming the focus of the social studies curriculum), assessment of program quality on the basis of its relationship to the job market (and later to college admission), the differentiated curriculum and curricular choice, and the perception of the school as an expression of the community's pride.

The progressive nature of Middletown lay in the enlargement of the school's domain and the elaboration of responsibility across an extraordinary array of adolescent activities. Indeed, given the confusion and uncertainty parents felt about childrearing, it appears that the high school was under constant pressure to do even more, to assume an even larger place in adolescent life. But progressivism in Middletown had a second dimension that involved a shift away from what was called "subject pattern domination," the view that academic disciplines tended to impose a tyranny on learning by demanding that teaching be rooted in the logic of a discipline. By shifting its curriculum toward the practical and the personal, Middletown could rightly claim that it was rejecting the tyranny of the academic disciplines. This was a progressivism that built upon utility.

The third dimension of that progressivism involved enlarging the realm of choice, and allowing for diversity in the curriculum and the differentiation of students based on interest, abilities, and needs. The high school curriculum was not electivism gone rampant; all of the twelve courses of study had a number of required courses. But in contrast to what had existed before, the notions that curricular differentiation and expanded course offerings were essential to the good high school were already well established.

Despite some criticism, it appears that the people of Middletown were proud of their high school. It seemed to be a reflection of the varied and conflicting expectations of their community. Although the Lynds never asked the question, I believe that had they done so, they would have discovered that the people of Middletown viewed their high school as democratic and progressive.[2]

If Middletown and the thousands of high schools like it appeared democratic and progressive, and seemed to engage the high regard of their communities, what happened to make them such targets of criticism? Since the mid-1950s, secondary education has faced harsher criticism than at any time since the turn of the century. The criticism has been bifurcated—the high school viewed as too progressive and excessively democratic, *and* as insufficiently progressive and democratic. How are we to understand these attacks?

The nature of the criticism and Middletown itself provide part of the answer. By the late 1920s, the high school was already becoming an all-encompassing institution. There was almost no purpose which secondary education could not address. Some specific programs might affront enough members of a community to restrict their implementation—sex education courses, for example. But the elaboration of an institution designed to treat the "whole person," to provide for intellectual, social, personal, and emotional growth by adding responsibilities, led communities and educators to deal with the tensions inherent in trying to be all things to all people by simply adding more. "More is better" became the prevailing ideology and practice of secondary education.

In practice, of course, there was always tension and ambivalence over these all-embracing tendencies. Some teachers and parents in Middletown complained that vocational education classes were undermining academic standards for the college bound. Some questioned whether the comprehensive social life found in the school—where the power of the peer group was consolidated—was overwhelming parental authority. The elongation of adolescence that went with extended secondary schooling exaggerated tensions over dependency and increased the ambivalence parents felt toward their teenagers—the Lynds labeled them "junior adults"—whose primary obligation to their families was to do well at school. The confused relationships between parents and teenagers led Middletown's parents to seek in the schools greater certitude, hoping that they would be firm places of discipline. But in so doing, they asked the impossible and increased their own insecurities. As the high school added more and more responsibilities, parents became more insecure and more prepared to lash out at the school's failure to affirm parental authority and worth.

Two other conditions further exacerbated the likelihood of conflict over schooling. The first lay in the expectation that secondary education would lead to economic success. The second lay in the expectation that the high school would create social solidarity and a common citizenship. Economic success and civic patriotism were essential to the high school's place in the community.

The first was paramount. For many parents of Middletown's youth, this was what the high school was all about. The economic returns of schooling justified the trials and tribulations of family life, and the day-in and day-out struggle to make a living. Parents in Middletown expected that children staying in school would have a better life. Over and over, the Lynds (1929) found both parents working with the hope that their children would continue in school. A business class mother reported: "The two boys want to go to college, and I want them to. I graduated from high school myself, but I feel if I can't give my boys a little more all my work will have been useless" (p. 29). Another mother stated: "If children don't have a good education they'll never know anything except hard work. Their father wants them to have just as much schooling as he can afford" (p. 187). A working class father said: "I don't know how we're going to get the children through college, but we're *going* to. A boy without an education today just ain't *anywhere!*" (p. 187). Across the class spectrum, the Lynds found the same intensity. Schooling was necessary to their children's success, and therein lay the legitimacy of sacrifice.

This economic expectation already so firmly in place in Middletown was rapidly becoming a *raison d'etre* of schooling. It was fundamental to why Americans placed so much hope in the school, to why they were so willing to allow the extraordinary elaboration of responsibilities by the secondary school. It was at the heart of the view that the school was a democratic institution. But it was also an expectation that opened the school to the deepest hostility. Parents began to believe that the school was not enhancing economic opportunity for their children. They believed, for instance, that they saw discrimination against their children, academic standards too lax to allow their children to get into the best colleges, decisions being made to boost other people's children at the expense of one's own. This belief that schooling was not being translated into personal economic gain meant that the schools were obviously not doing their job. The reforms that would be recommended would take on an edge of hostility from people who found their most cherished aims abused.

The expectations about civic solidarity were also weighted with the seeds of conflict. Much of the rationale for the extracurriculum and the proliferation of interest in the teaching of American history and civics that marked Middletown's high school exemplified the belief that schools should be "theaters of civic virtue" (Hampel, 1986).

There were two ironies about this that ultimately provided the basis for heated criticism. Social solidarity in the community and within the school was based on divisions, differentiation, and inequalities. High schools developed a host of mechanisms for distinguishing among youth. These included differentiating the curriculum, developing tracks, placing students into ability-grouped classrooms, dividing courses by gender, and keeping those of different races in separate wings of the school or requiring them to attend separate schools. If many high schools were more varied communities than those represented in segregated housing, labor markets, and recreational organizations, they nonetheless fell far short of the ideal of solidarity they claimed to be working toward. The democracy of choice within high schools was often a world divided by race, social class, gender, and age. In the 1960s, these divisions were challenged, and attempts were made to make high schools truly integrated communities in order to achieve a common and shared citizenship among equals. Those efforts fell short, leaving the reformers dissatisfied. But the attempts to increase integration also left those who had flourished in the divided high school worried and angry.

The second irony about the search for civic solidarity in the high school was that it was based on boosterism and a patriotism that denied a place for social criticism. The Lynds (1929) point out how tense Middletown's boosters were about those who criticized the town and its institutions. What Americans have meant by patriotism has a long and complicated history. But in the context of the school, what emerged was a tension between education as a process whereby youth learned to think for themselves—that was, after all, an essential feature of the entrepreneurialism that has so marked American life— and a valuing of "American first." To the extent that the latter was the dominant expectation built into the values being taught in the school, dissent and criticism were a measure of the school's failure. Not surprisingly, when youth in the 1960s and 1970s turned to social criticism, adult anger focused not simply on the young but on the institutions from which so much was expected— the secondary schools and the colleges. Social criticism was not what the adult sacrifices had been about.

There are, of course, other sources of the heated criticism of the secondary schools that have emerged in the last 25 years—the blight of our cities, the loss of identification with government and political leaders, the sharpened social class divisions, the nation's economic decline. But I think it is important to understand that the very arrangements that allowed the comprehensive high school to think of itself as democratic and progressive—its all embracing character, its commitment to the economic achievement of students, and its expectation that it would forge a common citizenship—held within it the seeds of conflict. We now fight over our proudest educational creation.

NOTES

[1] For a discussion of one high school's nineteenth century accommodation to markets and politics, see Labaree (1989).

[2] No historian, as far as I know, has made the connection between democracy, progressivism, and Middletown in precisely the terms I have done so here, but the analyses of David K. Cohen (1985), Patricia Albjerg Graham (1984), Diane Ravitch (1983), and Edward Krug (1972) are congruent with mine. Some suggestive support for this line of reasoning also comes from the brief discussions of high schools in John and Evelyn Dewey's (1915) *Schools of Tomorrow.* An alternative and much more common argument is that Middletown's high school was the antithesis of progressivism, a view strengthened by the remark of Progressive Education Association founder Stanwood Cobb that his aims were to avoid "Main Street minds, Middletown minds, mediocre minds" (Krug, 1972, p. 146). John Dewey (1984) commented on the contradictions in Middletown's values in "The

House Divided Against Itself," his review of the Lynds' book first published in the *New Republic* in 1929. See also Robert Lynd's (1930) discussion of *Middletown* in a speech to the Progressive Education Association.

REFERENCES

Cohen, D. K. (1985). "Origins." From *The Shopping Mall High School: Winners and Losers in the Educational Marketplace*. Edited by A. Powell, E. Farrar, and D. K. Cohen. Boston: Houghton Mifflin.

Commission on the Reorganization of Secondary Education (1918). Bulletin 1918, no. 35. U.S. Department of the Interior. Washington, D.C.: U.S. Government Printing Office.

Counts, G. (1926). *The Senior High School Curriculum*. Chicago: University of Chicago Press.

Dewey, J. (1984). "The House Divided Against Itself." From *John Dewey: The Later Works, 1925–1953*, Volume 5. Edited by J. A. Boydston. Carbondale: Southern Illinois University Press.

Dewey, J., and Dewey, E. (1915). *Schools of Tomorrow*. New York: E.P. Dutton.

Fox, R. W. (1983). "Epitaph for Middletown: Robert S. Lynd and the Analysis of Consumer Culture." From *The Culture of Consumption: Critical Essays in American History, 1880–1980*. Edited by R. W. Fox and T.J. Jackson Lears. New York: Pantheon.

Graham, P. A. (1984). "Schools: Cacophony About Practice, Silent About Purpose." *Daedalus* 113(4).

Hampel, R. (1986). *The Last Little Citadel: American Secondary Schools Since 1940*. Boston: Houghton Mifflin.

Krug, E. (1972). *The Shaping of the American High School, 1920–1941*. Madison, WI: University of Wisconsin Press.

Labaree, D. (1989). *The Making of an American High School*. New Haven, CT: Yale University Press.

Lynd, R. (1930). "Education and Some Realities of American Life." *Progressive Education* 7, May.

Lynd, R. S., and Lynd, H. M. (1929). *Middletown: A Study in American Culture*. New York: Harcourt, Brace, and World.

Ravitch, D. (1983). *The Troubled Crusade: American Education, 1945–1980*. New York: Basic Books.

5

THE EIGHT YEAR STUDY

KATHY IRWIN

The Eight Year Study emerged from a democratic tradition of struggle—a struggle for both change and the freedom to change. That struggle has a long history. If we stood on the steps of the original Jane Addams Hull House on Halsted Street in Chicago, we could see the outline of the Hart, Schaffner, and Marx building. Knowing the history of labor struggle in this country, we would be reminded of the battles that went on in the early years of the garment industry—in Chicago, New York, and elsewhere—to achieve adequate wages and decent working conditions.

As a pioneer in the American settlement house movement, Jane Addams found herself living and working in neighborhoods that were isolated, ethnic enclaves. Lithuanians claimed one section of Halsted, Greeks another, Italians yet another. These were people insisting upon remaining distinct and separate in terms of a positive cultural identity, yet at the same time needing to work together on the common problems of housing, work, health, and education. Hull House provided that place for working together.

One testimony of Hull House's ability to value differences while using them to build a common ground can be found in the maps drawn by community people that are today displayed in the front hallway of Hull House. Immigrants went out and canvassed the neighborhoods to discover who lived there. Their findings were then translated into beautiful color-coded maps. Today we can only imagine how such a project was organized. People from all the ethnic enclaves, speaking no common language, found the words, the time, and the energy to compile a record of who they were and where they lived.

It was a collective effort issuing from a common place. There was desperate need in those turn-of-the-century times for such common places and so, when Graham Taylor, his wife, their children, and a cluster of graduate students from the University of Chicago decided to establish a settlement house, they called it the Chicago Commons. What happened at Hull House and at the

Commons in Chicago was also what happened at the settlement houses in Boston, Baltimore, Des Moines, Jersey City, and Fort Worth. The conversation centered around human problems and the social values of a democracy that helped shape solutions to those problems. A kaleidoscopic range of people came together to exchange ideas, voice needs, and shape common action. To make the exchange as extensive and inclusive as possible was the challenge; Hull House met that challenge by numbering among its conversants such people as John Dewey, Florence Kelley, and W.E.B. DuBois, as well as Russian tailors, Italian factory workers, and Bohemian seamstresses.

When we stretch to identify a similar institution dedicated to many of the same ideals and values, only one comes immediately to mind: the common school. It comes, therefore, as no surprise that during the last decades of the nineteenth century and the early decades of the twentieth, as settlement houses cropped up in urban settings throughout the eastern and midwestern areas of America, we see as well the stirrings that were to lead to the formation of the Progressive Education Association and, in time, to the Eight Year Study organized under its auspices.

As the settlement house workers had an expansive notion of what education could do and be, so too did the pioneers of progressive education. Both were concerned with blunting the raw edges of industrial civilization and with reinvigorating the social sinews of human community. Both were concerned with discovering the forms of human association that could nurture individuality. They were concerned as well with demonstrating the necessity and efficacy of freedom as a wellspring of both individual and social growth. As the settlement house workers were impelled to deal with the destructive human consequences of harsh and mindless factory work, so the progressive educators were moved to eliminate the factory as a model for organizing the work of a classroom.

The growth of the progressive education movement really began in the years following the end of the First World War. In 1919 a group of educators organized the Progressive Education Association. In the same year, Carleton Washburne became superintendent of schools in Winnetka, Illinois, a post he held for a quarter of a century. The Winnetka Plan, which evolved under his leadership, enabled children to learn at their own pace. It eliminated failure based on age-linked standards, and placed strong emphasis on group activities that strengthened the individual school as a community (Cremin, 1964).

In this same period, Harold Rugg, director of research at the Lincoln School in New York City and professor at Columbia University's Teachers College, developed his Social Science Course—six volumes, complete with workbooks and teacher editions. The Winnetka schools were among the first to pilot the Rugg series (Rugg, 1929, 1930a, 1930b, 1931a, 1931b, 1932).

In his texts, Rugg asked students to think together about such issues as the invasion of Native American lands by the European peoples, the engineered dependence of Puerto Rico, and the contradiction of slavery as an institution in a democratic society. Not surprisingly, the series became notably controversial and was even burned in some American communities.

The explosion of experimental activities in American schools during these early years of the twentieth century is impossible to summarize in a few sentences. Perhaps the best way to capture some of the essential animating ideas of the progressive impulse is to cite the basic principles adopted by the Progressive Education Association at the moment of its birth in 1919:

1. Children should have the freedom to develop naturally.
2. The child's interests should be the basic motive for all his or her work.
3. The teacher should function as a guide, not a task master.
4. Record-keeping should serve the goal and methods of the scientific study of children's development.
5. Schools should pay equal attention to all facets of children's development, including the physical.
6. The school and the home must be active partners in meeting the needs of children.

These were the ideas and values that formed the platform for action in progressive education, the consensus that the ongoing conversation had reached by the end of the second decade of the twentieth century. That conversation continues today. Deborah Meier, founder of a cluster of new public elementary schools in New York's East Harlem, confronted the need for a high school that would be consistent with the values undergirding the new elementary schools and set about creating the Central Park East Secondary School. Her concerns echo those that led to the creation of the Eight Year Study.

The Study began as a conversation at the 1930 conference of the Progressive Education Association. Two years of further conversation followed. Initially there were no foundation dollars involved and people participated at their own expense. Beginning in 1932, support from the Carnegie Foundation and the General Education Board helped underwrite the expenses of what was called the Commission on the Relation of School and College. It was this commission, created by the Progressive Education Association, that designed and ran the Eight Year Study. Its first action was to conduct an assessment of American secondary education.

The Commission found that students were graduating with no sense of what it meant to be a citizen within a democratic social order. They found no connection between daily community life and the fundamental human values intended to guide that life. Student concerns and curricula were miles apart. Where to begin? What to change? How best to change it?

As a fundamental starting point, the Commission focused on the freedom to change. That may have been one of the wisest decisions it ever made. It was clear to the members at the time that secondary schools were most pow-erfully and extensively regulated by college admission criteria. So the Commission sought and won the agreement by some 300 colleges and universities to waive their existing criteria for graduates of an experimental group of high schools.

It was also clear to the Commission that experimentation could not and should not be the exclusive right of a few private and privileged schools; it required diversity of character, class, and geography. There is such diversity in the roster of participating public schools: Altoona Senior High School in Altoona, Pennsylvania; Roosevelt High School in Des Moines, Iowa; Tulsa Senior and Junior High Schools in Tulsa, Oklahoma; Eagle Rock High School in Los Angeles, California; and Shaker Heights High School, outside of Cleveland, Ohio, which elected to participate in the Study while still in the early stages of its own establishment as an operating school. On the private side were such schools as Francis Parker in Chicago, North Shore Country Day in the northern Chicago suburbs; several Quaker schools; lab schools at the University of Chicago, Ohio State, and University of Wisconsin; and such institutions as Milton Academy, Baldwin School, and Winsor School.

In the fall of 1933, all schools began the work of building new curricula. The process was intriguing and varied dramatically from school to school. Schools affiliated with the Progressive Education Association had been dealing explicitly with certain questions for years. What are democratic values? How do we recognize them in practice and test them publicly? How do we teach the ability to think deeply and critically about social issues and problems? How can we construct a descriptive yet dynamic portrait of a student's personality and character that will help us understand needs and actions in terms of that student's feelings and not exclusively in terms of our feelings about the student? Now, others were to join in that conversation.

Larger issues around authority and human agency arose. What were principals prepared to let teachers do? Should teachers be making decisions on course offerings? How would students help shape these same decisions?

Each school was free to pursue reconstruction on its own terms, but all agreed to be guided by two basic principles. School life and teaching method should conform to what was known about the ways in which human beings learn and grow, and the American high school "should rediscover its chief reason for existence."

At the end of a painful philosophical search, the schools concluded that their central purpose was to give students "an understanding and appreciation for the way of life we call democracy." What better path was there than to attempt to live out this appreciation within the daily ritual called school?

The struggle everywhere would be to try consciously to close the distance between belief and behavior. Distance varied. In one case, a principal walked into a faculty meeting and simply announced to his teachers that henceforth they would be involved in this thing called the Eight Year Study. Absolutely no one in the room agreed.

Then there was the principal who quite honestly said, "Look, I don't understand what all this is about. But we're going to do it anyway." He then chose four to six of those he considered the best and the brightest among the teachers and told them to take care of it.

Like charity, democracy quite literally began or did not begin at "home." It was reflected in the smallest habits of exchange, choice, and organization. The Eight Year Study educators would come to know it as an imperfect and confounding process which constantly tested values in both personal and collective ways.

The best situation was one in which the principal was confident enough to just sit down with teachers and say, "I don't know for sure what direction this Study is taking, but let's begin a conversation; let's agree to convene regularly and see where it takes us."

Once agreement was reached to participate in the Study, staff had to make arrangements to find time to work together—no mean feat, given the structure of schools. At one school, classes were dismissed at the usual hour and the entire faculty went out for an hour of exercise together. After that hour, they began reading, thinking, writing, and then concluded by having supper together. At another school, students began their day an hour later than usual and faculty used this time to meet. In every case, individuals and groups were pulling from their own resources, energies, and beliefs that the Eight Year Study was something important.

It was important, but it was also problematic, to work through just what it might mean to construct curricula that promoted a democratic way of life. Naturally, there was no immediate and shared clarity on what such a life meant or looked like. Schools found themselves proceeding without agreement but trusting that a willingness to be public and direct about any and all conflict would produce at least the amount of consensus needed for action and change.

The absence of conflict or outright confusion was never the goal. In fact, it was an acknowledged impossibility. It was enough that there was a group of people who wanted to identify democratic social values and determine what these meant for schools, wanted students to have their education in relation to one another, and wanted high schoolers to develop themselves and their understanding of themselves in relationship to the larger and immediate world.

Experimentation within a framework of ideas was the goal. There were alternatives to traditional ways of doing things, and choices had to be made. One faculty elected to take a Core Curriculum approach. They would base all curriculum on "the problems of living." Immediately, they plunged into debates over cutting across subject-matter lines, resisting cooperative planning and teaching, abandoning single periods in favor of larger blocks of time, and eliminating textbooks in favor of a wide range of source materials.

Another faculty chose the Unified Studies approach. Social Studies was to be paired with English. The result was supposed to be some shared and integrated focus. However, departmental dominance and rivalries die hard. English teachers felt trapped by history teachers who seemed to understand their discipline only in terms of sequence and chronology. What if the literature of a single period didn't make a good fit with the maturation and interest levels of the students? When would there be time for the necessary drill in grammar?

In situations where the Eight Year Study did not include the entire faculty, jealousies were aroused by teachers seen as receiving "special treatment" in the form of free periods for planning and record keeping, new materials for project use, and release time to attend meetings in distant cities.

Students in reorganized programs with two or three years of experience under the tutelage of able, progressive teachers eventually grew critical of other areas of their school experience which were more rigid and traditional. These students began talking about and criticizing the "autocrats" on the faculty.

So, as bold and fascinating as it all was, it also was a very human venture just as it would be today. Complexity and the frustration of false starts were all part of what was to be explored.

What succeeded and how was the "elbow room" that the Eight Year Study provided actually used? The English Department at Altoona High School replaced required reading lists and attendant book reports with discussion, literary parties, impersonations, and book clubs. It also designated one day a week as a free reading day—students chose their own books. "No one…read as few as the 14 books formerly required. They were reading because they wanted to read. Juniors read an average of 23 books a year" (Thirty Schools, 1943, p. 7).

A junior high school math teacher in Altoona organized a student-run insurance company that insured students against loss and damage to school books. The need to invest premiums "led to a study of banking and investment because the students had money to invest, not in order to 'learn something about banking'" (Giles, McCutcheon, and Zechiel, 1942, p. 65).

Schools in the Study recognized that "each pupil, of course, makes the decision as to what will be learned" (Giles, McCutcheon, and Zechiel, 1942, p. 77). So methods of planning evolved which supported the belief that students needed to learn how to make decisions and how to work in groups.

At Lincoln High School in Des Moines, one teacher regularly asked his class two questions at the beginning of a course: "What would you like to know about the unit we are to study?" and "What would you like to be able to do at the end of the unit that you cannot do now?" The answers helped shape both course content and method.

The Dalton School in New York City incorporated a nursery into its curriculum. Initially, students from all four high school grades worked in it. Later, inquiry revealed that the experience was more powerful for ninth graders that for any other grade—so an experimental course called "Nursery-Biology" was developed and proved so successful that it was continued.

Radnor High School in Pennsylvania addressed program needs for the noncollege-bound student by developing a senior curriculum known as the "cooperative course." These were "tryout" training opportunities for students in one or more vocational fields. Each "tryout" lasted two weeks. Local business people agreed to provide some form of introductory experience or training in their given field. These field experiences amounted to something between a part-time job and an apprenticeship, where instruction, supervision, evaluation, and reports to school were routine practice.

For years, the Francis Parker School had been operating what they called "Toy Shop" for two weeks in December. The shop made toys that were distributed to hospitals, settlement houses, and public schools in Chicago. With the Eight Year Study as an occasion for fresh thought, students and faculty decided it was time for everyone to get a little firsthand knowledge of the areas into which their products were being sent. A study of institutions and neighborhoods was begun. Groups spent five Saturdays working through one of the six Chicago settlement houses and then preparing reports on their work. Copies of student reports were sent to sponsoring agencies.

In 1936 a group of nine men, five from Ohio State University, began working around the country as consultants to the Eight Year Study. They served only at the invitation of individual schools. Scheduling was very tight—two or three days at one site, then on to the next. Each consultant had to discipline himself not to interfere with the curriculum-building process in place. There were moments when consultants reflected, "If only I had been available in 1932 or 1933, in the earliest stages of reconstruction." They did walk into situations where schools had gotten themselves onto a very sticky wicket. Their response was disciplined by the spirit of the Study: "What is happening?," "What are you most committed to?" and "What is not happening and why?"

It was not the role of a consultant to dictate or impose. Instead, the consultant assisted by having no axe to grind and no stake in the local broils. Each carried news of work in other schools. They visited classrooms, gave demonstration lessons, and served as a clearinghouse for research, ideas, and materials. Often they helped school people move their own mountains just by taking the time to leave a well-placed word of encouragement or understanding. In short, they were summoned to assist teachers in discovering their own ability to act and to change.

If the traditional pattern of college entrance requirements was not the key to how young Americans ought to be educated, then the Evaluation arm of the Study had to document the innovations. Evaluation had two focuses: one was the effect of the changes at the experimenting schools as revealed by the college performance of their graduates, the other was alternative means of tracking and assessing student progress in the experimental high schools.

The college career assessment was based on a sample of 1,500 graduates of Eight Year Study schools, beginning with the class of 1936 and ending with the class of 1939. Each graduate was matched with another student at his or her college so that comparisons could be made. Overall, the graduates of the experimenting schools did better in college than the comparison group. Moreover, the most pronounced differences were found in students who had graduated from the most radically changed experimental schools. When the graduates of the two most experimental schools were assessed, their superiority was "greater than any previous differences reported" (Chamberlin et al., 1942, p. 209).

The Evaluation Team's work in recording and appraising student progress came to be understood as integrally connected to curriculum development; the focus of the appraisal was to be the framework for curriculum experimentation and development. The Evaluation Team eventually settled on five areas of focus: *Aspects of Thinking* (logical reasoning and the ability to think critically), *Social Sensitivity* (beliefs on social and economic issues and the application of facts and generalizations to social problems), *Aspects of Appreciation* (art and literature), *Personal Interests*, and *Personal and Social Adjustment* (personality structures, effective or ineffective interactions in the social sphere).

These five dimensions marked out the areas of school life on which schools were to focus their attention. The accompanying traits and dispositions became the bond for everyone involved. Teachers learned to gather and interpret the technical data without advanced statistical qualifications. After all, they had the most sustained, personal contact with the subjects—the students—and therefore had the most immediate interest in the results.

The five volume record of the Eight Year Study was published in 1942–1943. Volume I, *The Story of the Eight Year Study* (Aikin, 1942), provides what we would call today a detailed executive summary of the whole enterprise. Volume II, *Exploring the Curriculum* (Giles, McCutcheon, and Zechiel, 1942), is an account of the curricular innovations tried and adopted. Volume III, *Appraising and Recording Student Progress* (Smith, Tyler, and the Evaluation Staff, 1942), captures the schools' struggle to find—with the help of the Evaluation Team—alternative methods of student assessment. Volume IV, *Did They Succeed in College* (Chamberlin et al., 1942), answers the question posed in the title and explains the methods by which answers were sought and found. In the fifth and final volume, *Thirty Schools Tell Their Story* (Thirty Schools, 1943), each school narrates its experience in the Study. Each volume is simply and clearly written, and reflects a conscious design to avoid educationese. The simplicity, directness, and candor of the volumes' language is at one with the sincerity of the Study's belief in democracy.

There is a renewal of interest in the Eight Year Study today because there are still progressive educators who believe that American schools must again become lively and innovative places. This destiny will not be realized by chance or by ill-conceived detours through educational trend or whimsy.

The Eight Year Study was not a banner under which all manner of research or innovation traveled. It was based on values that teachers came to believe in. Programmatic choices grew out of these values. The essential value was democracy. This feature, more than any other, sets the Study apart from contemporary movements for school reform propelled largely by vague appeals for increased test scores, increased accountability, or increased productivity. No alternative approach was selected by virtue of the popularity of the alternative. The litmus test was, and still should be, consistency with this framework of basic human values that we call democracy.

From that democratic framework flows specific imperatives for our work in schools. We think that students should be prepared to deal with—and to change if necessary—the world in which they live, and that teachers and students must be full partners in this process of preparation. We believe that we learn what we experience. If we want our students to believe that free and healthy human intelligence can prevail over discrimination, scarcity, and war, then they must learn in ways that allow them to discover that their own intelligence works best when combined with that of others.

We believe, too, that ethnic, racial, gender, and economic differences contribute positively to the development of children. We want students to explore and prize these differences. We want schools animated by those differences and dead set against any obstacle designed to frustrate the value of the contributions in any place or time. We want students who understand that learning and struggle never end and that there will always be new possibilities and new problems. We want students to act upon the notion that cooperatively generated wisdom and efficacy will meet the daily challenges of schooling and community-building.

These are not and never were abstract ideas. Eight Year Study teachers used them to move and mold classrooms, neighborhoods, and places of work and play. We need their ideas today. The Eight Year Study speaks to the present. We only have to listen.

Schools should be a further forge for democracy. The Eight Year Study proved that they *can* be. The purpose of schools is to nurture a democratic citizenry; it is not to manufacture technocrats adept at junk bond trading, corporate takeovers, and Savings and Loan bailouts, nor is it to lead America in world economic dominance. For those of us committed to the democratic tradition of struggle, the Eight Year Study is both our ancestor and friend, reminding us that the idea and broad practice of democracy must remain the centerpiece of our lives as citizens, teachers, and students.

REFERENCES

Aikin, W. M. (1942). *The Story of the Eight Year Study*. New York: Harper and Row.
Chamberlin, D., et al. (1942). *Did They Succeed In College? The Follow-Up Study of the Graduates of the Thirty Schools*. New York: Harper and Row.

Cremin, L. (1964). *The Transformation of the School: Progressivism in American Education, 1876–1957.* New York: Vintage Books.

Giles, H. H., McCutcheon, S. P., and Zechiel, A. N. (1942). *Exploring the Curriculum: The Work of the Thirty Schools from the Viewpoint of Curriculum Consultants.* New York: Harper and Row.

Rugg, H. (1929). *An Introduction to American Civilization: A Study of Economic Life in the United States.* Boston: Ginn and Company.

———. (1930a). *Changing Civilizations in the Modern World: A Textbook in World Geography with Historical Backgrounds.* Boston: Ginn and Company.

———. (1930b). *A History of American Civilization: Economic and Social.* Boston: Ginn and Company.

———. (1931a). *A History of American Government and Culture: America's March Toward Democracy.* Boston: Ginn and Company.

———. (1931b). *An Introduction to Problems of American Culture.* Boston: Ginn and Company.

———. (1932). *Changing Governments and Changing Cultures: The World's March Toward Democracy.* Boston: Ginn and Company.

Smith, E. R., Tyler, R. W., and the Evaluation Staff (1942). *Appraising and Recording Student Progress: Evaluation, Records, and Reports in the Thirty Schools.* New York: McGraw-Hill.

Thirty Schools (1943). *Thirty Schools Tell Their Story: Each School Writes of Its Participation in the Eight Year Study.* New York: Harper and Row.

6

JOHN DEWEY'S SCHOOL

JERALD KATCH

Future thought in America must go beyond Dewey...though it is difficult to see how it can avoid going through him. (Roth, 1962, p. 144)

This essay is intended to be one illustration of Roth's premise. Although the topic is Dewey's school, in a more fundamental way it concerns students' active learning, which Dewey brought to our attention. The curriculum at Dewey's school may be interesting to us now historically, but almost a century later it still raises critical questions about how children learn and about the place of child-generated activity in schools for a democratic society.

In 1894, when the University of Chicago was only two years old, its president, William Rainey Harper, invited Dewey to head a combined philosophy, psychology, and pedagogy department. Soon Dewey decided that a school was essential to evaluate his educational philosophy if his ideas were to be taken seriously. With Harper's support, he founded a separate department of pedagogy and established the University Elementary School in 1896, serving as its director until 1904. Dewey also thought a university that took the initiative in establishing a school would move to the forward ranks of educational leadership in the United States (Dewey, 1896a, p. 433).

In addition, there is some indication that Dewey had another reason for starting the school: his wife may have insisted upon it. Consider the following anecdote from Max Eastman's *Great Companions* (1942):

Dewey would never have started a Dewey School if it hadn't been for Alice Chipman [Dewey]. Dewey never did anything except to think—at least it often looked that way to Alice—unless he got kicked into it. Nothing seemed important to him but thinking. He was as complete an extrovert as ever lived, but the extroversion all took place in his head. Ideas were real objects to him, and they were the only objects that engaged his passionate interest. If he got hold of a new idea, he would sneak around the house with it like a dog with a bone, glancing up with half an eye at the unavoidable human beings and their chatter, hoping they wouldn't bother him, and that's all. Only a man of this temperament who nevertheless took human lives and problems for his subject matter could have made the contribution Dewey did.

Mrs. Dewey would grab Dewey's ideas—and grab him—and insist that something be done. She had herself a brilliant mind and a far better gift of expression than his. And she was a zealot. She was on fire to reform people as well as ideas. She had an adoring admiration of his genius, but she had also a female impatience of the cumbersome load of ideological considerations he had to carry along when arriving at a decision. Her own decisions were swift, direct, and harshly realistic....Dewey's view of his wife's influence was that she put "guts and stuffing" into what had been with him mere intellectual conclusions. (Eastman, 1942, p. 273)

This is not only provocative as an anecdote, but is telling because Dewey apparently did rely heavily on the teachers to maintain the everyday operations of the school, with his wife as teacher and later principal. Further, after Dewey left the university there is no indication that he worked regularly with a school again, which may have been a sign of his discomfort with some of that "guts and stuffing." Dewey's lack of involvement with the nitty-gritty of school life may also provide a clue as to why his philosophy did not appear to be fully coordinated with his school's practice.

Dewey's writings have given us the idea that his school evolved consistently from his thought. That was not entirely the case. For example, shortly before Dewey founded the school, he articulated a "fundamental principle" of child psychology:

The child is always a being with activities of his own, which are present and urgent and do not require to be "induced," "drawn out," or "developed," etc.; that the work of the educator, whether parent or teacher, consists solely in ascertaining and in connecting with these activities, furnishing them appropriate opportunities and conditions. (Dewey, 1895, p. 204)

But no evidence exists that children at Dewey's school could choose their subject matter or decide how to approach a teacher-chosen activity, even though Dewey's initial idea of teachers "connecting with" student activity would lead us to believe that such choices would be an integral part of the curriculum. However, there is evidence that the students did have some freedom of activity within the extensive range of flexible programs which were provided, and it is these activities which merit our interest. A vivid sense of them comes through in an article by Laura Runyon (1900) in the *Chautauguan*. She wrote as if she were a parent observer interested in enrolling her children (which she did), but by 1900 she had taught English and history at the school and eventually became its dean. She tells of being dissatisfied with letting her "children go on getting only a fiftieth part of the attention of a teacher in the public schools...." (p. 585). Her husband had heard of the "Dewey" school to which professors of the University were sending their children and so Runyon arranged a visit. Her description starts with the beginning of the school day.

> None of the children seemed to have any books as they came up. I didn't see even a geography or a reader among the older children....One child had a basket of fruit, and another a package which I heard him tell the teacher contained "sandwiches." As he gave them into her charge, a smaller boy, who had been following him, asked pleadingly, "Aren't you going to invite me, George?"
>
> I concluded that this must be an off day with the school; but thought that I might as well stay and see them start—they seemed to be having such a good time.
>
> At nine o'clock a bell rang, and the children went to various rooms, where I saw some one was marking their attendance. I was surprised to find that there were not more than ten children with any one teacher; and that instead of the absolute silence I had considered the proper beginning of school, the children merely took their places in what seemed to be a recognized order, and continued their conversation. Then the "leader" was given a program for the day.
>
> I concluded that not all were going to the picnic and that I would stay and see what I could. I followed the children to the gymnasium, where seats were arranged for the morning exercises, which consisted chiefly of singing. One or two groups of children were asked to sing their "Group Song." Upon inquiry I was told that the charming little melody and the words of the songs I heard were composed by the children who sang them. All the "leaders" as they took their groups to various rooms after the singing seemed to have programs for the day; and I concluded that the picnic had been postponed, and felt sorry for the children with the sandwiches and fruit.
>
> Upstairs I found a group of children about ten years old engaged in setting up electric bells. I recognized one of the children as a boy from our neighborhood, and wondered if I could get him to fix our bell, since we had had a sign "Please knock; bell don't [sic] ring" on the door for two days while waiting for the repair man.
>
> A group of younger children had a sheepskin from which they were taking the wool. They spread the wool out thin with their hands and let the dirt fall out, then pulled the fibers straight and wound them on a stick which they called their "distaff." One little girl who had her distaff full was spinning the wool into yarn with the help of a spindle she said she "made in the shop." Around the room were primitive looms being "warped" by the children, and I was shown designs of their own which were to be woven into small blankets. In another room I found one of the large old-fashioned looms of which I had heard but had never seen before. Two of the older boys were at work "setting it up," as they called it. (Runyon, 1900, pp. 589–590)

Later in the day Runyon sought out one of the teachers to explain the purpose of the foregoing activity.

> The teacher who had consented to enlighten me said that Dr. Dewey had
> no thought of training…factory hands, but that he believed there was an
> educational value in handling the raw materials from which our food,
> clothing, and comforts are derived, and a mental training in reinventing
> each stage of these industries. (1900, p. 591)

At this point, the visitor was beginning to get some idea of the curricular
structure, especially in the core program of history and literature. These subjects were often combined in the pursuit of understanding cultural industries
by reinventing them. Mayhew and Edwards (1936), who also had taught at the
school, provide a chronology. Stories encouraged the children to take on
occupational roles. During play, the four- and five-year-olds spontaneously
imitated household chores such as cooking, cleaning, and mending, and
neighborhood occupations such as milkman, grocer, iceman, postman, and
coalman. The six-year-olds found out about various professions by visiting
them and "became" farmers, for example, by planting and harvesting various
foods in their outdoor gardens and making models of farms, ranches, and
mills. About age seven, the children would be asked how they thought people
invented these industries and thus the investigation of primitive people would
begin, leading to such activities as the clothmaking and metal production
which have already been observed. By age eight, the children started to follow
the expansion of the new industries to different parts of the world by hearing
and reading stories about traders such as the Phoenicians and then by acting
out their own dramas about them. The nine-year-olds began to explore one
result of trade and exploration: colonization; and one area of colonization: the
local history of Chicago and surroundings. About age 10, the emphasis shifted
to colonial history and the revolution, and a year and more later the topic centered around the European background of the colonists which provided an
introduction to the study of other societies.

As might be expected, the topics of historical discussion in the school's
milieu often diverged from that accepted in conventional schools. Laura Runyon had become increasingly bewildered.

> Everywhere the children were busy, but the morning was half gone and I
> had heard nothing that reminded me of a school except a class taking
> Latin as I passed. I had heard a class discussing whether John Smith or
> George Washington were the greater man, and another group, with a
> relief map, trying to decide where it would be best to erect forts to protect
> the English colonies from the French aggressions from the north and west.
> But I always know at home when the children get on those subjects that
> they are *not* studying their lessons. I wondered why the teacher did not

tell them, if she thought it worthwhile, and then have them bound states and name the capitals and principal cities. In all the classes the children talked—sometimes two at once; but with a freedom of expression and an ability to stick to the point which surprised me.

I met one of the teachers in the hall and besought her to tell me about the school; whether they had days, or hours, when they really used books; whether Dr. Dewey believed children ought to learn how to read, write and cipher, or whether the new education was a preparation for Tolstoy's socialism. She said that Dr. Dewey believed the time spent in an elementary school on reading, writing, and arithmetic could be more profitably spent; an average child could learn these in doing other things.

She directed me to a class in primitive life where the children had spent some weeks working out, with the aid of the teacher, what the earliest people must have done when they had no clothing, or food, or shelter, or means of defense. She told me how they had thought of a spear by fastening a stick between the split ends of a club; how they had made bowls out of clay, and discussed caves as the first homes, and skins as the first clothing. How they had moulded in clay their ideas of man and animals in those days, and had become so interested that they had begged to write a report of their work for the school paper. [sic] This report had been dictated to the teacher, as none of the class could write. [Judging by the subject matter, as discussed earlier, the children were probably about age seven.] It was then typewritten and all read what the whole group had agreed should be a record of their work. (Runyon, 1900, pp. 590–591)

In the interest of combining the quantitative aspect of the curriculum with cultural industry, the teachers engaged the children in cooking activities, as Runyon found out during her visit.

As I passed through the dining room the boy I had seen with the sandwiches and the girl with the fruit were setting the table. Each had a high white apron on and said they were the "waiters," and that this was their "day for the group luncheon;" that the rest of the group were [sic] cooking in the kitchen.

I found my way to the kitchen, which I had previously mistaken for the laboratory, with its rows of gas fixtures and asbestos mats. I learned that earlier in the morning the group had had a cooking lesson in which they experimented with the food given them. Each child had cooked one third of a cup of flaked wheat in two thirds of a cup of water. Each had calculated how much water he would need if he cooked half a cup, and then one child was told to find out how much he would need for the whole group and to cook it, while other tasks were assigned to the rest. Some were cooking a food which they had missed by absence, or which they had failed to cook properly. One child was making cocoa for all; another was making out a tabular statement showing the proportion of water needed for each of the various preparations of wheat, oats, and corn they had studied.

I thought how Fred [their son] worried over his fractions, and here were children two years younger [probably about eight years old] working out the number of cupfuls of water and cereal that would be needed for a family of three, five, or eight, on the basis of the number for which one third of a cupful would be sufficient.

The teacher told me that after they had used various weights and measures until they were familiar with them, they arranged them in tables for convenient reference; that after they had added by threes, fives, sevens, etc., they arranged these in the multiplication tables.

As I went back through the dining room to the reception room where one of the teachers had promised to answer some of my questions, the children sat down to the luncheon they had prepared. The sandwiches and fruit appeared, and the small boy who had begged an invitation was there, as a guest. A teacher had also been invited, and served the cereal brought her by the waiters.

From time to time during the morning, a line from Dr. Dewey's book had come into my mind: "Education is a process of living, not a preparation for future living" [1897, p. 87]. (Runyon, 1900, p. 591)

Thus, a wide variety of activities were continually taking place according to Runyon. The question is, what kind? Some researchers, for example, Melvin Baker (1955), concluded that the school functioned as a democratic community.

We know that the school was to be organized as a democratic social community. In any functioning community, including a democratic one, there must be leadership. The task, then, is to see how this requirement of leadership functioned in the Dewey School.

...The teacher's leadership function is exercised to set the stage for group discussion and to draw out the contribution of each child's point of view. The teacher, too, contributes his own perspective to the planning. But the teacher is not the only leader; for his leadership was such that leaders arose from among the children. We learn that "the children developed their own methods of distributing important privileges" [Mayhew and Edwards, 1936, p. 377]. (Baker, 1955, pp. 138, 140)

But Baker doesn't say what those "important privileges" were. Mayhew and Edwards (1936) do, however. They reveal that "the children developed their own impersonal methods of distributing important privileges, assigning the waiter at luncheon or the leader of the class for the day, etc., by alphabetical order" (p. 377).

Useful as this choice-making may have been, it does not begin to include the decisions about the curriculum that Dewey's active child would be presumed capable of making. Yet the activities Runyon described seemed permeated with the children's own sense of purpose, indicating that they almost surely had a significant amount of flexibility in their activity, not only compared to conventional schools of a century ago, but even to most current schools.

Once again, Dewey's own early statements support such flexibility, as, for example, when he maintained that when the child was ready, he would make the necessary academic progress.

Reading, writing, and spelling are usually taught too soon, since the brain centers called into exercise by these studies are not sufficiently developed to make their use pleasurable and profitable. It is one of the great mistakes of education to make reading and writing constitute the bulk of the school work the first two years. The true way is to teach them incidently as the outgrowth of the social activities at this time. Thus language is not primarily the expression of thought, but the means of social communication. By its use the child keeps track of his work from day to day; by it he gives to others the results of his own special activity, and his own consciousness is widened by knowing what others have thought and done in the same lines. If language is abstracted from social activity, and made an end in itself, it will not give its whole value as a means of development. When the same reading lesson is given to forty children and each one knows that all the others know it, and all know that the teacher knows it, the social element is effectively eliminated. When each one has something individual to express, the social stimulus is an effective motive to acquisition. It is not claimed that by the method suggested, the child will learn to read as much, nor perhaps as readily in a given period as by the usual methods. That he will make more rapid progress later when the true language interest develops, and that the break in the continuity of the child's life will be prevented, can be claimed with confidence. (Dewey, 1896b, pp. 439–440)

The Mayhew Papers—source materials for *The Dewey School*, Mayhew and Edwards (1936)—contain about 1,300 pages of weekly teacher report fragments done for the school. They reveal that teachers did not always agree with Dewey's eloquent sentiments about waiting for the child to be ready. For example, in one of the reports, C.S. Osborn, a mathematics teacher for the 12-year-old group, wrote on October 5, 1900:

It may be worthwhile to state, that compared to the public schools, the children of this group seem to me...more spontaneous and quicker in grasping new ideas. They also seem less skillful in the mechanical operations. I have given practice examples in the fundamental operations so that they may acquire more skill in these processes....

On October 12, 1900, Osborn continued.

This group has just purchased McLellan and Ames' Public School Arithmetic. The children of this group are not easily interested, and I have spent most of the time in persuading them that it is worthwhile to separate work and play for a part of the time.

> We discussed the origin of the digits, and the children were much interested. They have brought in actual bills of actual business transactions and have verified the computations on these bills....(Mayhew Papers, 4: 74)

Osborn was a new teacher at the school when he wrote the report, but even experienced teachers in most academic areas of the school voiced similar concerns. For example, Georgia Bacon, who was supervisor of instruction and head of the history department at the school noted on January 18, 1901 that her group of 11-year-olds was "pitifully ignorant" as to the relative positions of the states and so she had the group study political geography to remedy the problem (Mayhew Papers, 5: 150).

The conflict between Dewey's faith in children's ability to learn through their own self-paced interests, and Osborn's and Bacon's beliefs in mastering basic information is still with us. One resolution is to do what Osborn did: try to make the work relevant and interesting but also insist upon basic skills. If this sounds like a time-honored progressive tradition, it is no coincidence. Programs proliferating in various forms over recent decades have taken this road. These include the courses concerning the Holocaust of the 1940s, the science courses initiated after the post-Sputnik excitement in the early 1960s, the African–American and peace studies of the later 1960s, and the career-oriented courses of the 1970s. In content these programs seem to embody the spirit of investigation which was a hallmark of the University School's curriculum.

But the content does not provide an indication of how much freedom of activity students may have. Here, too, Dewey's thought may be having its effect on school settings ranging from staunchly traditional to staunchly alternative.

In traditional settings it has gradually become more common for students to have some input into an English paper's topic, for example, or even into the method of study for a history topic. More often than before, several methods of study, in addition to textbooks, may be used for the same topic, including field trips, dramatizations, and model building.

In progressive settings, there are schools which specifically continue to make use of a curriculum like Dewey's, such as the Little Red School House in New York City. Dewey even wrote an introduction for De Lima's (1942) book on the school.

Finally, alternative schools have taken Dewey's early faith in child-generated activity the furthest. Because less is known about such schools, I will take a moment to briefly describe one which is at the cutting edge of such faith.

A highly flexible contemporary school has functioned for over 20 years and an initial follow-up study has been undertaken. In the *American Journal of Education* (1986), Gray and Chanoff have reported upon a survey of 69 available graduates (from 82 total) of a private day school in a middle class community. The Sudbury Valley School (SVS) in Framingham, Massachusetts had an open enrollment and served children from ages 4 to 19. Gray and Chanoff describe their purpose:

> What would happen to young people who are truly allowed to take charge of their own education, who...are provided with ample opportunities for learning but are free to use them in whatever way they choose or not to use them at all? Would they acquire the knowledge and develop the skills and work habits necessary to be happy, responsible, contributing members of our society?
>
> ...One purpose here is to present the results of a follow-up study of the graduates of a democratically organized school called the Sudbury Valley School. To the best of our knowledge, Sudbury Valley is the only school in the United States that satisfies the following criteria: (1) it is administered entirely through democratic procedures by the students and staff equally, (2) it places absolutely no academic requirements on students and establishes no academic standards for graduation, and (3) it has survived long enough so that there are graduates (albeit few) who have done all of their elementary and secondary schooling there. (pp. 184, 185)

In brief, the investigators found that slightly over half of these SVS graduates are attending or have matriculated from college and graduate school, and both this group and those who did not choose higher education have succeeded in a wide variety of professions. SVS graduates reported that the school was helpful "by fostering such traits as personal responsibility, initiative, curiosity, ability to communicate well with people regardless of status, and continued appreciation and practice of democratic values" (Gray and Chanoff, 1986, p. 182).

In the interest of space, the reader must be referred to the study for more information. The value of mentioning such an unusual school is to make clear that a wide range of activity-oriented programs exists in American society almost a century after Dewey's school began, at least partly influenced by an appreciation of the child's power of expression which Dewey and his school brought to public attention. Hence the question of how much an activity-oriented curriculum will help students learn what they need as citizens in a democracy seems to be highly pertinent in the current search for more effective ways of educating our youth.

REFERENCES

Baker, M. (1955). *Foundations of John Dewey's Educational Theory.* New York: Kings Crown Press, Columbia University.

DeLima A. (1942). *The Little Red School House.* New York: Macmillan.

Dewey, J. (1969ff). *The Early Works*, J. Boydston, ed. Carbondale, IL: Southern Illinois University Press.

——. (1895). "Results of Child Study Applied to Education." From *The Early Works*, Volume 5.

——. (1896a). "The Need for a Laboratory School." From *The Early Works*, Volume 5.

——. (1896b). "The University School." From *The Early Works*, Volume 5.

——. (1897). "My Pedagogic Creed." From *The Early Works*, Volume 5.

Eastman, M. (1942). *Great Companions*. New York: Farrar, Strauss & Giroux.

Gray, P., and Chanoff, D. (1986). "Democratic Schooling: What Happens to Young People Who Have Charge of Their Own Education?" *American Journal of Education*, February.

Mayhew, K., and Edwards, A. (1936). *The Dewey School*. New York: D. Appleton-Century.

Mayhew Papers. Special Collections, Milbank Library, Teachers College, Columbia University.

Roth, R. (1962). *John Dewey and Self Realization*. Englewood Cliffs, NJ: Prentice-Hall.

Runyon, L. (1900). "A Day with the New Education." *Chautauguan*, Volume 30, Number 6, March.

PART 2

FOUNDATIONS FOR UNDERSTANDING

7

TWENTY-FOUR, FORTY-TWO, AND I LOVE YOU: KEEPING IT COMPLEX

ELEANOR DUCKWORTH

In my entire life as a student, I remember only twice being given the opportunity to come up with my own ideas, a fact I consider typical and terrible. I would like to start this paper by telling how I came to realize that schooling could be different from what I had experienced.

FIGURING OUT MY OWN IDEAS

After my university studies, I joined the Elementary Science Study, a curriculum development program. I had been hired because of my background with Piaget, studying how science and math ideas develop in children, and had no formal training in either education or science. While the first of these lacks was probably a liability, the second turned out to be a great boon. I was with a highly imaginative bunch of scientists and teachers of science, all trying to put together their favorite kinds of experience to entice children. Because I was innocent in science I made a great "sample child" for my colleagues, and I spent a lot of time exploring the materials and the issues that they came up with. Of the many areas I explored, three seemingly unrelated ones came together in a way that showed me what learning could be like. I got hooked and have been an educator ever since, trying to develop learning experiences of that sort for every child and every teacher. It was the first time—with two exceptions mentioned in the opening sentence—that I got excited about my own ideas. I had been excited about ideas before, but they had always been somebody else's ideas. My struggle had always been to get in on what I thought somebody else knew and knew to be important. This was the first time that I had a sense of what it was like to pay attention to my own ideas.

This essay is reproduced with permission from Duckworth, E. (1991). "Twenty-four, Forty-two, and I Love You: Keeping It Complex." *HER*, 61(1), 1–24.

It is, of course, exhilarating to find that your own ideas can lead you somewhere. Few feelings are likely to be more effective in getting you to keep on thinking about things on your own. I would like to focus here, though, not so much on my feelings as on the nature of my understanding.

One team of colleagues was developing ways to study balances. They posed problems with a simple balance that consisted of a strip of pegboard resting on a rounded support with metal washers as weights. In each case, they started with the balance in equilibrium, horizontal. Then, holding the balance, they moved one or more weights and asked me to adjust other weights so that when they let go, the balance arm would remain horizontal (see Elementary Science Study, 1967b).

For example, they set up a relatively easy problem with the balance, as shown here:

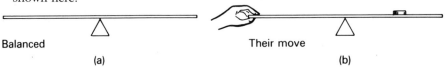

Balanced   Their move

(a)   (b)

Where should I add one washer, so the board would stay balanced? My solution was as follows:

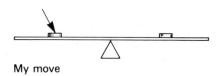

My move

They then gave me a problem that I found more difficult: they presented me with the board balanced with one washer on one side and two washers stacked on the other side, but closer to the middle. If they moved the single washer a certain distance to the right, how could I move *just one* of the other two washers, so the board would still balance?

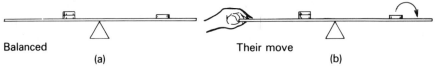

Balanced   Their move

(a)   (b)

I found that this solution worked:

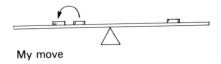

My move

Through this example and others similar to it, I found that it did not seem to matter where the washers started; I just had to move one of them the same distance the original had been moved on the other side, but in the opposite direction.

My grand triumph was the following problem. To start with, they put three washers in a pile on one side so as to balance one on the other:

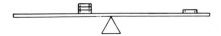

Then they moved the single one a long way—practically to the center. Again, how could I move *just one* of the others so it would still balance?

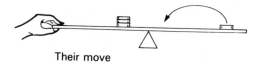

Their move

Well, I knew by now that I should try to move it just as far in the opposite direction. But there was no room. I ran into the middle almost right away. So what should I do? Move it in the *same* direction? That didn't seem right. Move it as far as I could towards the middle—just barely short of the middle? I thought I might try that. But the one I decided to try was my first idea—moving the washer in the opposite direction, even though it meant *crossing* the middle.

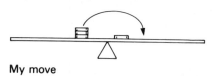

My move

It felt to me like a very daring move. And it worked! The rule worked, even across the middle. I remember saying to my colleagues at the time that I felt like Helen Keller.

I did not stop then. Among other things, I tried designing balances myself, and eventually even figured out what the differences were between a balance and a seesaw that accounted for the fact that the balance with nothing on it is horizontal, while a seesaw with nobody on it always has one end up in the air.

A second group was working on a study of what they called *Gases and "Airs"* (Elementary Science Study, 1967a). The tight sequence of reasoning demanded by this unit turned out not to work very well with elementary school children, but the unit did entail a wonderful variety of experiences that, for me, gave substance to what gases and airs are. It started from a close and critical look at the classic school science lab demonstration of burning a candle in a tube inverted over water: the water rises, the candle goes out, and one has "proven" that the atmosphere is 20 percent oxygen. But, there are some problems, as my colleagues pointed out. For one thing, the water doesn't rise gradually as the candle burns; it rises suddenly after the flame is out. If it were gradually using up the oxygen wouldn't it gradually rise? Another problem: the amount that it rises may indeed average about 20 percent, but it varies widely; in contrast, when wet steel wool is wedged into a tube above water and left to rust overnight, the water rises exactly the same amount in each tube.

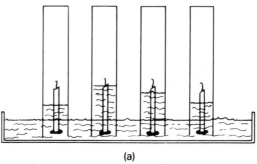

(a)
Water rise after 4 candles burned

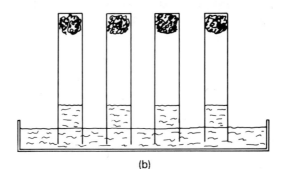

(b)
Water rise with steelwool overnight

The "demonstration" with a burning candle turns out to be a hoax, based on a totally different phenomenon. The candle actually goes out long before all the oxygen is used up (for various reasons). While the candle burns, it heats the air so that the air expands; some of it leaves the tube, bubbling out through the water in the dish. While the remaining air cools, the water rises to take the place of the air that bubbled out. As one who had been taken in by that demonstration in my own schooling, I was fascinated to explore the more complex relationships that had been covered up by it. To begin with, I was intrigued by the idea of different kinds of "airs" easily available to us: air that a candle had burned in; air that steel wool had rusted in; lung air; room air;

air that seeds had sprouted in. Could a candle burn in the steel wool air? Would another rusting steel wool ball pull up the same amount of water in steel wool air? Would seeds sprout in candle air?

I became very good at putting into a tube whatever kind of air I wanted to. Using a syringe, I could take air from any tube and put it into another tube that had no air in it (by virtue of being full of water). Bubbles came to be real things filled with some one kind of air—room air, lung air, steel wool air, or other. Putting an Alka Seltzer tablet under the lip of a water-filled tube, for example, did this:

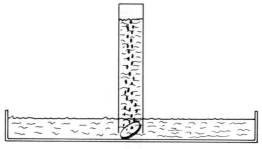

and I had a tube full of Alka Seltzer air.

I came to imagine the inverse of filling any container with liquid. As long as your container has no other liquid in it already, you can put it straight under the dripping liquid, and you'll capture all that is falling right over the opening. In the inverse, as in the case of some escaping Alka Seltzer air, you could think of it this way:

In a bucket of water, move a water-filled jar over the bubbles, and you will collect the escaping Alka Seltzer air.

This is not, I hasten to point out, intended as a practical example. I've never happened to be holding a water-filled jar upside down in a bucket of water when an Alka Seltzer tablet dropped into the bucket. But conceptually it helped me a lot: an "air" was for me as real as a liquid.

A third area that I explored originated in my attempts to build on my Piaget background. I thought of trying to find some situations for young children in which a certain order was maintained in spite of some striking change. It occurred to me to use the constant ordering of liquids floating on each other in a tube. Though the idea had less mileage in it for little children than I had thought it might, it did have some value (see Duckworth, 1964). More importantly for my education, however, it led me into a long series of explorations with liquids, starting with trying to make as many floating layers as I could in one tube. If I did not shake the tube, I could manage about six layers, and I experimented with dyes to keep the layers distinguishable. I expanded my horizons to include solid pieces—seeds, bits of plastic, bits of wood, bits of food. I don't recall any of these specifics, but a radish seed, say, would fall through three layers and sit on the fourth—and *every* radish seed would do that. One kind of plastic would sit on the second layer, another kind would fall through four, and so on. Some material (I do not now remember what and it took me a long time to find this material) stopped at the top of the top surface, and floated there.

I also tried to mix alcohol and water so that the resulting liquid would have exactly the same density as the salad oil I was working with—to see what would happen when neither liquid would necessarily float on top of the other. Would I be able to make stripes with them? Or would they stand side by side, with a vertical separation? Or what? I found that the oil always formed itself into a single enormous sphere in the middle of the water-alcohol liquid; and that this sphere *always* moved slowly either to the top or to the bottom of the water–alcohol liquid. No matter how delicately I added one drop of water or of alcohol, I could never get the sphere of oil to float right in the middle—it was always either *just* heavier or *just* lighter. (These explorations came back in my own teaching more than 10 years later; see Duckworth, 1986.)

Six or eight months after I started learning science like this, someone presented a puzzle that happened to draw on the three areas I had been exploring, and I think I was the only person around at the time who put together the right prediction. On the left-hand side of this balance is a plastic bag sealed airtight; an Alka Seltzer tablet is stuck in a piece of plasticene near the top, and some water is in the bottom. On the right-hand side is just enough weight to balance the arm. The question is, what will happen to the balance of the arm if the bag is shaken, and the tablet falls into the water?

Most of the people present knew that when the tablet fell into the water, a lot of "Alka Seltzer air" would be formed and the bag would fill out. Some

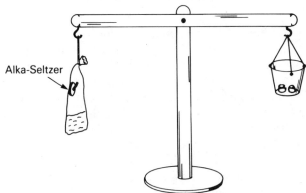

people thought that the arm would remain level, because the same matter that was in the bag to start with was still in it at the end, even if in a different form, so the weight would not change at all. Others thought that the left side would go down, because Alka Seltzer air (being, so they knew, carbon dioxide) is heavier than room air. My prediction, which turned out in fact to be the case, was that the left side would go *up*, because the filled-out bag would take up more space, while adding no more weight, thus being more buoyant in the surrounding sea of air.

I believe that it was because I started from my own ideas and found my own ways into these parts of the world that my understanding of balances, "airs," and floating belonged so thoroughly to me. Notice the difference between what usually happens in formal education—presenting the simplest, neatest explanation of "the law of moments," "the composition of the atmosphere," "density," "buoyancy," or whatever—and my experience of being enticed with the funny, frustrating, intriguing, unpredictable complexities of the world around me. Instead of disassociating myself from my own interests in my struggle to find out what whoever was supposed to "know" might have understood by the word "buoyancy," my learning was based on my own connections, within the idiosyncrasies of my own system of thoughts. The very complexities of the subject matters enabled me to connect with them, made them accessible, and the integrity of my own ideas enabled me to retrieve those connections when they could help me understand a new situation.

Lisa Schneier (1990) has put it this way, the relationship between complexity and accessibility:

> [W]e organize subject matter into a neat series of steps which assumes a profound uniformity among students. We sand away at the interesting edges of subject matter until it is so free from its natural complexities, so neat, that there is not a crevice left as an opening. All that is left is to hand it to them, scrubbed and smooth, so that they can view it as outsiders. (p. 4)

The experience of my science explorations was the exact opposite.

THE UNIVERSE IN A SENTENCE

My favorite radio show is "A Hitchhiker's Guide to the Galaxy." In one episode, a computer is built expressly for the purpose of answering the question, "What is the meaning of life, the universe, and everything?" When it is ready, they ask it if it can answer that question. It says, yes, it can, but that it will take, as I recall, seven million years. They say, "Well, OK, go to it." Seven million years later, whoever is around goes to learn the answer. The computer says that it does have the answer, but that they might be a little disappointed. "No, no," they say, "go ahead, what is it?" "Forty-two," it says.

Who knows? Maybe forty-two *is* the answer. But such an answer is of no more help to us than no answer at all. It does not speak to our level of interaction with the mysteries of our existence.

Note the parallels with the following story from Lisa Schneier's class in an urban high school:

> It had been a lively class, with the various Juliets taking turns standing on a table and the Romeos making elaborate and often comical gestures as they stood below.... A group of ninth graders and I were working on a scene from *Romeo and Juliet.* They had chosen to read the balcony scene aloud and were acting it out, taking turns with the parts. They took the difficult language and its foreign style into stride, at times staying true to the text and at others replacing or skipping words and phrases. It was clear as they spoke that at points the words held meaning for them and at others they hadn't a clue as to what it was that they were reading. But we didn't stop much for discussion; the students were enjoying this kind of involvement with each other, and there was a momentum in the reading that I didn't want to interrupt.
>
> But our last Romeo of the day finally did interrupt it. We had started the scene again to give more readers a turn, and he had begun to wade through his first speech. In the midst of it, he broke off, shook his head impatiently, and turned to me. "He loves her. *That's* what he's saying. So why all that other stuff? Why not just say it? I love you! (to the current Juliet). There!" And then in a memorable tone, a mixture of humor, frustration, and honest confusion: "Why can't he just say what he means?" (Schneier, 1990, pp. 1–2)

Why doesn't Shakespeare just say what he means? Of course that's what he *is* doing: "what he means" is complex. The words he chooses are the best he can choose to say what he wants to say. Poems and stories and paintings and dance and music are not just fancy ways of saying what could be said in a sentence. "I love you" does not quite express everything that Shakespeare meant, just as "forty-two" does not quite substitute for living our lives. There is a parallel here between a poet and a teacher: the universe is complex; science is complex; the poet's thoughts and feelings are complex. "Forty-two" doesn't do the trick. Neither does "buoyancy." Nor, in this case, does "I love you."

In this spirit, when studying a poem with a class, I start by asking students what they notice—an invitation to keep every complexity of the poem under consideration. People notice very different things, and almost every thing noticed leads to a question or another thought. Putting together what everyone notices and returning to the poem to try to look for answers to the questions leads to an understanding of the poem that is greatly expanded for each of us. Take, for instance, this Frost poem:

Design

I found a dimpled spider, fat and white,
On a white heal-all, holding up a moth
Like a white piece of rigid satin cloth—
Assorted characters of death and blight
Mixed ready to begin the morning right,
Like the ingredients of a witches' broth—
A snow-drop spider, a flower like froth,
And dead wings carried like a paper kite.

What had that flower to do with being white,
The wayside blue and innocent heal-all?
What brought the kindred spider to that height,
Then steered the white moth thither in the night?
What but design of darkness to appall?—
If design govern in a thing so small.[1]

Somebody will notice that there is a lot of white. Somebody will mention the rhyme scheme, or will imitate the rhythm. Somebody will mention that the first part of the poem seems to present a picture, and the second half seems to ask questions about it. Different people point out different possible plays on words: kindred and dreadful kin; appall and a funeral pall; a paper kite and a bird kite; morning right and morning rite; morning and mourning. Different people have different thoughts about whether the darkness is that which appalls, or that which is appalled. Arguments develop about why the flower is described as white in the first line, and blue in the ninth. This is a bare beginning. A group of adults can easily go on for more than an hour with increasing interest, and everybody's initial understanding is expanded by hearing from others.[2]

I have always been frightened by being asked: "What is the meaning of this poem?" My reaction is, "How could *I* know? I'm no good with poems!" But it is easy for me to point out something that I notice about it, and in turn to listen to what other people notice about it, and to figure out whether I think that what they say makes sense, and why, and what other thoughts their ideas provoke in me. Many students have feelings similar to these. One in particular said that she had determined when we started discussing the poem that she would not say a word, knowing nothing about poems and feeling scared by them. But as she heard the various things that people were saying, her own thoughts developed, and she finally couldn't contain herself, so much did she have to say and so strongly did she feel about it. One student referred to himself as a "poem-phobe," which prompted another student to say, "If Frost had been able to put what he had to say into a sentence, he would have. So don't worry that you can't."

I recognized that this was the same thought I had about the accessibility of science. It is in acknowledging the complexity of the poem, not "sand[ing] away at the interesting edges," to use Schneier's words, that we render it accessible. Our understanding seeks to do justice to the complexity that the poet sought to render, and by the same token it belongs to us. Just as the poet seeks to present his thoughts and feelings in all their complexity, and in so doing opens a multiplicity of paths into his meaning, likewise a teacher who presents a subject matter in all its complexity makes it more accessible by opening a multiplicity of paths into it.

"I KNOW THERE ARE TWENTY-FOUR"

I ask students to do the following: Take a fistful of four different kinds of markers (four colors of paper clips or four kinds of dried beans, for example) to represent four children who are going to the movies. Lay out the different arrangements in which they can sit in four adjacent seats. Some students ask, "Do I really have to do this? I know there are twenty-four." And I say, yes, you really have to; the question isn't how many arrangements, the question is *what are* the arrangements—each of them. (It happens, not infrequently, that someone who has impatiently affirmed that there will be twenty-four, because he or she knows a formula, has trouble generating the actual arrangements— which strikes me as not too different from knowing that the meaning of life is forty-two.) And the question behind that is, when you think you have laid out all the arrangements, how could you convince yourself or anybody else that you don't have any repeats, and that you are not missing any? I urge the reader to try this before continuing, and to see what system she or he comes up with.

Most nonmath people start this exercise more or less randomly, but many systems emerge when they think about whether they have generated all the possible arrangements. In what follows I will present some of these systems.

Some people make diagonals, such as the P in the following arrangements:

PBLM
MPBL
LMPB
BLMP

This could be called the "revolving" system, where the last letter to the right revolves around to appear on the left and everything moves over one. This looks systematic and promising, but when they follow this rule to a fifth step it turns out to be a repeat of the first (PBLM). So they have to side-step, and think about how to find the various different possible starting points.

Another system which keeps P on the diagonal is the "squeeze between" system:

PBLM
BPLM
BLPM
BLMP

Move P to the right by squeezing it in between the next two letters. Again, the question arises about what to do after the fourth.

You could reinterpret that system to be not "squeeze between" but "exchange": Keep P moving on the diagonal by exchanging it with whatever letter is in the place where it will be moving. That explains the four above, and allows you to keep going:

PLMB
LPMB
LMPB
LMBP
PMBL
MPBL
MBPL
MBLP

At this point, after twelve arrangements, we get back to the starting point. Is that, then, all there are? Is there a reason to think that this system would have generated all we could possibly get? Is there a reason to think it is inadequate? Or can't we tell anything about it at all?

Not all approaches use diagonals. For the next ones I will limit the discussion to three children in three seats in order to write out fewer arrangements.

Many people, as a system starts to emerge, lay out something like this:

LMB
LBM
MLB

By this time they have an idea about what they will put next, and most think that their idea is the only sensible, systematic possibility. The first surprise is that there are two different, almost equally popular, next moves:

MBL   or   BLM

And the two completed lists would look like this:

I	LMB	II	LMB
	LBM		LBM
	MLB		MLB
	MBL		BLM
	BLM		MBL
	BML		BML

The system on the left started with two L's in the first position, then put two M's in the first position, and then two B's. The system on the right started with the L's in the first position, then moved the L's to the second position, and then to the last position. In both cases, people can say, "Once I have one position filled, there are only two ways to fill the other two, so these are the only possible six ways for three children to sit." They are two very different systems, and yet they end up with the same exact arrangements.

Playing this out with four children and four seats, using, for example, system I, would give this result:

PLMB
PLBM
PMLB
PMBL
PBLM
PBML

There would be six different arrangements with P in the first position. There would, therefore, be six ways to put each of the four letters in the first position; that is, four times six ways altogether. (Playing out system II above, P would end up in each position six times—again, four times six ways altogether.)

One nine-year-old—no math whiz, he—after placing a few arrangements according to no system that I could see, started to make new ones by reversing pairs in the ones he already had. (From PLBM, say, he might make PBLM; or from MLPB he might make LMPB.) He worked slowly, and for a long time he would make a new arrangement and then check to see whether he already had it rather than generate a new one from some overall system he had in his mind. After a long time, though (he worked at this for close to an hour), and as he explained to me what he was doing, a system emerged; he started to know how to look for ones that were missing and to fill in the gaps. It was a system that was totally new to me. He never articulated it as clearly as I am about to here, but essentially his system was this: Start with one block, let's say P, and pair it up with each of the other blocks in turn. Let's start with the pair PL:

Put them in the middle, and put the two remaining blocks at either end. Then reverse the two on the ends. Then reverse the originals (PL becomes LP) and repeat: then put the end-ones in the middle and the middle-ones at the ends and start over.

BPLM
MPLB
BLPM
MLPB
PBML
LBMP
PMBL
LMBP

Now we have eight. Starting with PM gives us another eight and starting with PB gives us eight more. This way you get three times eight instead of four times six. Is there any reason that this system is a convincing one? When you've started with P and each of the other letters and done all the rearrangements as described, is there any reason to think that you would necessarily hit all the possibilities?

I could go on. Looking for relationships among the systems enhances our understanding even more: what is the relationship between a system that has four variations of six positions and a system that has three variations of eight positions? The point is that the more you look at this question, the more ways there are to see it. "Twenty-four" is a sadly impoverished version of all that can be understood about it. Just as with the poem, each different way of thinking about it illuminates all of the others—a wonderful pay-off for allowing for the complexities of the matter. Note that in this math problem *as with the poem*, individuals tend to think that their way is the one way to look at it, unless they are in a social context where other possibilities are presented; then it is not a matter of replacing their point of view, but of enhancing it.

Of course, many people raise for themselves the question of arrangements of five children, and work out a formula that applies to any number—a formula which, then, *represents* their understanding instead of substituting for it.

One further comment: Another nine-year-old pointed out to me that, once he had laid out all the arrangements (and he came up with twenty-four), if he removed the first item from all of them, the twenty-four arrangements of *three* items are still all different from each other. After some thought, I can more or less understand that this must be so. But it certainly brought me up short when he raised the idea.

EXTENDED CLINICAL INTERVIEWING

Now I want to move, with one last example, to develop the idea of a kind of research that such a view of teaching and learning leads to and calls for: extended clinical interviewing. Early in my work in education I found that the Piagetian methods I used to investigate learners' understanding—that is, having them take their own understanding seriously, pursue their own questions, and struggle through their own conflicts—was at the same time a way of engaging people in pursuing their own learning. People became avid learners, even in fields which had not interested them before, and my ways of trying to follow their thoughts were, in fact, excellent ways to help them learn.

Later I came to realize that the circle is full: This way of helping people learn is at the same time an important form of research about how people's ideas develop. It really amounts to Piaget's clinical interviewing, extended in two ways: it can be extended over time, and it can be carried out with more than one person at a time.

This approach requires, however, more than just an interviewer's questions. Many of the interviews in Piaget's early books used only the interviewee's previous experience as the basis of discussion (what makes the wind; where are thoughts located). In contrast, the questions that I found most often engaged interviewees in the pursuit of their own learning grew from his later work, where children tried to explain or predict or describe relationships in something which they had before them and could transform or otherwise keep returning to (the last example above is based on an investigation in Piaget and Inhelder, 1951/1975). The more surprises people encountered, and the more possibilities they became aware of, the more they wanted to continue to do and to think.

Extended clinical interviewing as a research approach requires just as much resourcefulness in finding appropriate materials, questions, and activities as any good curriculum development does. Whether it be poems, mathematical situations, historical documents, liquids, or music, our offerings must provide some accessible entry points, must present the subject matter from different angles, elicit different responses from different learners, open a variety of paths for exploration, engender conflicts, and provide surprises; we must encourage learners to open out beyond themselves, and help them realize that there are other points of view yet to be uncovered—that they have not yet exhausted the thoughts they might have about this matter.

Only if people *are* interested in expanding their views does one learn anything about how people's ideas actually develop. Curriculum development goes hand in hand with following the intricacies of the development of ideas. (This intertwined relationship led me first to refer to this research as "teaching-research," 1987.)

Once we are willing to accept the real complexities of subject matter, we find that they lurk even in the most unlikely places. One of the abilities I seek to develop in teachers is the ability to recognize unsuspected complexities in what seems like straightforward, even elementary, material. (David Hawkins, 1978, has pointed out how mistaken it is to think that "elementary" ideas are necessarily simple.) It is always in confronting such complexities that one develops real understanding.

"AND THAT'S HOW THEY DID THE LATITUDE LINES"...
"IT MAKES ME DIZZY"

I want to close with one detailed example of extended clinical interviewing that shows what can happen when learners confront, rather than cover complexities. I want to show the process as it actually takes place in a group over time. I hope to be able to convey the relationships—both interpersonal and ideational—that this approach to learning entails. I hope to reveal the interplay of thoughts and feelings, the tantalizing confusions, the tortuous development of new insights, and the crowning accomplishment possible when people struggle honestly with their own ideas. I think it is a rare picture of minds at work.

This account involves a group of adults that has spent eleven years pursuing a study of the habits of the moon. This group began at Massachusetts Institute of Technology as the Experiment in Teacher Development (Bamberger et al., 1981). After the official end of the two-year project, about 10 of the original 15 teachers wanted to keep going. We met periodically through a third year, as we tried to decide which strands of our work together we wanted to continue. For six of the teachers, moon-watching was really the most passionate interest. This was the experience that they felt had given them the greatest insights into themselves and their students as learners, and thus into themselves as teachers. (For more on moon-watching, see DiSchino, 1987, and Duckworth, 1986.) So, for the last eight years, seven of us have continued to meet with a focus on moonwatching.[3] There have been no drop-outs. We meet for a two-day study session every summer, for one or two all-day study sessions during the year, and for evening meetings about once a month. By now, the teachers are familiar with most of my thoughts on the motions of the moon, and I am a learner like everybody else. This, in fact, does not change my role very much. In all of my extended clinical interviewing I keep asking people to say what they mean again, please, more clearly. In this group I have no special standing in asking for such clarification.

I did not set up the conflict described below. It emerged on its own as we continued to try to understand the motions of the bodies in our solar system. I may have played a role in keeping the conflict on the floor as an issue worth trying to resolve, and in refusing to believe too readily that we had resolved it. The discussion presented here is about what "east" means, which at first blush seems like a pretty simple idea. Let me first try to present two different views, and then give some sense of the discussion that took place.

Both views put east in the general direction of the rising sun. ("Orient"ing literally means taking a bearing to the east, heading for the rising sun.) The first view is relatively simple: east is along a latitude, in the general direction of where the sun rises. The second view is more difficult to convey, and for us it came from two different sets of thoughts. The simpler of *these* is the following. East lies 90 degrees from north, in the general direction of the rising sun. If you look at the North Star (or to the earth underneath the North Star) and put your right arm out at a right angle, you'll point east. If you cut a 90-degree L-shape from a piece of paper, and lay it on a globe so that one tip of it is at the North Pole and the bend in the L is at Boston, then the arm that is heading east does *not* go along a latitude; it goes on a gentle slant from the latitude, so it ends up crossing the equator.

North Pole

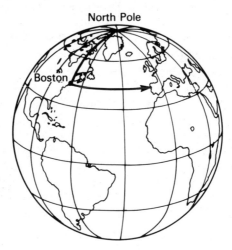

Our second way of getting to this view is the following. In September you may find the sun rising in a certain position, relative to your house, for instance, or to the end of your street. As the months go by, the sunrise point changes, moving to the right along the horizon until by Christmas it is very much further to the right. By mid-January it has started to move back, until some time in March it is again where it was in September; it then continues to move to the left for a couple of months. In June it begins to move to the right again, and by September it is back where it started. So where, in all this, is east? This group thought of the one in the middle of those extremes as a reasonable candidate—the place where it started in September and that it reached again in March. That is also the time when the sunrise and sunset divide the twenty-four hour period into exactly half. Everywhere in the world, that day, the twenty-four hour period is going to be divided exactly in half. Everyone in the world, that day, will look to the sunrise to find where the exact east is. And here's what that led us to think. If everyone on one north-south line from the North Pole to the South Pole is looking toward the sun at the same sunrise moment, they are all looking at the same place at the same moment. On that day, the sun is actually rising so as to keep going directly overhead *at the equator*, which means that we must all be looking, not directly along a latitude, but in a direction gently sloping towards the equator.

We had two reasons to think of east as tending toward the equator, rather than along a latitude parallel to the equator. And, of course, we also had common sense and pragmatic reasons to think of east as heading along a latitude. In order to proceed with an investigation that we were engaged in, we needed to know which of these easts to deal with.

This discussion lasted three long sessions, which are the essence of the following account. The first took place at one of our two-day summer retreats, in June 1987. It refers back to a conversation at a retreat three years earlier, when one central idea first emerged and left us perplexed. The second session took place in December at an all-day meeting, and then there is a follow-up to that. *Much* material has been cut, but I still hope to convey a sense of the nature of what can happen when complexity is accepted as a pedagogical resource, rather than avoided.

FERN: [one major protagonist in this discussion; always willing to take on a seemingly unlikely idea if it expands her/our understanding]...[T]here's always east, even if the sun isn't rising there. There's still due east...it's down there, because it's towards the equator.

WENDY: [another major protagonist] No. I'm not happy with that sentence, I'm sorry. Due east is *not* towards the equator....

FERN: Where is due east, even if the sun isn't there? It's towards where the sun rises on the equinox, which is...towards the equator....

WENDY: What makes you think that it tips towards the equator?...

ELEANOR: [altogether quite unsure of myself in the discussion] It's the 90 degree thing [the L-shape, which we had discussed earlier]—the latitudes·are not

90 degrees to the longitudes....

WENDY: I think I see what you're saying. You're saying that if I look due east eventually my eyes will...touch the equator...if I could look around the corner.

FERN: You know what it is? There's always due east. Whether or not the sun rises there. And what due east is, the definition of it is, where the sun rises on the equinox.

WENDY: I think of it very differently. I think of due east as, I drew a line from the North Pole to the South Pole and then went 90 degrees off...from that.

ELEANOR: OK, that would come to the same thing....

WENDY: But I don't like it....I don't like it ending up on the equator....It really makes me nervous....

WENDY: [taking a styrofoam ball] Well if I draw a line from there [A—point standing for the North Pole] to there [B—point standing for Boston] and go at a right angle [she starts to draw a line like a latitude].

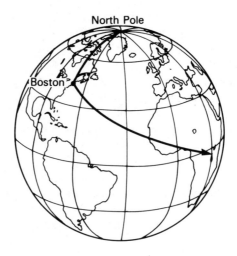

FERN: Nope, that's not a right angle, your right angle's going to go like that [tending toward the equator].

WENDY: Yeah, but I don't like that right angle. I'm having serious problems with that right angle....Well how come the latitudes don't tilt down? How come they don't bump into the equator?

FERN: Latitudes are latitudes, they're not east.

WENDY: You say Spain is due east from of us, and—

ELEANOR: That's a good point....

WENDY: If I get into a boat and I drive due east and I keep the compass on due east, I bump into Spain.

FERN: [stretching things a bit] You say Spain is on the same latitude, you don't say Spain is due east.

ELEANOR: [quite uncertain] Although we do say that....

FERN: They're not east–west lines, they're latitudes. If they were east–west lines we wouldn't need latitudes.

ELEANOR: Huh?

MARY RIZZUTO: Why? Why [then] do you have longitudes? They're [after all] north–south lines.

JINNY: [laughing] That *was* a little—cryptic! Go on!

MARY R.: Go on, we need to hear this.

[We all recognized that she had made a far-out comment, but had confidence that Fern would say something interesting about it.]

FERN: Ok, here we go. [Fern thought silently for a while, but, to our great disappointment, she decided she did not, after all, have something clear to say.] No....

WENDY: Alright, hang on. You're saying that if I got a compass, and I started walking in California, and I followed that compass wherever it said east, I would end up on the equator.

FERN: Right....

WENDY: You're saying that if I were a sailor, and my compass told me to sail due east, I would end up on the equator no matter what I did.

FERN: Right....

MARY R.: So which way would you have to go to get to Spain?

JINNY: You'd have to go—

MARY DISCHINO: North of east....

[with hilarity] So north isn't north and east isn't east....So if you want to stay in the Northern Hemisphere you have to keep going north....

WENDY: [arm around Fern's shoulder] This is the first time in eight years that I don't understand what you're saying. In eight years you're the only person who I've always, always understood....If I'm driving [east]...am I driving [on a latitude]?

JINNY: Probably if it's short enough. Because, right? it's going to take you a long time to get down to the equator. [This was the first inkling of a resolution—but nobody noticed.]

MARY R.: It's incredible. Well it's interesting, one of the kids last year in mapping asked me why there was an Eastern and a Western Hemisphere. Why did one get named one and the other one get named something else [given that they each get their turn at sunrise]. [She laughs.] I said, "I have no idea." I had no idea. I mean, why?...

MARY D.: What would happen if we took the crust off the earth and then started walking due east?...Lie it flat...It would be like the orange peels [another reference to an earlier session]....

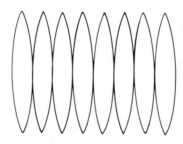

Wendy: Do you mean to say you don't believe that compasses tell you where
     due east is?
Fern: No, I do.
Wendy: So you think that if I were a sailor and I sailed whatever number of
     degrees due east is, 90 or whatever, that I would end up on the equator?
     [We acknowledge the need to adjust a compass for magnetic north, and
     proceed on the assumption that is done.]...
Fern: I think you'd go due east.
Wendy: And would you end up on the equator?
Fern: Yeah.
Eleanor: Instead of Spain.
Wendy: Instead of Spain. If Kevin who has sailed and navigated said that
     doesn't happen, would you say your due east is different from the com-
     pass due east? I don't know what he's gonna say, he might say, yes, you
     have to correct—...
Fern: This is the thing. This is the thing. I *think* maybe this is the thing. If you
     start—
     [Now here, Fern *is* able to articulate her insight, and it is related to Jinny's
     partially formed thought above. She comes to it, alas, just as the men and
     children arrive back for lunch, so the tape is stopped! I wrote down the
     following, in which Fern refers to an example we had used of walking
     along the 49th parallel.]
Fern: If you *walk* east, you walk along the [US–Canadian] border; if you *look*
     east, you look into the United States.
     [We get a brief respite from the children, to finish our discussion, and the
     tape is back on. I had not understood what Fern had said, and Jinny tries
     to recapture it for me.]
Jinny: ...Where were we. We were on the border. If you're going to walk,
     umm, if they, if you continue to adjust...90 degrees, so you stay consis-
     tently 90 degrees east of north, you know, 90 degrees in relationship to
     north, you'll stay on that border, and...[a new thought she has here now]
     and that's the definition of a latitude....
Eleanor: But I want to know, I just want to know the thing you said, about it
     keeps pushing up, could you say that part again.

Mary R.: Well it, it keeps, if you're just walking, [Eleanor: Yeah.] then you're just, you're constantly straying down. [Eleanor: Yeah.] But if, if you, if you keep yourself on the compass, and you constantly push the compass, then you're constantly keeping yourself at 90 degrees....

Eleanor: And what's the pushing up?...

Jinny: You have to adjust. You have to keep the adjustment happening. Because of...the sphere. That's what the pushing up is....

Eleanor: Yeah. I haven't quite got that. I'll keep thinking about it.

[In December, we started by watching some of the summer's videotape, and then the conversation went on this way.]

Joanne: [who had been running the videocamera in the summer session] The last thing you said there, [on the tape] do you know what it is? "There's always due east." [laughter]....

Fern: [reflecting her insight at the end of the last session] I think where we ended up was if you navigate, if you're a sailor and you navigate and you're heading due east you don't go to the equator. You go to Spain or whatever—

Eleanor: Any step is headed toward the equator, but the next step—...

Mary D.: It's due east from that step. Due east is due east from each step that you take. That's how you get across [to Spain]. As opposed to due east from your starting point. [Jinny: Mmhmm.] If you look at a compass when you begin, and you go due east, if that compass froze there at that moment, then you'd get to the equator, but the compass is heading due east even when you're ten steps ahead of where you started....

Mary R.: It corrects it sort of.

[I still do not follow the line of argument, and keep asking for more clarification.]....

[Fern starts drawing a picture.]

Wendy: If you were walking around a circle, around the top of the globe....It's telling you to go, like, due east is this way [she steps slightly outside the circle]. But really it's saying take a step this way and then it says, OK, now, north is over there.

[Wendy essentially outlines the argument that I finally understand a little later. I shall present it more clearly at that point.]

Jinny: It's like making a circle in Logo....

Wendy: East is pointing off the circle, down.

Eleanor: Yeah.

Wendy: But I don't believe it.

Eleanor: I believe it but I don't get it. You get it and you don't believe it....

Jinny: Well the only thing I said, just when Wendy just did that, is it's like making a circle in Logo....

Mary R.: With straight lines. You make a circle with straight lines.

Wendy: That's lovely.

[I try but fail to understand this analogy.]....
Mary D.: ...[Y]ou keep moving, also. That's part of it.
Fern: [Fern finishes her drawing] Something like that picture....

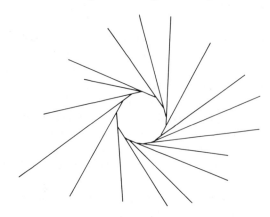

Eleanor: How come I go there [around the circle] when the compass says to
    go off into space, I don't know. How come I go there, that's my question.
    [Jinny and Eleanor laugh.]
Wendy: 'Cause the circle is big enough that you can take a step this w—I
    mean, if you think of, like, octagons, but with, like hundredsagons...You
    walk a little bit this way, and then you look and say, oh, north has moved
    from here to here, 'cause I've gone a little bit around....
Eleanor: 'Cause *north* moves.
Mary R.: It doesn't.
Eleanor: No, it does, with respect to *me.*
Wendy: Perhaps you move with respect to it.
Mary R.: Yeah.
Eleanor: Yeah. [I start walking with my left arm out to the side, supposedly
    pointing at the North Pole, and my right arm straight ahead of me, sup-
    posedly in the direction that my compass would indicate is east.] So I take
    this step now...*[top figure]* [ahead of me, essentially down one of Fern's
    lines] but I can't have...kept my hands like that,...'cause I have to stay like
    this.... *[bottom figure]*
    [I shift slightly left, so my left arm still points to a supposed North Pole.]
    So then I take this step here, [down another of Fern's lines] and then I
    have to move back [to the left] like that, [Mary R.: Right, right.] and then I
    take this step here [down another line]. [The others break out in
    applause.]....
And then I follow that one [another line], but if I take my left arm with me, it's
    left the North Pole, and it has to correct back again....
Mary R.: It keeps adjusting you. It's really neat....

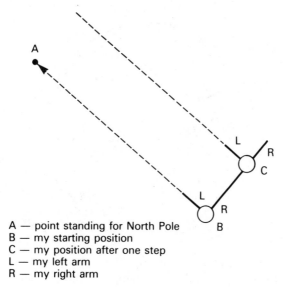

A — point standing for North Pole
B — my starting position
C — my position after one step
L — my left arm
R — my right arm

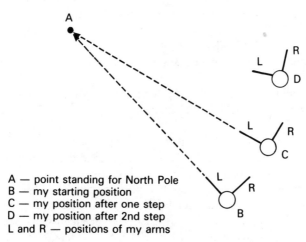

A — point standing for North Pole
B — my starting position
C — my position after one step
D — my position after 2nd step
L and R — positions of my arms

Wendy: But if you glued, if you could clamp the compass so it wouldn't move when you walk a little bit, suddenly north would be at a totally different place....

Fern: ...[T]his line that you're going around here is the latitude...that would bring you to Spain, as opposed to down there [down one of the lines], to the equator.... This shape, when you put this shape onto the globe [her drawing, with the North Pole at the center], this line [the circle] would set at a certain latitude....

Mary R.: Everything else would go down....

Fern: 'Course then they would keep going past the equator, I don't know about that.

[This introduces the third idea of east, which we did not resolve with the other two. The going-to-the-equator view of what east is had, as you recall, two sources. The L-shape *crosses* the equator, while in the other version, Fern's lines would wrap around the equator. I include a short bit of discussion of that idea.]....

Fern: [T]here's something wrong about the L, maybe...maybe it's not really an L....

Eleanor: Wouldn't it stay on the equator once it got to the equator?...

Mary D.: Because then if you're in the Southern Hemisphere, you'd do the opposite....

Joanne: What kind of a shape is that?

Eleanor: That is an amazing shape, though...a spiral that then reaches a circle, and stops getting bigger....

Fern: The only way you'd get this line [the one that would wrap around the equator] is if you had a laser beam, and you shot your laser beam from where you were standing, due east, and in an instant, the laser beam burns a trail on that line....

Joanne: This line is a continuation of one of those lines up there [in Fern's drawing], which eventually reaches the equator....

Wendy: If you could stand on the earth, on the equinox, and shoot one of those pistols that has a string with a sucker, and you could shoot it right at the sun...and have it "blip" on the sun, so you had this lovely string from you to the sun. And then the earth began to turn, that day, and the string would be wound—....

Mary D.: You could be putting this dot on the earth, as every point on the earth passes through sunrise. This is sunrise. As it passes through sunrise, if there were something spitting at the planet, making points on it,...when you went through, when the day was over, you'd have an equator on your planet...I see how the equator is made. Now the equator has a different meaning for me.

[We return to a discussion of our other two easts.]....

Wendy: I will not agree that that's due east, toward the equator....I want another word than due east for that....

Wendy: [If Fern's east is east] how can you say Spain is east of us? Spain is north of us [since the compass reading is corrected to the north].

Mary R.: No it's not!...

Wendy: But you have to constantly correct, after each step.

Mary R.: You don't have to correct, because your constant corrects for you. Either the north star, or the compass—one of those change for you. They keep you going in the direction, and that's how you, and that's how they did the latitude lines.

Wendy: But then, why—Then there are two easts.

Mary D.: Yes! We said that. There's Fern's east, and there's the latitude east.

Wendy: Right. But I don't—, I can't—, I don't feel comfortable with it...it makes me dizzy....

Wendy: What I would like to do is...I'd like to present that kind of information to somebody who deals with east and west....

Fern: I'm thinking, if he came in here right now, and said, you're right and I'm wrong, I would think he hadn't thought about this problem long enough....

Wendy: ...Now we have two different words for east.

Eleanor: Different meanings for east.

Wendy: Right. And one word.

Jinny: In two different lang—I mean it's like two different worlds, it's a flat world and a spherical world....

Eleanor: You'd like a map-maker.

Wendy: Yeah, or somebody who sails....

Fern: I don't think any of those people would have had to resolve this issue in order to be able to do what they do....

Wendy: ...What I understood today doesn't fit with what I've understood from all of that learning and all the things that I understand about east so far. Or believe about east, have read about east, hold about east...

I'm trying to think if there's another way to resolve it that wouldn't have two easts....

Fern: The two views that we have right now are not, one, that east is Spain and the other one that east is something else. We have two views. One is that east is Spain. And the other is that east is both Spain and something else....They're not two conflicting things. One is part of the other....Do you

know what I mean? Like one has more parts to the explanation...
Wendy: I don't think that anyone will agree—
Mary D.: Then why aren't we the experts?

We did go off to see Philip and Phylis Morrison, creators of PBS's *The Ring of Truth*, which included one episode on map-making. And there we learned, to our extraordinary satisfaction, how Charles Mason, astronomer, and Jeremiah Dixon, mathematician and surveyor, laid out the Mason–Dixon line. At night they fixed north, by the stars. By day they cut through the trees at 90 degrees from north. At night, they fixed north again, and when they started each new day, returning, in Jinny's terms, to the "flat world," they had to adjust their continuing swath slightly to the north. It was just like Wendy's walking circle. As Mary R. had said, "And that's how they did the latitude lines."

CONCLUSION

This is an exceptional group, admittedly; not in its make-up at the outset, but in its history of learning together. That is one reason I wanted to present an impression of their work together. They know it pays off to stick with a complex issue. They know the value to each person of starting from her own set of ideas and points of engagement and relating new ideas to that base— Piaget's fundamental point, but so rarely really acted on in formal education. And they know the value of paying attention to each other's ideas, to see how they can expand their own through making the accommodations necessary to assimilate other points of view—classic Piaget again.

Any one of us in this group might have dismissed the discussion by saying that, of course, Spain is east, so let's get on with it. Or, well, we know that east is where the sun rises, so let's get on with it. Instead, by recognizing that this was a complex issue, we pushed our ideas into a construction of a fairly sophisticated understanding of relationships between a flat world and a round world. This took us into map-making, surveying, history, geography (as we talked about this issue with various people we learned that the east–west highways in the Canadian prairies have periodic small-angle turns—like Wendy's hundredsagons—having been set out in a fashion similar to the Mason–Dixon line), and math (what is the mathematical nature of that third version of east, a curve which approaches the equator and wraps around it?).

Our delving into these areas grew out of the simple question of what east is, which itself grew out of the simple question of what can we see the moon do in the sky—a question that has engaged this group for eleven years. This exaggerated example is the strongest way to make my point: most areas of study that are at all worth our attention entail far more complexity than is acknowledged in our curriculum; and, further, people's intellectual engagement, when they are given the chance to pursue these complexities according to their own lights, is extraordinary. Our challenge as curriculum developers is to find the ways to engage learners, young or old, in the complexities of the areas we think it is important for them to know about. As researchers who are interested in how ideas actually develop, I think we have exactly the same challenge. I hope I have made clear how intertwined these challenges are.

I am under no illusion that, in the current climate of oversimplification, curriculum activity that celebrates the complexities of subject matter will be readily received. The point of this article is to rail against that climate, and to offer an idea of what our schools, our teachers, and our students may be missing by being subjected to that oversimplified view of the nature of teaching and learning.

I would like to end with some high school students' points of view, that poignantly express their awareness of how they are short-changed by current curriculum. With Candace Julyan (1988), they studied trees changing color in the fall. They were watching the trees themselves, in all their complexity, and trying to relate what they saw to their textbook course on chlorophyll and photosynthesis. The quotes exemplify their feelings about details that make a complex study accessible; about being able to figure out complex things in their own ways; and about the futility of trying to over-simplify curriculum.

> "It took me a while to get it...[to get] all my ideas together and see what I think. Once I got it was good....This is fun. I like it. It's neat that I figured all this out."
>
> "I was thinking how the wind takes the tree and the leaves...and when the tree bends, it stops feeding the leaves. Did you ever think of that?"
>
> "I love this project....I can never come up with ideas like this during labs....But *this*, it seems like I can come up with ideas really well. I don't know. I like this so much. I love it...."
>
> "You have to think. I don't think a lot of people like to think....[This study takes] a lot of figuring out. It's fun, but it's hard."
>
> "They throw something new at me and I can't stand it, and I have to do it their way. That's what I don't like about science, everything has already been figured out ahead of time. But if you find something different it's wrong."
>
> "I don't know why we *read* about trees in science class. It seems stupid not to come outside and really study 'em, don'tcha think?"

NOTES

[1]From *The Poetry of Robert Frost* edited by Edward Connery Lathem. Copyright 1936 by Robert Frost. Copyright © 1964 by Lesley Frost Ballantine. Copyright © 1969 by Holt, Rinehart and Winston. Reprinted by permission of Henry Holt and Company, Inc.

[2]For an analysis of one high school student's developing understanding of this poem, see Schneier, 1990.

[3]The members of the group besides myself are: Virginia Chalmers, Eliot Pearson School, Medford; Joanne Cleary, Tobin Elementary School, Cambridge; Mary DiSchino, Graham and Parks Elementary School, Cambridge; Fern Fisher, Consultant; Wendy Postlethwaite, Consultant; Mary Rizzuto, Graham and Parks, Cambridge).

REFERENCES

Bamberger, J., Duckworth, E., and Lampert, M. (1981). *An Experiment in Teacher Development: Final Report* (Contract No. B-81-0042). Washington, DC: National Institute of Education.

DiSchino, M. (1987). "The Many Phases of Growth." *The Journal of Teaching and Learning, 1*(3), 12–28.

Duckworth, E. (1964). "Floating Color Tubes." *Nature and Children, 1*(2), 6–7.

Duckworth, E. (1986). *Inventing Density.* Grand Forks, ND: North Dakota Study Group on Evaluation.

Duckworth, E. (1987). *The Having of Wonderful Ideas and Other Essays on Teaching and Learning.* New York: Teachers College Press.

Elementary Science Study. (1967a). *Gases and "Airs".* St. Louis: McGraw-Hill.

Elementary Science Study. (1967b). *Senior Balancing.* St. Louis: McGraw-Hill.

Hawkins, D. (1978). "Critical Barriers to Science Learning." *Outlook, 29,* 3–23.

Julyan, C. (1988). *Understanding Trees: Four Case Studies.* Unpublished doctoral dissertation, Harvard University.

Piaget, J., and Inhelder, B. (1975). *The Origin of the Idea of Chance in Children* (L. Leake, Jr., P. Burrell, H. Fishbein, Trans.). New York: W. W. Norton. (Original work published 1951)

Schneier, L. (1990). *Why Not Just Say It?.* Unpublished manuscript, Harvard University, Graduate School of Education.

8

ASSESSING "IMPERFECT" CONCEPTIONS

HUBERT DYASI

A VIEW OF ELEMENTARY SCHOOL SCIENCE

Assessment of children's progress in elementary science is embedded in an educational approach and serves clear purposes. In this article I shall describe my preferred approach to elementary science learning and outline what I think are appropriate data for assessment.

Children achieve a better understanding of the world by continually building and reinterpreting their direct knowledge. Their conceptions of the world undergo change as they grow and gain more direct experience with the physical world and with the world of symbols and ideas. Conceptual imperfection and continual refinement are, therefore, part and parcel of elementary school science learning. At the City College Workshop Center in New York, we view children's learning of elementary school science as encompassing content and approach. The content is found in common materials and phenomena that we encounter, and the approach is inquiry built around making meaning from observations and experience.

Direct experience with phenomena of the world connects the content of elementary science with children's experiences and observations outside the classroom. This connection reconfirms that science is a continuing search for underlying commonalities in apparently disparate phenomena, and an intense engagement with things that arouse our curiosity.

In an illustration of this approach, Jos Elsgeest (1969), a Dutch science educator who worked for many years in African science education, engaged African children studying the larval stage of the ant lion, an insect that resembles a dragonfly. The children's curiosity had led them to wonder about

An earlier version of this article appears in Hein, Ed. (1990). The Assessment of Hands-On Elementary Science Programs. *NDSG*, August, pp. 248–262.

observable characteristics of the ant lion, and to devise ways to answer their own questions. A transcript of a class discussion held after several observation sessions gives a flavor of the approach (T refers to the teacher; C1–C5 refer to five children) (Elsgeest, 1969, p. 3):

> T: Do you remember what you have already learnt about the ant lion [from the ant lion itself]?
> C1: They live in the soil.
> C2: They move backwards.
> C3: They like the sand.
> C4: They cannot live outside the sand.
> T: How do you know?
> C4: I tried it. I put it in my tin without sand, and it died.
> T: After how long did it die?
> C4: After three days.
> T: Why do you think it died outside the sand?
> C4: It cannot live outside the sand.
> C5: It could not eat.
> T: Now, that is a big problem: what do ant lions eat?

The children learned directly where the ant lion lives and about its locomotion. The record went on to show that among other things, they had also learned what the ant lion eats, how it catches its prey, whether it can see, and about how many legs it has.

Prominent, experienced scientists support our view of elementary school science as a precursor to authentic science inquiry and practice. Philip and Phylis Morrison (1984) have said quite simply, "You can't talk about science and remain solely in the domain of symbolic discourse. You require some contact with that substance of which science is a symbolic representation" (p. 4). Arons (1983) expressed the point in these words:

> Experience makes it increasingly clear that verbal presentations—lecturing to large groups of intellectually passive students and having them read text material—leave virtually nothing in the student's mind that is permanent or significant. Much less do they help the student attain what I consider the marks of a significantly literate person. (p. 92)

David Hawkins (1983) put the issue as follows: "There is a marvelous continuity between the worlds of children's experience and the adult worlds of the arts, of the sciences and mathematics, of conduct and social life. This community is one of cumulative learning" (p. 65).

At the City College Workshop Center, elementary school science learning encompasses three related processes: primary inquiry into a phenomenon of nature, symbolic representation of observations, and the ability to see patterns.

Inquiry involves direct, first-hand experiences with a selected piece of the natural world. If the selection is pendulums, children have direct experiences with pendulums by making and examining them, thus getting to know the parts of the pendulum. They observe pendulum motion and how it varies under different configurations, and identify periodic motion in nonclassical pendulums, perhaps by looking at the arms of a runner.

Observations children make may initially be general, but will often be refined as a result of a teacher's quest for greater specificity. For example, children will describe an insect with wings and legs and then begin to see an insect with so many pairs of wings, a specific shape, patterns of colors, and venation, and with specific points of attachment to the insects' body. They likewise arrive at detailed observations of legs: jointedness, number of pairs, smoothness or roughness, softness or hardness, and so on. The overall significance of primary inquiry is that children devise valid and reliable ways of obtaining information directly from nature, and actually do obtain it.

The second part of the process—symbolic representation—takes various forms: words, drawings, sound recordings, numbers, tracings, and photos. Asking children to represent some aspect of nature in symbolic form encourages them to observe details more closely for the purpose of keeping an accurate record and communicating observations.

The final process, children describing patterns as a result of their observations and representations of nature, engages them in generating knowledge and in developing concepts. At one level, children might see similarities among different things, and at a slightly deeper level, they may invent categories of attributes shared by objects or organisms. They may also begin to see patterns emerge under varying conditions or configurations. As children go beyond trial and error, the process involves studying descriptions, manipulating variables, and conducting tests to yield more descriptions. Children then create an organizing scheme to establish order from the descriptions, and draw conclusions or abstractions based on evidence. The abstractions go further than lists of observations and representations to careful operational statements that provide a basis for making predictions and for developing additional understandings.

There is a difference, of course, between scientists' science and children's science. The difference resides in children's ideas and frames of reference on the one hand, and of scientists on the other. A classroom example in which children were allowed to reveal their science understandings shows the relationship between observation and a frame of reference. Hein (1970) followed fifth graders studying linear motion of differently shaped objects down an inclined plane. The children had been asked to compare ways the different objects moved down the inclined plane; and they did, but not in ways the science educators expected them to do. The children raced the objects against one another to see who the winners and who the losers were. No matter what

Figure 8.1. Children's Scheme for Classifying Insects

CATEGORY	CHARACTERISTIC	EXAMPLES
Live communally	Very small, build houses	Wasp, white ant
Attack intruders	Eat other insects or powdery things	Bee, safari ant
Do not bite	Humble	Mantids, butterfly, ant lion, earthworm
Make honey	Lay eggs, obtain food from flowers, suck food, hairy legs	Bee, butterfly
Have three parts	Short wings, eat tender leaves, big eyes, winged	Wasp, house fly, termite, bee
Live underground	No eyes	Ant lion, white ant, small black ant, safari ant
Live in trees	Eat fruits, bite	White ant

questions the educators asked or in what direction they tried to lead the children, the children persisted in looking at the events as races. Within the frame of "races," children observed some events and failed to notice others which would be important in a different frame of reference. The important observation to children was spotting the winners; ties were irrelevant. Hein concluded logically and reasonably: "These children do not have a statistical view of data and scientific observation. Instead they have a particulate view of events. Each observation has its independent existence, each observation could decide the contest" (p. 87). Looking for winners in this activity is not what a scientist would do. Scientists would attend to "ties" in their frame of reference because they are interested in probabilities of independent events.

Children's science tends to draw understandings directly from the nonidealized conditions we all know, whereas scientists' views relate to established canons of knowledge drawn from idealized or controlled laboratory conditions. For example, children know that in free fall, heavy objects fall faster than lighter ones. Scientists make the same observations; but children's explanations of this phenomenon will differ from the scientists' because children's frame of reference is centered only on the weight of the objects and does not encompass observations of free fall in a vacuum. The different frames of reference or presuppositions with which children and scientists approach this observation result in different "facts," different trials of one factor or another, and different degrees of elaborateness of investigations.

If children's frame of reference of winners and losers is flawed as a basis for scientific understanding of rolling objects down inclined planes, it has to be improved by creating an interest in examining ties which still need to be

Figure 8.2. A Child's Classification of Caterpillars

COLOR	FATNESS	HAIRY	FOUND ON	SAMENESS
Green	Thin	Not hairy	Hawthorn	Not the same
Yellow and grey	Fat	Bit hairy	Hawthorn	
Brown	Fat	Hairy	Dock leaf	Not the same
Brown	Medium	Bit hairy	Hawthorn	Same

explained. Such an examination might lead children to consider frames of reference that allow for a more comprehensive and reliable description of observed events. They might go beyond "naive" notions or theories to careful operational statements that lay ground for predictions and for broader understandings. A close look suggests that children's work is important in assessing their progress in science inquiry.

Children's Work

A fifth grade class which had been looking at insects for several lessons developed its own classification scheme (see Figure 8.1) and a "key" for identifying insects found locally. A person looking at the children's classification scheme might be struck by its unusual basis and by errors it contains. For example, a person might think that the first column is not necessary—that the categories are actually also characteristics in some sense. One notices also that some of the organisms belong to more than one "class." From the Linnean frame of classification (the genus and species frame of reference) earthworms should not be included because they are not insects. These are legitimate sources of concern but the concern must not overshadow the power of the children's creation of a scheme (Science Education Program for Africa, 1978).

Independently of these fifth grade children, other children in an elementary school class in England engaged in a similar science learning activity. One of them developed the classification scheme shown in Figure 8.2 (Rowland, 1984, p. 27).

In this classification activity the teacher reported that the child *first thought* about the attributes he wanted to use and then examined the specimens over and over again and selected those that share the attribute. This thinking about an embracing attribute from discrete observations is a very bold and constructive intellectual activity whether it is done at the frontiers of a discipline or, as in this case, at earlier stages of learning. The action signifies the interpretations of nature on the basis of observations, representations, and understanding of the selected organisms in the environment.

The creation of an interpretive scheme shows that the children have gone beyond particular examples to think of generalizations that can be supported by demonstrable observations. What remains to be done to further their science development is no small task; it is to encourage them to be willing to refine and modify their scheme, and to make finer distinctions. Before children can evaluate the usefulness of any scheme, however, they would have to use it extensively. From that use, perhaps they would recognize problems with a scheme that does not, for example, discriminate well among things that are very different from one another in some important respects. In time, they might see the value of seeking guidance from schemes developed by others. Perhaps as they observe other living things closely, they will look at the structural characteristics of the organisms in order to make fine classification distinctions. They will recognize their earlier schemes as first approximations that were useful for gaining a general idea and for laying a foundation for a coherent picture.

Observations need not be represented only in prose, drawings, and tables; they can be represented in verse, as the 10-year-old Leo's poem show. (Leo—not his real name—did this work at the Prospect School, Bennington, Vermont [The Prospect Archive, 1984]):

It's a Spider

Moving through the night
As if always in flight
From some unseen enemy.
In the summer webs on trees
In the fall webs in the leaves
In the winter you die on out
In the spring your children
Search for a new home.

There is a sense here that Leo has focused on the spider not momentarily, but over an expanse of time and space. He has arrived at the notion of the physical home (the web) located in a broader habitat—the tree at one time and the leaf at another. The life cycle is captured by the child: life of the spider in the summer, fall, and winter and then the young ones appear in the spring. Unstated, but understood is that in the summer they become adults, that will presumably die in the winter. The young ones have the task of building a home or searching for one. The great explosion of life in the spring and the end of a lifetime in the winter have been duly noticed and recorded by the child. *That* is the essence of observation to make meaning (Carini, 1979).

Documenting Children's Inquiry Work

Children have a natural inclination to make connections and to create schemes that account for perceived relationships. Previous examples of children's work indicate that children can generate knowledge directly from objects of nature; such knowledge goes beyond mere speculation and guessing. Children can obtain information from direct experience with concrete natural phenomena through systematic manipulation and observation. They can utilize symbolic material to represent the observations faithfully, and make relevant abstractions from the representations. The challenge for assessment is to find strategies and mechanisms that portray this development in elementary science learning.

Documentation of children's work over *significantly long periods of time* is one of the best sources for assessing children's progress in elementary school science inquiry. The documentation can be obtained through the research technique of observing and recording a single child's experiences and responses. Although this method yields invaluable information for assessment purposes, it cannot be used consistently by classroom teachers who have responsibility for *all* children in their class for *only* nine months. But this technique can be modified to meet these constraints. The records of children's work at The Prospect Archive and Center for Education and Research are an excellent example of such a modification.

The Prospect Archive is a unique collection of individual children's drawings, writings, constructions, and other artifacts spanning an average of six to eight years of a child's school experience. The material on each child also includes a teacher's weekly statements about the child's educational activities, as well as a general summary covering each term. Below is an excerpt from a teacher's general summary about Leo, the child whose work has been cited above:

> He (Leo) builds intricate structures all of which have long explanations to go with them. One building of (Leo's) was...a building on another planet complete with laboratory, energy sources, water systems, solar collectors, secret passageways with trap doors. (Leo) has a natural sense of balance and symmetry....He is very inventive with wood and thinks up very original projects for himself to do. He built a base for a star ship. For this he invented a pivotal cannon that could move up and down and around. It was very impressive because he had come up with the whole thing completely independently. (The Prospect Archive, 1984, p. 54)

These evaluative statements are part of the data attached to the child's work. Interested persons can have access to the entire portfolio to make their own judgments. The teacher's statements do not make reference to the inquiry process associated with these activities, but there could have been such reference had the teacher included science inquiry as a major focus of the child's activities. However, the teacher did view making representations of objects as a very important activity for the child, hence the following comments:

(Leo's) drawings often express his mechanical interests. They are often cross sections of buildings revealing all the inner networks of stairways, water systems, energy systems, and structural supports. His drawings are striking for the detail and depth. (p. 54)

The teacher's comments indicate quite vividly what a close observer Leo is; the comments lead us to look at the child's work directly to satisfy our curiosity about it.

Another mechanism for assessing development in elementary science learning is the documentation of group activities within a class over extended periods in the form of a "teacher's journal." In this case, work of groups of children is accumulated over time, thus creating a "bank" of detailed material encompassing their science learning activities. Included with the children's work are their teachers' perceptions and reflections about the work. The children's work cited above can be used to make inferences about the children's progress in science learning. *Juba Beach* (1971), a teacher's journal prepared for and published by the African Primary Science Program, is an example of such a journal. The journal includes children's descriptions of their science inquiry activities complete with written accounts, diagrams, and questions related to the organisms the children studied along a beach. The teacher's comments, interspersed in the children's own accounts, are informative. For example, in *Juba Beach* the teacher wrote:

> The general topic of beaches and sea integrated many experiences of learning. The children found and observed a wide variety of animals. They examined rocks and shells and sand. They tasted and tested water for salt content. They counted waves and the flow of rivers and talked to fishermen. The challenges were without limit...The events of this unit encouraged them to find answers to new questions. They wanted to learn and because of this they used and developed their skills—they measured, weighed, compared and counted, they kept notes and discussed their findings. For me, their own evaluations and this record book tell more about the progress of the children than any written examination I might have given them.

Computer technology can be used to build a data bank based on children's work which can provide evidence of the quality of their participation in science inquiry activities. In such cases the computer is a tool that children use to record the observations, experiments, and abstractions derived from their science investigations. The records can be retrieved by the children, the teacher, or by someone else interested in them. The Bank Street College of Education's Center for Children and Technology in New York City has done interesting work in this respect. In the *Earth Lab* project, children work in groups to do earth science inquiries; they collect data and later share their findings. The Center's project *INQUIRE* is a software design that makes it possible for children to keep notes, and record their ideas, plans, guesses of expected findings, and findings while engaged in inquiry activities on sports physics. As a result, it is possible for children to create their portfolios as they progress in their elementary school science learning activities during science investigations (McCarthy, 1989).

Another interesting use of computer technology in elementary school science learning which has a great potential as a documenting mechanism for assessment purposes is *The National Geographic Kids Network*. This project for grades four through six is carried out by Technical Education Research Centers and combines the use of computers with telecommunications. Children in the network conduct experiments in their local areas, such as collecting data on acid rain. The telecommunications network links them with children in other localities by sending the results of their local experiments to a central computer. Through the network, children in various parts of the world can discuss their findings with their peers and work collaboratively in a manner similar to how a research team works together. Although many classrooms might not have easy access to a telephone line, the computer component of the activities can be good for recordkeeping.

The question is: Who assesses this work? The answer is teachers. Most documentation described here can be done by suitably educated teachers enjoying unfettered professional judgments. They would use prepared assessment guidelines indicating how the children's work is to be judged. The guidelines would be faithful to the advocated science approach, both sufficiently flexible and unambiguous. Carefully selected panels including teachers, science educators, child development specialists, leading scientists, and school children would prepare these crucially important guidelines. Since community schools are local institutions, groups of teachers at the local level, assessment specialists, science educators, and if possible, outstanding scientists would come together to examine children's work. Based on that examination they would prepare detailed reports describing the work and indicating how it was assessed. It would be left to the local school districts' or the state's discretion to make assessments by child, grade, school, district, or a combination of all those elements. For purposes of comparison across school districts, samples of assessed children's work could be examined by panels of teachers and assessment specialists drawn from the districts, with additional members drawn from other states. These panels would also prepare detailed reports on the documents they examined. These informative reports would be used widely to improve elementary school science instruction. Tests would not be eliminated; instead they would be restructured to focus on children's demonstrated capability to make sense of observations derived from physical materials presented to them.

I have portrayed elementary science education as focusing on children's engagement in organized inquiry with natural phenomena in their surroundings. I have also implied that science inquiry requires a considerable density of often repeated experience over long periods of time. I view one major purpose of assessment as support for quality instruction in science inquiry. The examples of children's work indicate that children are capable of conducting inquiries into nature, but are still developing "imperfect" conceptions by adult scientific standards. Through children's work, one gains insight into their developing art, skill, and knowledge of doing science. I am calling, therefore, for assessment that portrays children's continuing development in science inquiry through appropriate, practical, concrete investigative activities; and children's capacity to communicate their understanding by the questions they raise about nature, by the observations they choose to make, and through the symbols they devise. The willingness to document such data will not come about until it is accepted that elementary school children's inquiries are valuable starting and continuing points for science inquiry instruction, and that teachers can play a large role in assessment activities.

REFERENCES

Arons, A. B. (1983). "Achieving Wider Scientific Literacy." *Daedalus*, 112(2).

Carini, P. F. (1979). *The Art of Seeing and the Visibility of the Person*. Grand Forks, ND: University of North Dakota Press.

Elsgeest, J. (1969). "Ask the Ant Lion." From *African Primary Science Program*. Newton, MA: Education Development Center.

Science Education Program for Africa. (1978). *Handbook for Science Teachers*. Accra, Ghana: Author.

Hawkins, D. (1983). "Nature Closely Observed." *Daedalus*, 112(2).

Hein, G. E. (1970). "Children's Science Is Another Culture." From *ESS Reader*. Newton, MA: Education Development Center.

Juba Beach, A Unit of the African Primary Science Program (1971). Newton, MA: Education Development Center.

McCarthy, R. (1989). "Behind the Scenes at Bank Street College." *Electronic Learning*, October, pp. 30–34.

Morrison, P., and Morrison, P. (1984). *Primary Science: Symbol or Substance?* New York: Workshop Center.

The Prospect Archive. (1984). *(LEO)*. Unpublished manuscript, North Bennington, VT: The Prospect Archive and Center for Education and Research, Inc.

Rowland, S. (1984). *The Enquiring Classroom*. London: The Falmer Press.

9

JASON AND MATT
KAY HIBL

As an elementary school teacher, differences in problem-solving approaches fascinate me and I take every opportunity to explore them. One of my favorite experiences came while working with two fifth-grade boys, Jason and Matt. I wrote down this story to illustrate how diverse two children's thinking can be about the same situation.

I had worked on the chessboard problem before with groups of adults and children. On this occasion, using a chessboard and beans, I told the boys the legend from Jacobs (1970):

> There is a legend about the king of Persia and the inventor of the game of chess. According to the legend, the king of Persia, out of gratitude to the inventor of the chess, offered him anything he would like for a reward. The inventor requested that one grain of wheat be placed upon the first square of the chessboard, two grains be placed on the second square, four grains on the third square, continuing in this manner, doubling the number of grains for each successive square on the board. This request seemed reasonable enough to the king and he sent one of his servants off for a bag of wheat. As the king soon realized, one bag of wheat would simply not be enough. By continually doubling the amount of wheat on each square of the board until the sixty-fourth square is reached, more than nine quintillion grains of wheat are needed. That is enough wheat to cover the state of California with one foot of wheat. Another way to consider the amount is, 500 times the 1976 *annual* world harvest of wheat, which is probably more wheat than has been harvested by man in history! The inventor, no doubt, was compensated in another way. (p. 54)

Jason and Matt began computing straight away. Matt added first on his fingers, then on paper. Jason, in contrast, sounded like a metronome saying the numbers out loud: 1, 2, 4, 8, 16, 32, 64, his perfect rhythm broken only slightly for the next two numbers in the sequence. Matt stopped adding and counting

111

to suggest that we figure out the number of beans for the first row of the chessboard and then multiply by 2. Jason wasted no time in telling Matt that his idea would not work and then reminded him that the number *doubled* on *each* successive square. Matt went back to counting. He counted out beans, put them in a cup, and added in the new amount. When he had filled his cup halfway, I asked him how full the cup would be when he doubled the amount in it. I knew that Matt had been working with fractions in class and was surprised when he struggled with ½ cup + ½ cup. Later it became evident that Matt had a very strong need to be precise; he was unwilling to make the mental leap from 128 beans = ½ cup of beans, 128 beans + 128 beans = 256 beans, therefore ½ cup of beans + ½ cup of beans = 1 cup of beans or 256 beans. He argued that measuring by cups was imprecise because he could not *always* be completely certain that one cup had exactly 256 beans!

At one point Matt's addition and self-checking fascinated me. He added two six-digit numerals, looked at the sum, and muttered, "That can't be right." He then counted the digits in his answer for verification, said, "No, that's not right," and added again. Matt also had difficulty reading large numbers. Having only as an adult mastered reading six or seven-digit numerals, I sympathized with Matt and offered help. My offer was shunned and Matt continued to add.

Both boys became interested in calculating how many containers of beans it would take to actually fill one quarter of the room in which we were sitting. Jason sprung to action immediately: the bottom of the bean container was roughly the size of one floor tile, or one square foot, and the container's height was about one foot. He began counting the floor tiles to figure the area of the room and then multiplied to obtain the room's volume. His math was completely mental and incredibly quick. So swift, in fact, that my brow was knitted and I was saying, "Wait a minute! I need to figure this one out on paper!" Jason's arithmetic was accurate. I asked him if he could tell me what his mental process was.

In his serious way, he carefully told me that he had counted a length of 32 tiles and a width of 50 tiles. "Since half of 30 is 15, then half of 32 is 16, then add the zeros to get 1,600 square feet." I needed to write *that* down and think a bit! Jason knew that there was a connection between multiplying by five and dividing by two (did *I* know that connection?). He was very comfortable with ignoring zeros while computing mentally and inserting them when finished. My mental approach for multiplying 32 × 50 would have been to first multiply 50 × 30 = 1,500; then multiply 2 × 50 = 100; and then add 1,500 + 100 = 1,600. For me to re-create what Jason had done so quickly, I had to think about it being easier to multiply 32 by 100 instead of multiplying 32 by 50 resulting in 3,200, or twice the answer. Once double the answer is arrived at I only needed to divide 3,200 by 2 to 1,600. Since Jason ignored all zeros from the start, he multiplied by 1 instead of 100, then divided his answer by 2, and then added two zeros. Jason's comment, "Since half of 30 is 15, then half of 32 is 16," puzzled me until I realized that Jason did not know immediately what half of 32 was, but he did know that half of 30 was 15; thus, 32 ÷ 2 had to be 16.

The area of half the room was 1,600 square feet. To arrive at a figure for one quarter of the room's volume, Jason estimated the height of the room as 10 feet, and calculated the volume for one half of that space. To figure volume for a space that is 1,600 square feet and five feet high, Jason knew that he needed to know what five 1,600's are. His approach, once again, was to take the zeros off 1,600 and add 16 five times: 16 + 16 = 32, 32 + 32 = 64, 64 + 16 = 80, replace the zeros and Jason had 8,000 cubic feet!

Matt was committed to proving Jason's square footage wrong. Matt counted tiles and argued that there were some partial tiles in the area where Jason had counted. He also pointed out that Jason had not counted every bean in the container and therefore would be unable to compute *exactly* how many beans there would be in one quarter of the room. Jason looked at him incredulously and said calmly, at first, "The exact number of beans does not matter, we have a good idea how many beans there are and who really cares with beans, anyway?" Matt continued to needle Jason until Jason left in utter disgust. I talked with Matt about the importance of accuracy in certain situations, but felt that my words fell on deaf ears. I began to wonder if Matt's demand for accuracy was a cover. He had been most comfortable doing the routine operations of addition and counting. He was less comfortable with reasoning and problem solving, and very often unsuccessful in these situations. Jason estimated a great deal and was very comfortable with ball park estimates. Matt was safe when he shifted the arena for debate from problem solving and estimation to computation based upon certain, not estimated numbers.

REFERENCES

Jacobs, H. R. (1970). *Mathematics: A Human Endeavor.* San Francisco: W.H. Freeman and Company.

10

LOOKING AT A CHILD'S WORK
KATHE JERVIS AND ANN WIENER

We must be attentive to children. Whether it is in modeling clay or solving problems, we must pay attention, heartfelt deeply caring attention, to how children learn. We should study children and their work and then share what we see with each other—(Patricia Carini, quoted in Jervis, 1983, p. 30)

KESHANA—THE ELUSIVE FASHION PRINCESS

At the first faculty meeting, we chose Keshana (as we are calling her here) at random. We knew nothing about her except that she was one of 40 fifth graders new to our small alternative urban public fifth through eighth grade middle school. Some children are easy to know, but not Keshana. She might have remained an invisible presence in the school if she had not been the subject of our teacher research project, a study designed to observe closely one child's transition from elementary to middle school over a two year period.[1] Had we selected a different child to illustrate how our school serves children—perhaps a noisy boy or a cerebral over-achieving girl—our study would have illuminated other corners of the educational landscape. The choice of Keshana, however, was fortuitous; rarely do low profile children command such careful and sustained attention.

When Keshana came to our school her physical presence was her most striking characteristic. "Cutie Keshana" is how she identified herself in an introduction game the first week. From the first year notes:

Keshana is a petite, small boned, medium dark-skinned child with wide eyes, a high forehead, and prominent cheek bones. Her teeth are straight and even, but her wide smile reveals a gap where her molars will eventu-

114

ally be. Characteristically, she is noticeable in a group for the way she holds her body—straight back, chin resting pensively in her hand, legs delicately crossed at the ankles. Her graceful presence and beautiful posture are extraordinary. Hair in corn rows or a french braid gives her an always-cared-for look. More fashionably dressed than many fifth graders, she also looks more adult, perhaps because her clothes—long skirts and tucked in shirts—hang particularly well on her. She coordinates her sock color with her outfit—even her shoe laces match. Other children take an acute interest in her wardrobe.

In our social studies/science class of 28 untracked racially and economically diverse fifth through eighth graders, she sat day after day, her legs daintily crossed, saying nothing to us or to peers, and rarely making her presence felt. We took weekly notes on her as we went along, but at the end of the first trimester, she was one of two children who made so little impact that we could say nothing significant on her report card. We knew almost nothing about the way she thought or how she viewed the course content. Her written work was sketchy—typical of many first trimester fifth graders—but what was she taking in? She certainly wasn't putting anything out, but what was she taking in? We looked in vain for points of connection to school.

Yet, after receiving her conspicuously bland report card, she was one of the few children who wrote comments back to each of her teachers. It was a first clue that the written word might be an avenue to understanding more about her. Written with a breezy equality, her lively comments revealed a more responsive and connected child than we saw in class. About social studies she said, "I feel that the assignment on ROOTS is a good one. It is very interesting and I find it fun for the whole class." To the math teacher, "I like the way you teach the class and how you play games with your class and you make it seem interesting. " In Writers Workshop, "I like the class and I think you teach it well. *But* do you mind when people/your students ask you questions? Because when I ask you questions I get in trouble."

The "Attitued" of a Fledgling Philosopher

Sometimes an "attitued" (as she spelled it) leaked out, almost against her will, as if she had lost her self-control and strong feelings just overwhelmed her. An anecdote, recorded by an astute student teacher, captures the flavor of the faculty complaint:

Keshana is in math and working on "The Problem of the Day": You are having a party with 36 guests. You have three pizzas. How would you divide them to have enough for everyone?

She wouldn't budge on her thinking. First she asked, "What if there are drugs on the pizza?"

Then she refused to divide the three pizzas, and only divided one. When I asked her what she did with the other two, she said, "I put them in the refrigerator for later."

When I pushed her further about the slices being uneven, she said, "Who said we have to have pizza anyway? Why can't we order Chinese food?" I continued to press her about the different size slices, and she said, "Who said I would invite you?"

Unlike predictably rude or excitable children, Keshana did not openly bait teachers, but asking "What if there are drugs on the pizza?" is surely designed to drive a teacher mad. For Keshana this is not a math problem, but a practical (and more compelling) problem of how to arrange a party. Pizza may not be the right thing to serve; Chinese food may be better. In many instances, Keshana's own concerns and the proffered academic agenda did not fit, and the result was the adults' plausible conclusion that she was uncooperative and had limited academic potential.

Our concern was Keshana's lack of engagement with academics. How could she reach her potential—whatever that meant—if she continued to produce schoolwork that teachers found mechanically done, careless, and incomplete? She often complained she was bored, and therefore didn't spend any time on her work. Right before our eyes we saw her disengaged from the curriculum, but we were helpless to tinker with the system to make it better for her. Her compelling interest was social and the magnetic properties her friends exerted on her were hard to counteract. In formal academics, a consistent picture emerged. Her report cards noted that she was often behind in work, "appeared lost," and had trouble understanding concepts. "Unfocused," "distracted," and "lacking concentration," her academic progress inspired no faith in her ability. Homework and school work seemed equally uneven. We didn't have a clue where to begin.

Quiet Keshana would not have been noticed had we not been on a campaign to notice her. On the spectrum of children who demanded our attention, Keshana ranked at the bottom. We even wondered if her "attitued" was more visible because we kept the focus on her. Generally, she stayed out of any teacher's way and kept a low profile. Some faculty resisted the time spent on this "unintriguing" child when many more needy children could have benefited by our study. But we persisted in collecting "inadequate" work samples and anecdotes about her "bad attitude." We were actually tantalized by the possibilities that her random selection would bring us new understanding of a child we would never have noticed.

Then in April she took the New York City Standardized Writing Test. We were stunned by what she wrote:

Who Are You?

One day I was riding my bike in the park. You would never guess what happened to me. We both crashed into each other.

"Hello, my name is Keshana. What's yours?"

"My name is LaToya"

I asked her where she lived. She replied "I live in Brooklyn." I started asking her so many questions that she got tired of it and said "Buzz off & mind your own bee'swax!"

Boy was I ever shocked. She rode her bike off to I don't know where!

There was one thing she forgot. I asked her her phone number. I called her house, she answered the phone and said "Hello who's speaking?" In such a nice way. I answered, "Keshana."

"Keshana who?" she replied. "The girl who you met in the park? She hung up. If there was one thing I hated about that girl it was her attitued.

I went home that night and thought am I going to be like her when I grow up? Is she going to be like me when she grows up?

If you think about it we might grow up to have switched personalities. I went back to the park to see if she was there. She wasn't. I thought to myself, "I'm glad I didn't see her."

But it gets you to wondering, will I be like her when I'm grown up. Will she be like me?

The world will
never know!

Here (with her own errors retained throughout this article) Keshana writes with directness, honesty, and a storyteller's skill that could hardly be improved, qualities which the faculty did not see in her classroom work. Where was she hiding this skill? The Keshana of this story is perceptive, philosophical, and intensely curious. Her language is vivid and lively.

We looked carefully at "Who Are You?" with several colleagues according to the formal Descriptive Processes developed at the Prospect Center in North Bennington, VT. We read the work aloud with colleagues many times in order to extract as much meaning as we could from Keshana's story line, word choice, sentence structure, and rhythm. We tried to hear her voice clearly. We could have used a piece of art, a social studies project, or a conversation, but the first vehicle that stood out as having meaning for Keshana happened to be writing.

In this essay, Keshana is struggling to understand and communicate who she is. New York City required that she take a standardized writing test, but she made this formal structure her own. She gave herself the opportunity to think of herself as a grown up and to explore what kind of person she will become. Significantly, she wrote for an impersonal audience. This "intimate" writing is the first time she began to tell her story at school in a way that we heard it.

Risky Questions

A sense of unease permeates the essay's topic and its execution. A bicycle crash initiates the action. Keshana shoots a barrage of questions at LaToya, who responds with an unwanted, rude abruptness. Keshana pursues this other self, but her own curiosity thwarts a potential connection as she comes up against LaToya's unforgiving "attitued."

Keshana's harmless social questions are the center of this essay on self-doubt. She has transformed the universal identity question from "Who am I?" to "Who are You?" and devised a double to personify her own uncertainty about adulthood. In this story she makes it clear that asking questions is risky and answering even riskier. She asks *ten* questions in this short piece, beginning and ending with the deeply philosophical and unanswerable. In between she courteously inquires about socially acceptable topics only to get an immediate and quaintly old fashioned response: "Buzz off & mind your own bee'swax." She contrasts her own gracious persona with this rude double. She demonstrates her own social skills by politely courting LaToya "in such a nice way," and concludes judgmentally: LaToya has an "attitued." That strong feeling draws the reader further into the story, but also pushes the limits of Keshana's graciousness. Socially skilled, but impotent, she cannot achieve her desired goal of connecting with LaToya.

Keshana's central identity question may be unanswered, but the essay's end implies that eventually she will reach responsible adulthood. That Keshana might grow up to have this unpleasant child's "attitued" is a dreaded, but possible outcome which she resolves temporarily by absenting LaToya from the park. In good narrative style, she leaves the question open.

For reasons of gender, temperament, a particular vulnerability, or a combination of all three, Keshana has concluded that asking questions may not be safe. In person, Keshana is not an abrasive badgerer or tiresome provocateur children and teachers loathe, but questions vex her not only in her imagined neighborhood park, but in her real middle school classroom. "*But* do you mind when people/your students ask you questions? Because when I ask you questions I get in trouble." This comment from her report card is the quintessential articulation of this stance. Indeed, we heard very few questions in class.

Teachers thought that the striking *absence* of Keshana's questions prevented her from learning classroom material. An unusual number of references to questions and questioning appear on Keshana's fifth- and sixth-grade report cards. Among them, her math teacher writes, "Occasionally she comes up with the right questions. It's questions more than the answers that are the key to her success. She must become involved in her own education." A science teacher, who found that Keshana "didn't quite get a grasp of ideas and concepts," said, "Participation in discussion and questioning would have helped her understanding."

We know asking questions is an important way of acquiring knowledge about one's identity, and about the larger world. It seems obvious enough that if asking questions in the classroom is too threatening, or classroom work not compelling enough to provoke questions, academic success can be tenuous. It is also possible Keshana lacked the confidence to ask. More likely, Keshana had questions, but we just didn't hear them until we listened hard.

We recognized the worth of "Who Are You?" as good "data," but at that time we did not look so carefully at other written work. Rather, we kept trying to disentangle more salient school behavior. We knew more and more about how she was manipulating the system and the adults. Keshana negotiated the gray areas masterfully according to her whim. She never reported her conflict between math and Writer's Workshop winter trimester, and missed out on three months of writing class. The next term, this same child came 20 minutes late to class saying without a flicker of hesitation that she was "there all the time." All-day shadowing revealed that she had no written permission to leave the school grounds, but we discovered she was putting the free school lunch in her coat pocket and leaving with peers whose parents permitted lunchtime outings. Had low profile Keshana not been a study child, no one might have known. She managed to be almost invisible, even as the focus of a study. As we mulled over the ethics of uncovering her deceptions, and wondered how many other children found ways around the most basic rules, other information rose up to perplex us.

Keshana as the Author of Her Life

Midway through the first year, we discovered this "nonachieving" child was sustaining soul-wrenching losses in her family. The faculty looked for openings to get her to talk, but not even when she was assigned to the school counselor's small group did she refer to any of her losses, large or small. That led us to conjecture that Keshana's muted impact was due to masked feelings, and that her "stalled" academic progress came from lack of emotional energy. This tempting avenue of exploration kept us from focusing on the daily classroom work that teachers found so deficient.

But later, when we looked at more of her written work, we found that Keshana wrote frequently about her losses. We had missed the point. That oversight underscored our growing certainty that were we to know her at all, it would be through her writing. Her second essay on the fifth grade standardized writing test specified the topic of loss, but Keshana's resolution is typical of many of her examples. Keshana wrote "Where is it?" about a lost necklace. After looking everywhere she finally stopped searching for this lost jewelry, and the essay ends with her mother giving her a new necklace for her birthday, "and it looked better than the old one."

Keshana frequently wrote about families and loss, and her pattern was to resolve each setback or disappointment at the end of the story and move on. In response to an assignment to write about something that happened to her over vacation, she wrote this story:

The EASTER That Never Was

My name is Audrey. I'm 12 years old and I live in Brooklyn N.Y. Yesterday was EASTER Sunday and most people go to church with their families and mabey go see their relatives. But not US. I can tell you what I DID in one sentence. Almost nothing. I woke up put on my robe, and my slippers and brushed my hair into a ponytail. Then I washed up. Got dressed while watching T.V. in my room brought the papers for my mother, made my mom some coffee, and ate breakfast, took a shower, put on my easter clothes and fixed my hair. And then after all that I went threw I found out that we weren't going anywhere. Everybody except my Mother & Father were disappointed. But for the first time I wasn't surprised. I mean it's not like this had never happened before. Because once we were going to Rye-playland but my mom thought that it was too hot. I mean it was a beauti-ful day amost 100 degrees, so instead we went to Yonkers to see my friends and family. What was the diffence we still had to go out in the heat anyway. So anyway I put on my jeans and colored some eggs with my sister. I guess you could say that that was an easter never to be.

   My father and mother spoil my sister and I alot. Whatever we ask for we get. I mean their not even our parents their our grandparents. My sis-ters name is Julian we get along most of the time. When we were coloring the eggs we had lots of fun, and when we ate them it was even better.

Keshana did not reveal herself to the adults in school except in her writ-ing. Even then, it was all too easy to miss her voice. This piece—so complete and vivid as a story—had to be extracted by threat. It was so overdue some teachers might have given her no credit and ceased to insist that it be done. Indeed, her invisibility made it easy to ignore delinquent work.

Keshana made this assignment her own. As usual, she chose not to write a straightforward answer to "Something I Did Over Easter Vacation." Like much of her other writing, this breezy piece has a powerful aural quality. The mechanical mistakes convey some of the meaning. *EASTER* takes on bold importance at the beginning, but as she writes, the urgency drains out, and her intense disappoint-ment fades. Her writing serves as a coping mechanism. Keshana does live with her paternal grandparents, and she does have a sister, but as the first part of this story makes clear, she does not get everything she wants. So she has written an alternative ending to this nonexistent Easter in which her discontent is manage-able and she even admits that "when we were coloring the eggs we had lots of fun, and when we ate them it was even better."

She took personal meaning from an academic assignment when she wrote a book report on a biography of Arthur Ashe that is a chronicle of loss and family strength. Again, we brought Keshana's work to a group of colleagues for collaborative analysis, this time at the 1989 Chicago Conference on Progressive Education. Keshana "owns" this book. She is indeed the "author" of this life of Arthur Ashe and even begins, "*My* book is about...," foregoing the more usual "*This* book is about...." She has personalized the assignment for her own purposes. Is this not what we want of children in school?

Author Ashe Tennis Champion, by Louie Robinson, Jr.

My book is about a tennis champion Author Ashe. When Author was really young his favorite sport was baseball. He hit the ball very high and some people wondered where he got the strength from. At the time he was three '3': he had '1' brother Johnny. Johnny was younger than Author.

When Author was about 4-5 yrs. old his mother passed away. Author took it hard and didn't understand why? his mother passed away. One day Author went down to the tennis court to see all the players in action, and get his mind off of his mother's death. A man named *Ronald Charity* was playing and happed to notice Author. He had asked Author if he knew how to play? Author replied "No Sir I don't." "Will you watch me? He hit the ball so high that Mister Charity started laughing. He caught on to this game really soon. Mr. Charity knew that Author was one day going to be a star! When Author was about 6 his father had got a *new* mother for Johnny & him. His father made them call her mother.

She was an old lady but with lots of knowledge.

Pretty soon Author made it to the tennis tournaments & and even won a few games. People would say that he was the greatest that's played tennis in along time. Author's family gave him alot of back up and showed him that they cared. Author Ashe is still playing tennis today. He will always be good at it.

Arthur could hit the ball so high some people wondered where he got his strength, but what interests her is sibling birth order, maternal death, remarriage, and stepmothers. Keshana asks the eternal question of why Arthur's mother had to die. Keshana treats his loss as she does her own. She identifies the loss, mourns it, and moves on. The *deus ex machina*, Ronald Charity, couldn't be more aptly named in fiction. He recognizes five-year-old Ashe's star quality—high hitting and catching on easily—but again, as in the first paragraph, Keshana focuses on family. Arthur's athletic prowess is downplayed: "He made it to the tennis tournaments & even won a few games." Missing from this personal essay is anything about hard work and long hours of practice. Still, "People would say he was the greatest." She ends with Arthur as an adult, still active and always good at tennis.

Though the book report begins and ends superficially with tennis, Keshana has distilled a deeper message from Arthur Ashe's life: bad things happen to Arthur, but he survives with the support of his family. His mother dies, but as he copes with his grief on the tennis court, Mr. Charity appears. Arthur's father "got" him a *new* mother with knowledge. "Author's family gave him a lot of back up and showed him that they cared." Even this standard school assignment can be a vehicle for growth if teachers can recognize that Keshana's questions—both personal and philosophical—are embedded in her responses.

But no matter how important this personalized assignment was for Keshana, it is easy to see how a teacher's first response might be (as ours was), "When you do a biographical book report you should at least spell the subject's name right," and further dismiss it for its emphasis on jumbled details irrelevant to Ashe's tennis. As Keshana wrote this book report, her own (estranged) father had just set his wedding date. She would have a *new* mother. Would she be required to call this woman "mother?" Would this "mother" be as supportive as Arthur Ashe's mother? As knowledgeable? As caring? The crucial point for Keshana is that Arthur Ashe's family kept him going by care and backup.

As we looked at this piece of work with colleagues, we saw that rather than deficient book reporting, it reflected her strength in coping. She connected to academics through her feelings, a perfectly valid way to learn. She is using her school work to be the author of her life. Keshana has taken from the reading what is meaningful to her. Is this not what we strive for in our classrooms?

Gaps and Misperceptions

Keshana and the school adults misperceive each other across a large distance. Perhaps teachers need to meet Keshana more than half way if the distance is to be narrowed. In order to reflect back to her how she appears to adults we need to make adults more visible to her. She needs to expand the audience for her work and be convinced that teachers can be a part of it.

Keshana finds teachers just as perplexing as they find her. She is piqued at how teachers are treating her, and her sixth grade journal reflects her exasperation:

> What do you mean I've got an attitude. I can't be like someone else. I'd rather be just like me; not loud, not quiet. I'm just tired of everyone saying that I should change and act like whoever.
>
> Not to argue, but I still think that if there's something that I don't like, or don't want to do, I shouldn't be forced to do it. As a kid I feel this way but as an adult you feel (another) way. I still don't understand Mr. C. I walked out of the room like he told me and I still got in trouble. Was it the way that I walked? Please don't take this too seriously.

She protests she doesn't get why Mr. C. objected to her coming into his classroom against the rules. This is only one occasion among many where she has no insight into how adults see her. Her question "Was it the way I walked?" is genuine, but the answer—too risky to pursue—might spoil the happy ending of the author's story.

Keshana has shown in more examples than we have told here that she will personalize school tasks beyond reason. This leaves too great a distance between Keshana's work and school expectations, between Keshana's assessment and how teachers assess her. Keshana doesn't understand why teachers criticize her work. "But I thought it *was* good," she will retort. On a self-evaluation she wrote, "The people I sit with help me with what I don't understand and then I help them out." An eloquent statement, but at odds with teachers' perceptions: "Talked to friends"; "Hard to keep track of in class"; "Less talk and more concentration would help." In the same way she ends her stories happily, she idealizes how teachers see her. About a teacher who said several trimesters ago that her writing in Writer's Workshop was "unproductive," Keshana remembers only that "Ms. F. really made me work. I did all my homework." That she distances herself from the criticism also keeps her from hearing it.

Adults who educate Keshana find the distance hard to negotiate, too. The more choice in the open-ended work they assign, the less likely Keshana's products are "acceptable." Yet Keshana dismisses tasks which leave her no space for personalizing her effort. Her answers to teachers' specific questions on a social studies sheet or literature book are misunderstood, hastily done, and incomplete. Yet when we pay close attention to any of Keshana's completed assignments, we can see the pattern of personal purpose. It is now clear to us that rather than rejecting her efforts, we have to value her own purposes, be respectful of her agenda, and refrain from labeling her as inadequate when she does not meet school expectations.

Part of Keshana's complex relation to school is that she doesn't know for whom she is doing this work. Teachers criticize work that she thinks is good. Keshana needs to hear adults reflect back to her how powerful her questions are. She writes—as most of us do—to know who she is and to make herself more visible to others. As she puts her thoughts on paper, she is poking obliquely at the eternal questions, conjuring up adulthood, and examining her family and friends. None of this is for the benefit of teachers.

The Continuing Saga of a Low Profile Child

Keshana is now a seventh grader. As beautiful as ever, she makes more impact in the halls, if not the classrooms. School is for her a social event. Fashionably coordinated clothes have given way to more relaxed dressing, which we take to be a sign of increased security. But still, in her value system, what matters most is that her hair is fixed and her clothes are right. She is taller than many classmates and has kept her exquisite posture and carriage. She flirts more openly. For the first time, she joined in the Halloween costume parade, wearing a headscarf and the label "gangsterette." As she danced at the party with her peers, we realized how much our careful attention to her writing has allowed us to see under her mask without requiring her to take it off.

Our close observation has magnified Keshana's presence, and amplified her voice for our faculty. We have gained insight into her school persona, and by implication, understood more about other preadolescent girls who similarly distance themselves from school adults. We have learned from Keshana, not because she confides or makes her academic self in any way visible, but because we made the effort to look and keep looking.

NOTES

[1]Kathe Jervis and Ann Wiener conceived this project, collected the data, and analyzed it with the assistance of Diane Mullins. This work has been supported by a teacher–researcher grant from the National Council of Teachers of English.

REFERENCES

Jervis, K. (ed.) (1983). *Reunion, Reaffirmation, Resurgence: Proceedings from the Miquon Conference on Progressive Education.* Miquon, PA: The Miquon School.

11

GROUNDED INSIGHT
WILLIAM AYERS

We are once more midstream in a movement to reform the nation's schools. I say "once more" because school reform in the United States is as regular as rain—it comes and it goes, but it is never far away. We can predict with near certainty that as the intensity of the current reform effort breaks up and moves into the distance, a new reform front is gathering strength just over the horizon. It won't be long before the next reform begins to sweep across the schools and the educational community, warm winds or cold, on a mission of change.

Some will argue that the perennial attention to educational reform is all obfuscation and lies. A host of critics point out that the fundamental mission of public education is far from altruistic, and that the basic structures of privilege and oppression, of predetermined success and failure remain intact through virtually every reform effort. Schools, even those in crisis, are not "failing" in this view, but are, rather, fulfilling a clear if brutal function: sorting youngsters to fit neatly into the realities of an unjust society and simultaneously convincing them that they deserve whatever befalls them. These critics further note that the public schools are really government schools, that they are not "public" in any meaningful sense. Still others reiterate an easily observable fact about various attempts to improve the schools: the more things change, the more they stay the same.

None of this explains the popularity of educational reform in our cultural life, the enthusiasm with which Americans embrace each impulse toward school improvement. The roots of this passion can be found in what some might call the myth of public education: it is through education, we still believe, that people can transform themselves and their situations; it is by means of education that we hope to widen horizons, open perspectives, discover possibilities, and overcome obstacles. Education, we think, is the most certain road to empowerment, intelligence, and freedom. Acknowledging the

125

complexities of change, and noting that schools are in some way captive to larger social designs, it is this deeply grounded passion for education that makes public schools one legitimate area for ongoing popular struggles.

Myth or reality, every season of reform is a time of hope. For those of us who work for the transformative and liberating potential of education, school reform brings with it a wider dialogue, an extended audience, and an intensified debate. It is in this expanding space that possibilities are disclosed, rebellions staged, and actions undertaken. Even in the current dismal season of reform—a time of smug self-satisfaction, unprecedented elitism, unquestioning obedience to tradition, and an insistent blame-the-victim chorus—important questions become the focus of national discussion: What is schooling for? What contexts make possible or constrain effective teaching and learning? What knowledge and experiences are of most value?

The central assumptions underlying the current flurry of national and state reports on school improvement are universally and patently wrong—the assumption, for example, that teaching produces learning, that the measure of what is taught is apparent in what is learned; or that, in spite of decades of contrary evidence, the drama of learning is characterized by active teachers and passive students. Still, the space opened by those reports provides possibilities for rethinking much that is taken for granted in schools; and for revisiting important questions about the roles of teachers and parents, and the nature of curriculum and teaching. For me it has been an occasion to challenge the traditional conceptualization and practice of teaching teachers, a time for struggling to forge something new (or, perhaps, to recapture something lost) in teacher education.

What has been lost is, in part, a focus on the teachers as thinking, feeling human beings who are choice-makers and the instrument of their own practice. What is missing is a central belief in teaching as intellectual and ethical work. In its place has been an over-reliance on psychology and social science, and a corresponding diminished sense of teaching. The big debate in teacher education has been between those who would transfer research-generated knowledge to passive practitioners-to-be, and those who favor a more practical, methods—heavy, connect-the-dots approach to preparing future teachers. This is, in reality, a nondebate since neither position goes to the heart of the problem, neither looks to the teacher as a moral agent, a reflective practitioner, a critical thinker, or a transformative intellectual. Both positions posit teaching as the straightforward application of someone else's thought and judgment. Each sits comfortably alongside the tidy but rather tight definition of teaching provided by Diane Ravitch and Chester Finn (1987): "explaining, questioning, coaching, cajoling until children understand what adults want them to understand" (p. 204).

Teaching teachers is, of course, still teaching. What we know about teaching youngsters, or anyone else, should apply to teaching teachers. For example, if we believe, as Eleanor Duckworth (1987) argues, that "the essence of intellectual development" is "the having of wonderful ideas" (p. 1)—the setting of tasks, the search for answers, and the surprise of discovery—then we are required to somehow figure out how to create that possibility for youngsters as well as for students of teaching. For a teacher of young children it might mean creating an environment where working at the easel allows for the astonishing discovery that red and yellow make orange. A wonderful idea! For a teacher of teachers it might mean providing multiple opportunities for direct, hands-on experiences with children in classrooms, allowing for the emergence of problems and the thoughtful and collective search for answers. If we throw out the easels and instead instruct children in primary and secondary colors we deny them their wonderful ideas; if we more or less isolate students of teaching from the laboratory of the school and instead deliver research-generated knowledge about classroom management, for example, or disconnected skills in lesson planning, we deny them their own specific search for meaning and perspective, and the power of discovering teaching.

It is more difficult to set down a curriculum, *a priori*, for such an undertaking. This more problematic view of teaching creates a more complex set of tasks for teacher educators. We can begin to move away from a sense that teacher education (any more than teaching elementary school) is best captured in lesson plans, course descriptions, or curriculum guides. And we can pursue several devalued, often invisible areas of importance in the discovery of teaching and the education of teachers. These essential if elusive areas could include inquiry, reflection, action, autobiography, and community.

INQUIRY

Because no two teaching situations are quite identical, successful teaching cannot be completely prescribed, but must be the result of a teacher's ability to extract knowledge from unique and messy situations, to make specific choices and judgments, and then to act on what is known in an imperfect world. Teachers, if they are to become more than clerks, need to understand as much as possible about themselves, the children they teach, and the social and historical contexts that enable and constrain their teaching. Even within the walls of a classroom, teaching is uncertain. Outstanding teachers probe their classroom situations, interrogate their practice, and continually search for other, better ways to perfect their craft. It is insufficient in this view to begin teaching as if school reality is given, immutable, or the center of all action and growth, with children's lives, experiences, and contexts irrelevant or deficient. Nor is it acceptable to gear teaching toward definitive, sometimes punitive judgments of children's abilities. Inquiring teachers tend to develop formative evaluations of children, always in the service of framing teaching problems, deciding what is to be done, directing action to be tried, and assessing the problems again.

Teaching is not essentially performance; it is not the delivery of the goods. Teaching is an interactive practice that begins and ends with "seeing" the student. This is quite complicated, for it demands an awareness of culture and history, thought and feeling, affect and intellect, social context and idiosyncrasy. "Seeing" the student is something that is ongoing and never completely finished. The student grows, the teacher learns, the situation changes, and "seeing" becomes an evolving challenge. As layers of mystification and obfuscation are peeled away, and as the student becomes more fully present to the teacher, experiences and intelligences that were initially obscure become the ground upon which real teaching can be constructed. This is as true in a college of education as it is in the kindergarten.

Because teaching is complex and kaleidoscopic—an endeavor that requires continuous awareness, re-evaluation, and adjustment on many levels simultaneously—knowing how to look into unique situations is indispensable. Teaching is a craft in which there are degrees of mastery and competence, but no final point beyond which one cannot grow. There is, therefore, always something more to learn. Sustained inquiry, formal and informal, is an important part of learning how to teach.

REFLECTION

Donald Schön (1983) describes teachers (as well as nurses, architects, and city planners) as "reflective practitioners" (p. 14), people whose work leads them to have an infinite number of reflective conversations with unique situations. Reflective practitioners rely less on positivistic science or technical rationality and more on thoughtful reflection rooted in experiential knowledge. This practical knowledge is neither easily accessible to outsiders nor easily codified. Schön recasts intuition as a legitimate though undervalued form of knowledge, and he resists the tendency to force professional knowledge into a prescribed technical vocabulary.

All teaching, consciously or unconsciously, explicitly or implicitly, deals with two questions: What knowledge and experiences are most worthwhile? What are the means to strengthen, invigorate, and enable each person to take full advantage of those worthwhile experiences and that valuable knowledge? Of course neither question has a straightforward or universal answer for every individual in every situation. This is a central challenge of teaching. These questions cannot be resolved by referring alone to fact or empirical data; they have no single, provable answer. There are several possible answers and courses of action to follow. We are left to probe the particulars, to draw on our own experiences and knowledge as we craft solutions, and to think about what ought to be and what ought not to be. We are left to choose, and choosing well requires reflecting critically and intensely about possible courses and outcomes.

Teaching involves moral, ethical, intellectual, and social choices, dimensions that are difficult to teach and assess in straightforward ways, and are more suited to being achieved through reflection. Teaching also involves synthesizing experiential and scientific knowledge. Reflection is a process that can allow teachers to integrate personal, implicit knowledge with objective knowledge, and along the way to render choices more controllable. Reflection is more than thinking; it is thinking rigorously, critically, and systematically about practices and problems of importance to further growth. Reflection is also linked to conduct, the ground from which it arises and into which it must flow. Reflection is a disciplined way of assessing situations, imagining a different future, and preparing to act on that thought.

ACTION

For an inquiring, reflective person, teaching is thoughtful and ethical action. Teaching can involve resistance to the machinery of schooling, the institutional realities seemingly designed to interrupt authentic education. Creative insubordination and guerrilla tactics in the classroom are rarely taught but regularly practiced. Losing forms, cutting the wires to the intercom, asking forgiveness rather than permission—these kinds of strategies are basic to successful teachers. Teaching always involves constructing an environment for learning that nurtures and challenges a wide range of learners, and building bridges from what students know to deeper and wider ways of knowing. Teaching involves insight and decision, understanding and action. To be aware of the social and moral universe we share, as well as what has yet to be achieved in terms of human possibility, is to be a teacher capable of being a public person. A teacher's work is more than inducting the young into a given world; it's also opening them up to inquiry, imagination, and invention. Outstanding teaching goes beyond passing down the wisdom of the ages, and involves also teaching for transformation. Where tradition has been debilitating or oppressive, teaching includes opening students to ways of breaking the power tradition exerts on their lives. Outstanding teachers are passionate, fervent people who are advocates for and allies of children, and therefore naturally socially responsive, political, and activist.

Students of teaching can learn to oppose the banal and the petty, to protest both brutality and patronizing in schools. Certainly they can oppose a weak and wishy-washy curriculum that disengages and disempowers children. They can also learn to separate institutional constraints from human capacity, a history of injustice from the natural order of things. Students can understand schools as human constructions, and as such institutions that can be "deconstructed" or reconstructed by them. Society itself is a human creation, and it is also subject to human re-creation.

AUTOBIOGRAPHY

Because no teacher can or should entirely escape or transcend subjectivity, teachers, whatever else they teach, teach themselves. Teaching involves a meeting of subjects, intentions, agendas, maps, dreams, desires, hopes, fears, loves, and pains, and in that meeting teachers necessarily live and promote what they themselves value. Making explicit one's values and priorities, becoming aware of oneself as the instrument of one's teaching, and the story that makes one's life sensible, allows for greater change and growth as well as greater intentionality in teaching choices. Working on autobiographical texts is working on the heart of teaching; it is a way to open and examine the question of ethics.

Constructing an autobiography can be a way of making values, beliefs, and choices accessible to teachers and prospective teachers. Each autobiography—complex, idiosyncratic, alive, and changing—provides the kind of detail from which one can interpret practice. Autobiography is a way to engage the intricate interaction of inner and outer—the worlds of feeling, thought, experience, belief, and action. Autobiography even partially realized, can become a tool for improving practice.

Teaching is self-construction. Knowing one's own pathway to teaching well allows teachers to take the next step, to lay the next stone. Autobiography connects thought with feelings and intentions, a connection that is essential in education. It relates being and knowing, existence and education. Personal knowledge is not easily described or examined, and yet teaching practice is most often constructed precisely on personal knowledge. Autobiography is a potentially useful method for helping teachers connect with personal knowledge, making it accessible in their own search for understanding and meaning in their practical work.

COMMUNITY

Teachers must live and participate in the manifold of diverse ideas and people; they must combine the insights and the energies of many, and create consensus and harmony in the classroom. Learning how to build a sense of community involves working with different publics and developing an understanding of fellowship and cooperation as a fundamental human need.

Community, which implies cooperation, shared values, and an ethics of caring, must somehow be forged inside institutions—those places which are rule-driven, bureaucratic, and goal-oriented. Society posits a romanticized view of the dedicated, caring, inspiring teacher who is also brilliant, creative, and self-activated. But we know that the harsh reality in many schools is a structure that disempowers and de-skills, a system that prespecifies teachers thoughts and oversees and constrains activities. In large, impersonal systems, teachers become obedient and conforming; they are expected to deliver the curriculum without much thought, and control the students without much feeling. Students are expected, in turn, to follow the rules and go along with whatever is put before them. The crucial lessons for everyone in such a school system, top to bottom, are about hierarchy and one's place in it, convention and one's obligation to it, unquestioning passivity in the face of authority. Building community, then, is an act of resistance.

Community building opens opportunities for sharing and overcoming problems, making productive connections, and acquiring deeper, more meaningful knowledge. It allows for democracy to be practiced and not merely discussed, and can be a particularly important factor in helping teachers to successfully overcome obstacles and difficulties encountered in practice. Community can be realized—if only partially and contingently—when teachers assume a spirit of cooperation, caring, and compassion among themselves and with students.

CONCLUSION

None of these areas of knowledge can be taught in direct, didactic ways; none can be transmitted to passive students as discrete skills or behaviors. But each area can be valued, practiced, and examined. For example, public and private space can be created for reflection. Students can be encouraged to write autobiographical texts, and to view those texts as complex, idiosyncratic, organic, and dynamic. The concrete situations and ideas of students can be taken seriously, fostering an environment that provides opportunities for inquiry, cooperative learning, and action. Students can learn by doing, by being immersed in life in classrooms, and by juxtaposing ideas in dialogue with the actual problems they themselves pose.

Discovering teaching is more an act of faith than a rational pursuit. It requires the willingness to suspend disbelief, the courage to plunge into the unknown, and the imagination to create something unique in a world where there are few valid general principles. Honoring and validating the lives of students and setting the environment for learning are the main tasks of teacher educators, as they are for other teachers, as well as inviting the kinds of people who can fully share the adventure of teaching to come along.

REFERENCES

Duckworth, E. (1987). *The Having of Wonderful Ideas*. New York: Teachers College Press.

Greene, M. (1978). *Landscapes of Learning*. New York: Teachers College Press.

Ravitch, D., and Finn, Jr., C. E. (1987). *What Do Our 17-Year-Olds Know?* New York: Harper and Row.

Schön, D. A. (1983). *The Reflective Practitioner: How Professionals Think in Action*. New York: Basic Books.

PART 3

THE PROGRESSIVE HIGH SCHOOL

12

THE KINDERGARTEN TRADITION IN THE HIGH SCHOOL

DEBORAH MEIER

Returning to Chicago is always a voyage of nostalgia. This is where the best things in my life—the things I hold most dear—got started. All three of my children were born in this city, and that alone gives one a special feeling for a place. In addition, this is where my teaching career began. And while at first this hardly seemed a blessing, teaching has turned out to be a labor of love.

In the mid-1950s, I graduated from the University of Chicago with a Master's degree, dead set against teaching. I had resisted taking courses in education, despite strong encouragement, precisely because this was the kind of thing women were urged to do just "in case," or for pin money, or while their children were young. I was not going to fall into that trap. But a few years later I did just that, and for just those reasons. It was to be a temporary measure until my kids were older.

I had been the product of an independent private school, and attended Antioch and then the University of Chicago. I'd had, in short, a sheltered idea of what school life was like. My entry into Chicago's public schools was, therefore, a stunning shock to be repeated again and again as I moved first to Philadelphia and then New York. The first and most striking reaction I had to Chicago's public schools was that they were, and still are (although I'm somewhat more numb to it now), the most disrespectful environments—even for adults—that I had ever experienced. I had no prior experience of being treated with such little respect or common courtesy, even as a child. Since my children started in the Chicago public schools at the same time that I began to teach in them, I got a double dose of disrespect.

I recently came upon a letter I wrote during my first year as a substitute in Chicago's South Side schools. I had two stories to tell. The first was about my feeling of personal humiliation at the way I was treated and my difficulty in knowing how to respond to it. I wanted to walk out indignantly, making clear that I refused to be associated with an institution that could treat anyone so badly. But I simultaneously felt feisty: "They're not going to get rid of me so easily." The second story was about my shock at a simple truth that I had never before faced so squarely: some of us grew up in schools like those I had experienced as a child and others experienced schools like those I was subbing in daily—and we were all citizens of the same country. Recently, this indignation was reignited as I shared my own two children's experiences as elementary school teachers: one working in Williamstown, Massachusetts, and the other in Oakland, California. Could it be that both school systems they described were intended to produce citizens of the same country?

I entered teaching accidentally, and became a kindergarten teacher for the same reason: it was the only teaching job available part time. I didn't want to teach, but above all I didn't have much respect for teaching little children. And there I was doing both and finding myself plain wrong on all counts. This fortuitous opportunity to work with young children developed in me a particular viewpoint and perspective that has, as much as anything else, shaped all of my subsequent efforts. I have carried a kindergarten teacher's perspective with me, first into elementary school as a whole and now into high school.

When I went to get my high school principal's license, three high school principals sat in the audience to rate me. As the final exercise in a long examination procedure, I was supposed to explain what in my background fitted me for such a license. Since my resume indicated that I had never worked in a high school, and had, in fact, only taught three to six-year-olds, I suspected my audience thought I had a lot of nerve applying for a high school principalship. I told them, in some detail, why I believed the kindergarten tradition was the most appropriate basis for all schooling.

Kindergarten was the one place—maybe the last place—where you were expected to know children well, even if they didn't hand in their homework, finish their Friday tests, or pay attention. Kindergarten teachers know that learning must be personalized, just because kids are idiosyncratic. (I speak here of the old-fashioned kindergarten which did not yet look like a first grade.) Kindergarten teachers know that helping children learn to become more self-reliant is part of their task—starting with tying shoes and going to the bathroom. Catering to children's growing independence is a natural part of a kindergarten child's classroom life. It is, alas, the last time children are given independence, encouraged to make choices, and allowed to move about on their own steam. The older they get the less we take into account the importance of their own interests. In kindergarten we design our rooms for real work—not just passive listening. We put things in the room that will appeal to children, grab their interests, and engage their minds and hearts. Teachers in kindergarten are editors, critics, cheerleaders, and caretakers, not just lecturers or deliverers of instruction. The value of what Ted Sizer (1984) calls "coaching" (p. 3) is second nature in the kindergarten classroom.

In between kindergarten and postgraduate school something else happens. People who work with doctoral candidates rediscover that they can't handle more than five or six students at a time, because they have to get to know their students and their student's work well. But in between, there is a vastly different mind-set about teaching and learning. The more difficulties students have in learning, the vaster that difference becomes. Teachers who work in community colleges teach five courses for every one or two expected of a professor at the University of Chicago. For most teachers, school is a sorting and screening out institution, where everything we know about teaching and learning tends to go out the window. Layers upon layers of time-honored institutional malpractice, and ingrained modes of thought and language make it hard to think about schooling any other way.

The jargon of our profession is hard to escape. Grade levels, norms, and even the "developmentalist" clichés of early childhood educators can be both misleading and dangerous. Are five, 15, and 50-year-olds really that different? In stressing the differences we often forget our common humanity. Amazingly, what is true about how five-year-olds learn is equally true of how I still learn. And not, I think, because I'm such a peculiar adult. Few things annoy me about 15-year-olds that don't apply also to the adults at school. It's hard at staff meetings for us to listen to each other. We interrupt, get up and walk around, read a book, pass notes, or even fall asleep when the agenda gets boring. It's not a wonder that my favorite Piagetian, Eleanor Duckworth, seems almost entirely uninterested in Piagetian stages, and treats adults as though they were still concrete thinkers. I'm not suggesting that there are no differences between me and a five-year-old, but if we reflected on ourselves as learners we would design schools more learner-friendly for kids. We don't have to design them differently *just* because they are five years old. Schools need to be restructured because we're human learners. Period.

What we did at Central Park East, and what we did in District #4, was build a network of elementary schools based on good nursery school and kindergarten practice. Ten years later, after celebrating a decade of growth, Ted Sizer came to visit and said: "Why don't you just keep this going through twelfth grade?" What he recognized was the similarity between good high school practice and good nursery school practice. Dare we? Could we take on teenagers? Isn't that an impossible age? I had spent a lot of time avoiding adolescents in groups of more than two. If I was going to start a secondary school, I'd certainly need to think in terms of at least three.

We read Sizer's book (1984), *Horace's Compromise.* We examined the high schools our own elementary school graduates had attended. Most of our kids, after all, had survived and even graduated from high school. As we looked over the data, the miracle was that virtually no children had dropped out. We didn't think it was due to the strength of their academic preparation, although it wasn't bad. But we thought our kids started high school with an extraordinary head start: they felt comfortable in a world that included adults, they found the people who could help them get through the system, and their families also knew how to negotiate on their behalf. They knew how to cope.

As we listened to their individual stories (as well as the stories of the children in our own families), we realized that the high schools they attended were peculiar institutions designed as though intended to drive kids to the edge of their sanity, into numbness and mindlessness. The schools removed the very adult role models they most needed; all the interesting and strong adult/student interactions used by young people to test their ideas and their new strengths were absent from high school. Gone were powerful adults of any sort. We placed them, instead, in a most vulnerable relationship to hordes of peers, without guidance or nurture to handle peer pressures. Then we said: "Look how weak and bad they are." We removed all healthy risk-taking, all serious and sustained opportunities for thought, and then complained about their short attention span and unhealthy risk-taking. We gave them seven, eight, even nine different periods a day in randomly ordered short snippets—English, Home Economics, Math, Social Studies, Gym, Science.

Imagine an endless conference with many plenary sessions, long speeches, short (if any) question periods, no chance to talk to colleagues, no breaks: that's school. Unlike a conference, you can't sneak out in the middle of a session to go to the bathroom or light a cigarette or whatever else we all do to break the tedium and tension. Imagine if any conference you've attended had lasted for 185 days. When we go to conferences we look forward to seeing old friends, or finding a job. That's why kids keep coming back to school, too—to see their friends, to make connections. It's in the bathrooms, the halls, the corridors, and the playing field where the real life of school is taking place—just as it does at professional conferences. We teachers frown on it; we're even infuriated by it. "Why aren't they interested in the really important stuff?" We blame it on their impoverished backgrounds or hormones or parental disinterest. If we went into high school education, we knew we would have to change all of this.

Kids need to be immersed in a world where powerful adults are at work—and at work collegially. They need to experience—see and hear—adults thinking aloud, making decisions, utilizing judgment, organizing to resolve differences, and expressing their care about ideas as well as each other. We tell them they should take ideas seriously. Then we rush them through a curriculum in which serious ideas never appear. I am familiar with many teachers who care about history, politics, and literature, but there's no way their students could know it. We wanted, instead, to create a place that might cause at least some kids to envy us for the life we led, and to want to join our club. Growing up ought to seem attractive, after all. We decided that students needed lots of opportunities to practice science, not just to hear about it; to be writers, not just do writing exercises; to read books, not just practice becoming readers; as well as to do history, make ideas, and care about their world by working in it.

We began in a muddle ourselves; we weren't sure what the final product might look like. We didn't have the rich examples that were available when we began our elementary schools. There were progressive high schools, but they were generally elite institutions that solved problems by selecting the kids who fit. We didn't intend to limit ourselves to families who believed in progressive theories, or to kids who were already independent learners, or prepared for "our kind" of school. We wanted to demonstrate that all or any of our East Harlem kids deserved and could benefit by the kind of schooling that only 5 to 10 percent of our nation's children had hitherto received. We knew this was a scary proposition; that we wouldn't get it right immediately. However, we felt the challenge was worth taking. We solaced ourselves by saying that the alternative for most of our kids couldn't be worse, so why not try to make it better.

To start, we acknowledged three cardinal principles: (1) everything is connected, we couldn't just change one thing and leave the rest alone; (2) one could never attend to only one thing at a time, common sense to the contrary—we couldn't take up Sizer's nine principles in order, one this year and the rest later, we would have to tackle them all at once; and (3) all solutions have unintended side effects and we couldn't resolve all the side effects at the same time. We realized that the third principle contradicted the first and second. We would have to learn by doing. What we did was bound to be partly wrong. We would not be able to put it right until it had worked itself out in ways we couldn't anticipate.

We needed to be bold and revolutionary on one hand. On the other, we needed to remember that all human beings—adolescents above all—cherish conformity and familiarity. For lasting change to occur, we had to imbed the new into the old and build the future on the past. If we made too few changes, we'd find ourselves slipping back; if we made too many changes too fast, we'd lose the confidence of our families and students, and cause unproductive anxiety.

We would survive only if we could build a foundation of mutual respect and trust among the adult faculty, between the school and its students, and between the school and the students and their families. Such a foundation couldn't be built overnight. There would be setbacks and traumas. In the long run a solid foundation was essential. We had to do it with families who normally expected to be told—almost to their relief—"Forget it. Your children are teens now. Your role is over. Go home." But we were saying the opposite: "Your kids need you as much as ever, only differently." We were also telling them: "Don't second-guess us all the time. Trust us even if you don't always agree." In short, we were going to have to be compromisers while also being uncompromising; steadfast and yet flexible; reassuring and also open to doubt.

Teachers can't educate if they don't have the respect of their students and their families. They can't get such respect if they don't give it. They can't give it if they don't have a chance to get to know each other. We needed to find ways to figure out how our kids were interpreting their lives and our school, what they were attending to and what they were ignoring, and how they made sense of the world "out there." To do this meant we had to greatly reduce the ratios between teachers and students—without enormously increased finding. We had to find a way of going from the usual high school arrangement where a teacher "sees" 150 to 160 students a day, to something closer to what elementary school people know is already too high—40 to 80 students daily. Oddly, high school teachers think these smaller figures are some utopian ideal. We knew that these ratios were necessary, but in and of themselves hardly sufficient.

To learn to use one's mind well one must be placed in an environment where, at the very least, the adults are doing that. We knew that teachers needed to make decisions about almost everything critical to their work, and have control over the major forces affecting their daily school lives. Time and structure for collegiality needed to be built into the day without being an add-on or a time-waster. Teachers needed time to see each other in a variety of contexts, interdisciplinary as well as intradisciplinary. Teachers who worked with the same kids needed to talk about kids; teachers who were teaching the same subject needed to discuss subject and pedagogy, and all teachers needed time to work out school-wide issues. Decisions would have to be made quickly and efficiently, circumventing vast arrays of committees, subcommittees, delegated bodies, representatives, and task forces. We needed a schedule so simple that we could focus on what was the real complexity—kids. We needed to make democratic life a pleasure, not another exercise in bureaucratic life. Staff empowerment would be so attractive that teachers could get on with teaching and wouldn't long for top-down mandated school administration.

In fact, teacher empowerment had to stop being the goal and become a necessary prerequisite for the real reforms—a changed relationship between teachers, learners, and subject matter. The case for having schools run by those who work in them is not a matter of principle. Many different parties to our society have equally valid rationales for school governance roles. The rationale for the empowerment of the school's staff rests upon assumptions about the nature of being human, the aims of democratic education, and the connections between means and ends. The importance of the teacher's role in school decision making rests upon the simple fact that there isn't another way to do "it." People work best when they're valued; to be valued requires respect and respect requires being "listened to." But there's no point in listening to people who can't do anything about what they hear. Expert teachers aren't valuable if they can't exercise their expertise.

People are never powerless, of course. Empowerment is perhaps an inaccurate term. Even devalued and disrespected people remain powerful, but they are forced to exercise their powers in odd, distorted, and limited ways. You can't make people powerless, but you can remove many of the choices and options available for the exercise of their powers, the way they can show what they think and feel, and want. Children have been exercising their powers for years, without the formal right to do so. Ditto for teachers. Teachers know how limited their powers are; how the best and most wonderful lesson plan in the world is helpless in the face of real live kids. Teachers are in the same position. They can sabotage the best-laid reforms.

We shouldn't bemoan this. It's a saving grace. A virtue! It's our humanity we're describing and protecting, and it keeps us from being brainwashed by every dictator who comes to power. When we feel helpless we hide our mistakes, avoid exposure, resent outsiders, and play dumb. We pay a heavy price for such helplessness, but we do so whenever we suspect we'll play an even bigger price for not engaging in such sabotage. Teachers, like many of our fellow citizens, sabotage reforms—the best and the worst—when they feel imposed upon and helpless.

When we don't tap the knowledge and intelligence of those who know our schools best, our reforms are endlessly repetitive. We are bound to invent unworkable reforms until we trust practitioners. Of course, reform is also going to be unworkable until practitioners trust parents, and both extend greater trust to students. Similarly, only respected practitioners truly extend their provisional trust to other experts whose ideas may help inform their work. A mighty team emerges once we can all hear each other. It takes many viewpoints to see what's really happening.

If I hire a babysitter and I want to increase the odds of my child's safety, I need to create conditions that encourage the sitter to use intelligence and good judgment. This is as true for babysitting as it is for teaching. We have to act *as if* we trust the babysitter, hoping we've done a good job checking out references beforehand, spending sufficient time going over mutual concerns, providing him or her with the appropriate tools and resources, and leaving little reason for the sitter to be afraid to call for help. It won't improve the odds if we hem this sitter in with lots of laws, threaten dire penalties if things go wrong, and tell the kids to keep their eyes open because the sitter may be dangerous. So too with teachers.

That's why we need "teacher power"—not as a reward for our good behavior, not because we've proven to be professionals, not in return for a wage increase or merit pay, but merely because it's an essential prerequisite for sound education. Parents must have the same opportunities they have in hiring babysitters. They need to be able to check the school's references, observe the school in operation, and interview the staff. They have a right to be sure that the school has the appropriate tools and that its teachers can call for help without being afraid. As in choosing babysitters, parents need educational choices—because you and I may not agree on who's the best sitter in town. Only then is it fair to ask them to offer provisional trust, not too much and not too little. There's an acceptable level of trust without which schools cannot do right by children. That right amount generally takes time to develop.

At Central Park East Secondary School (CPESS), teachers needed a framework that enabled them to know their students well, and to know that their students and parents were offering them at least a provisional trust and respect. Because families came to us by choice, at least some modest basis for mutual trust was built into the system. Teachers also needed to know what they were expected to teach, and how their teaching and kid's learning would be assessed. We refused to let our work be judged on the basis of our students' capacity to collect trivia, but instead wanted it to be judged on intellectual habits of mind, such as the demonstrable capacity to weigh evidence, take on more complex responsibilities, make difficult judgements, and see finer distinctions. We wanted to demand improved performance at real, worthwhile tasks. We needed to devote ourselves to covering less, not more, and to develop standards that were no less tough and no less rigorous; not lower, but different.

Respect between children's families, their community, and the school is an end in itself, as well as an essential means to the education we had in mind. Education isn't merely a question of good and frequent contact between school and family. The gap between the social, ethnic, and class histories of the school's staff and the school's families is often substantial. It's a gap we cannot bridge entirely. However, at minimum parents need to know that we will not undermine their authority, their values, or their standards. They need to believe that we're not frustrating the aspirations they have for their kids, nor blaming them for what goes wrong for their kids.

When school people complain that parents don't show up at Parent/ Teacher Conferences, especially in high schools, I remember my own experiences as a parent attending school conferences. At best, the teachers restated what I already knew: my child was doing fine. Bad news at the conference was more than useless. I left such meetings feeling more inadequate, more guilty, and more helpless. I learned to stop going. It was an act of intelligence and survival, not lack of concern, that led me to stay away. Without an adequate level of trust, children pay the sometimes paralyzing price. Children are stuck between the two suspicious, warring parties to their education—their parents and their teachers.

At CPESS we tried to reverse this distrust. One obvious first step was to create a small rather than a large school. My own high school had under 500 students, but in New York's public schools anything under 2,000 is small. To them, 500 is hardly a school at all. Fortunately, we existed in decentralized District #4, which already had a sympathetic view toward smallness. We were also buttressed by a current interest in smallness and considerable research about small schools. Finally, we had 10 years of District #4 experience to show us how to have small schools in big buildings. District #4 has 20 buildings and

52 schools. A building is not a school. More than one school can be located in a single building. Our high school building houses nearly a thousand students, but there are three schools in one building, not one.

Our high school enrollment—actually 450—is too big. Maybe we should have remained smaller, but instead we settled on subdividing. (Incidentally, 450 kids can fit into our auditorium, which is not a bad criteria for maximum size. The other useful criteria is whether or not the entire staff can fit into a single room, preferably in a single circle.) We subdivided the school into three major Divisions, each with about 150 kids. The Divisions are further subdivided into two Houses of 75 to 80 students. A House has its own faculty of four or five staff members, thus a Division has a faculty of about nine teachers covering all the basic subjects. Most teachers also teach more than a single discipline, so we can combine courses such as math and science. We have cut the number of children teachers see each day from 160 to only 40. The 40 includes about 15 students who teachers see daily for an extended Advisory period.

Students spend two years in each division. Division I is the equivalent of grades seven and eight, and Division II consists of grades nine and ten. The last division, called the Senior Institute, lasts as long as students need to get a diploma and be prepared for the next step in their lives. Within each Division, no distinctions are made by grade level; everyone takes the same courses together.

We decided on the simplest of schedules: two hours each day in Humanities (art, history, literature, social studies), two hours daily of Math/Science, and one hour of something we call Advisory. That's it, folks—day after day, with virtually no change for the first four years, from grades seven to 10. Some kids attend Humanities first, while the others have Math/Science; then it reverses. Within each two-hour block, the staff makes whatever decisions it wants about time and grouping. They can decide to do one thing on Monday and change their minds on Tuesday. When the kids and teachers complained that no one seemed really prepared to study hard after lunch, we all grumbled about it until the kids suggested a simple solution: no after lunch. So we run four hours straight, eat lunch late, and put Advisory at the end of the day. Everyone prefers it, at least for now. This was a decision we were able to make on Monday and put into effect within the same week. In most New York high schools, it would take a task force months to study an idea like this and months or years to put it into effect. But we just sat in our circle, listened to the kids' proposal, and said, "Let's try it."

Actually, there is one day a week in which the kids' and teacher's schedules differ. One morning per week each student spends half a day in community service, which allows for collegial planning time. Also, between 8:00 and 9:00 each morning we offer foreign language—with a mostly auxiliary staff of Spanish language teachers. The kids think 8:00 A.M. is outrageously early and they are still giving us a hard time about promptness. But being on time is a necessity for our kind of schedule, so we aren't budging. Besides, we've discovered that most kids in America start high school at such an early hour. This logic has not yet been persuasive, however.

We also have an hour for lunch, longer than is typical. It gives the staff time together, and it gives the students time to eat, attend options such as sports and computer classes, as well as use the library for independent study. Finally, from 3:00 to 5:00 P.M. the building is open for sports programs, study and homework in the well-staffed library, and a few student-initiated clubs. This kind of schedule is not only simple, but it also provides time for faculty to meet and talk to each other—to do collegially what people who work together need to do.

We are creating a staff-run school with high standards—the staff must know each other well, be familiar with each other's work, and know how the school operates. Each team of teachers that works with the same students and the same curriculum teaches at the same time. The school's structure, from the placement of classes to the scheduling of the day, is organized to enable teachers to visit each other's rooms, to reflect on their own and their colleagues' practice, and to give each other full support. Curricular teams (four to five people), for example, have a full morning each week to plan together. For the same reason, those who teach the same kids—the faculty of each House— have an hour and a half extended lunch together every week. The entire staff meets from 3:00 to 5:00 P.M. every Monday to make collective, school-wide decisions and discuss ideas. Thus, decisions are made by curricular teams, Houses, Divisions, or when appropriate, at school-wide meetings. The staff is responsible for hiring their own members, assessing their own colleagues, and when dissatisfied, for confronting colleagues with their concerns. They are responsible for developing and assessing both the curriculum and their students' success with it. Above all, the teachers are responsible for defining the criteria for receiving a CPESS diploma. Together, this constitutes a powerful staff development project.

Every visitor who comes to CPESS has trouble accepting our claim that our students are a typical cross-section of New York City. But it's a fact. The students are largely African–American and Latino; about 15 percent are white, and a few are Asian. Twenty percent come to us designated as "in special need" of additional services, mostly with a label of learning disabled. Many are students who would otherwise qualify for self-contained special education classes. There is no easy way to distinguish such students in our school. In addition, two out of three students are eligible for free or reduced-price lunches: read "poor." About half of our incoming seventh graders spent at least part of their elementary years at one of the three Central Park East schools; the others attended more typical public elementary schools.

We're getting more comfortable with what we're doing and so are our students. There are plenty of unresolved issues. How do we know if we've developed sufficiently high standards for graduation? What does it mean to tell kids the content of their final exam at the beginning of a course? How can we deal with questions of racism—even among ourselves as a staff—honestly and yet carefully? How can we insure that we don't tear ourselves apart as we pick our way through dangerous waters? We must solve these issues if we are to help kids who desperately need to be able to talk with adults about such things. How does democratic school governance work? What are the limits on a faculty's legitimate rights to make decisions versus the necessary controls exercised by a community, school board, or parent organization? In what capacity, and at what age, should students play a role in governing their own schools?

These are just a few of the unresolved issues. Many will never be resolved. But as we struggle with them we've seen dramatic changes. The deep immersion in a value system that places mutual respect first and encourages a climate of diversity and disagreement is enormously powerful over time. The kids know we're serious. Sometimes we fear that they are just parroting our ideas, but mostly we can't help but be impressed. They are less engaged in battling with us over every imposed limit on their freedom, and more engaged with us in the battle to become well educated. They get down to business faster and are more cheerful about more things. They read and write a lot. They talk a lot about their own learning and schooling. Yes, it's partly glibness, but even the glibness is a triumph.

Is it working? We've grown accustomed to that question. Our answer is not always satisfying. We don't yet have data on the high school graduates, achievement tests, or college acceptances. We generally rely on classroom observation and discussion with students. The limited data we have, however, looks promising. It's hardly surprising that our rate of retention is very high. Students neither transfer, nor move, nor drop out. Attendance is extraordinarily high. kids and parents show up at family conferences, complain about things to our faces, and risk the necessary confrontations. We think that's a plus. The children are willing to let us catch them acting like nice young people who want to be smart. By tenth grade, they say "I'm bored" a bit less, and admit to being interested in the idea of becoming truly well-rounded citizens.

All this reinforces our belief that what makes a school good for the least advantaged is no mystery. It's not much different from a good school for the most advantaged. We don't need research on this astounding proposition. The main difference between the advantaged and the disadvantaged is that the latter need good schools even more. When people think "those kids" need something special, the reply we offer at CPESS is: "Just give them what you have always offered those who have the money to buy the best, which is mostly a matter of respect." After society does that, then let's talk "special."

Schools face obvious burdens when children come from families without social, political, and economic power; but such schools also face some less obvious hazards. Young people coming from families that have suffered from severe forms of powerlessness and disrespect need a school that offers more than ordinary reasons for why they should try to join what psycholinguist Frank Smith (1988) calls "the literacy club" (p. 3). Unless we make that club very attractive, students are unlikely to join it. Unless it appears to be a club that accepts people "like them," they are not likely to view it as a serious option. If they expect to be excluded anyway, they're likely to avoid rejection by rejecting it first. Above all, if belonging to this literacy club requires quitting all the other clubs they know of and now belong to, particularly those their parents and loved ones are members of, then the takers will be few. We could, on the other hand, offer them a family membership plan. Or, at least, we could assure them that people can belong to lots of different clubs. They might be more willing to join if we assured them that choosing one club does not mean having to drop all the others.

I think we've created a framework at CPESS to tackle these questions, day by day. I don't know how far we'll get in answering them, or the degree of success we can expect. We don't create all the conditions; I can't stop the world they live in while we do our work. That world beyond our control places crushing burdens on far too many of our young people. We have no guarantees to offer our kids, our families, or the wider public beyond trying our best to make CPESS a place that at least temporarily makes life seem more interesting and more worth the effort.

Several events have reinforced my confidence that we're on the right track. I had the good fortune to drop in on the ninth and tenth graders as they were presenting their scenes from *Macbeth* in the school auditorium. They had spent many months working over their ideas about the play, and now they were presenting these ideas to each other. The keen sense of ownership they displayed over the material was astounding to me. It was the product of the kind of leisurely pacing only a school like ours can afford, and they were able to show it off to each other without fear of being ridiculed. They knew that the laughter from the audience was the laughter of colleagues working with, not against them. It was a wonderful few hours.

Another confirmation came under less happy circumstances. The infamous, so-called "wilding" assault on a Central Park jogger occurred just a few blocks from our building. That event had a particularly powerful impact on the sensitivities of East Harlem residents. As I came to school after the four-day holiday in which the assault occurred, I knew one thing: we needed time to work out together how to deal with the youngsters' reactions. The staff met at lunch to talk about what the kids were saying, and how we might respond. We knew we had to address not only the children's reactions, but our own fears and angers. We had to face our different responses and learn from them. We also had to help kids deal with a hungry press, and to prevent their unwitting exploitation as cameras, microphones, and newsmen with pencils and pads pushed into their lives in order to get first-hand "reactions." Our response, atypical for a New York City high school, was based on our ability to set priorities. Our size, our simple schedule, and our collegial organization made this feasible.

Then came the third event: the death of one of the most beloved members of our larger school community, Josie Hernandez. Her children were in our first graduating class fifteen years ago. She had become the secretary at one of our elementary schools eight years ago. She was important to all of us in many different ways. Her sudden death could not go by unnoted. We stopped to take stock of her life and its meaning. We knew we had to respond to her death, personally and individually. We had to be sure that those students who had known her could attend her memorial service. We had to pay attention to details, not just good intentions.

We could do such things not because more caring than other teachers or other schools. Not at all. It's because we have a structure and style that enables us to show our care effectively. What could a high school principal with 4,000 students possibly do in the face of such a situation? In such schools, a death a day is commonplace. To take cognizance of individual tragedies would be to lapse into a state of perpetual grief and mourning. The distancing and numbing required in most schools is a fact of life, a necessary coping strategy.

If we want children to be caring and compassionate, then we must provide a place for growing up in which caring is feasible. Creating such intimate schools is possible even in our existing system of large buildings. That's what I think the visitors who come to our schools recognize and acknowledge. That is what is visibly obvious.

It's harder to convince people that what we do is do-able by others—in their own way. People often have a whole string of "well, buts" for why our situation is different than theirs. I want to argue strongly that it is not Deborah Meier, not our unique staff, not extra funds that makes us different. It's our wanting it badly enough. Principals come and say: "Ah, but you have only 500 students. I could do it too if I only had 500." I say, terrific, you can divide your building into a bunch of smaller schools and you too will have schools of only 500. They say: "Well, you have so much more freedom than I do." I remind them that no one actually gave it to me or to us. We have what we took. They say: "You have an unusual staff." I agree, but it's not because they went to unusual colleges, taught longer, or have exceptional gifts. What's unusual is that they are practicing what they believe in. And me? If I'm unusual it's because I had the perseverance to put up with a tenaciously irritating bureaucracy, and still keep trying to put into practice the concerns and convictions of a kindergarten teacher. That kindergarten perspective is replicable, too. It's a perspective that does not merely tolerate, but exults in diversity.

If what we've done is to have wider applicability, we need to look upon our story as an example, not a model. We'll need to be tolerant toward the different strategies for change that friends and colleagues try out. We need to insist that there cannot be just one right, perfectly crafted, expertly designed solution. Good schools, like good societies and good families, celebrate and cherish this diversity. Since we don't know the ending ahead of time, life's unpredictability is a given. After accepting some guiding principles and a firm direction, we must say hurrah, not alas, to the fact that there is no single way toward a better future.

What makes me hopeful about life, no matter what tomorrow brings, is our infinite capacity for inventing the future. It's what allows me to remain optimistic even though there's presently more racism and more hostility to the poor in my home town than I've witnessed in a long time. There are opportunities out there; things are stirring. It's up to us to come out of the cocoon we built during the 1970s and early 1980s to protect and nurture our fragile educational practices, and join in the fray for a more powerful democratic schooling.

REFERENCES

Sizer, T. (1984). *Horace's Compromise: The Dilemma of the American High School.* Boston: Houghton Mifflin.

Smith, F. (1988). *Joining the Literacy Club.* New York: Heineman.

13

THE HIGH SCHOOL INQUIRY CLASSROOM

ANN COOK

Inquiry Teaching seeks to promote active learning. Its goal is to encourage students to use their minds well: to formulate appropriate questions, identify relevant sources of information, recognize multiple perspectives, listen and observe critically, exchange views, and participate in shaping the focus of investigation. While Inquiry Teaching by its very nature supports considerable leeway in how each teacher specifically develops curriculum, the inquiry approach is characterized overall by an intensive investigation of central issues or problems, and strives for a balanced interweaving of process and content.

At the Urban Academy, an alternative high school created as the working laboratory for the Inquiry Demonstration Project, inquiry courses are offered in most subject matter areas, including math, biology, chemistry, physics, history, social studies, puzzles, astronomy, calculus, foreign language, art, and English. In an attempt to challenge students to think about the questions and content focus within each course, inquiry teachers draw on a repertoire of approaches: guest speakers, panels, debates, mock trials, "sorts," interviews, surveys, presentations—all such techniques are employed to spark discussion and deepen understanding. Such techniques are the stuff of all good teaching. It is, however, the particular use to which these techniques are put which differentiates inquiry from more traditional approaches to teaching and learning. Some examples follow.

Traditionally, guest speakers are invited to classrooms as experts in a given field. Generally, they are asked to make a presentation followed by a question and answer period. Students are expected to take notes and then to ask (hopefully) intelligent questions usually prepared in advance. While such an approach may be more lively than a textbook, there are other, more dynamic ways to utilize a speaker. In an inquiry ethics course, for example, a hospital administrator was invited to class as an expert who could provide students with authentic dilemmas faced by someone in his profession. Each case involved an ethical decision which had to be made, often on short notice, sometimes involving life and death situations. The expert presented each situation without resolution and the students were invited to formulate their own conclusions based on the evidence at hand, along with legal and moral judgments. One dilemma presented involved a Jehovah's Witness who had signed a document requesting no blood transfusions. The hospital agreed to perform the elective surgery because of its apparent safety. However, when during the operation an artery was nicked, the transfusion became a life and death necessity. Students were asked to consider the situation, request whatever information they felt necessary, and finally, make a decision. Only after students had responded did the speaker discuss his own decision. While it was possible to present such dilemmas to students from written descriptions, having the expert on hand provided an urgency and authenticity which might have been missed otherwise.

Similarly, a panel discussion focusing on the question "What is a good museum?" involved two teachers and a professional museum consultant. The two teachers took divergent points of view—one arguing that museum-goers have the major responsibility to get something out of an exhibit; the other arguing that it was the museum's responsibility to present the material in a way that first lured the museum-goer, then educated the visitor in an entertaining and lively way. The museum consultant presented the view that the museum and museum-goer had dual responsibilities: the former to provide a thoughtful and attractive exhibit, the latter to be receptive to the material presented.and to think about what might be on hand to discover. The discussion and questions were lively and passionate, with one student finally asking the panel to address the question: does the museum exist for the visitor, or vice versa?

In still another example, a research scientist whose specialty is the study of monkeys was invited to a biology class studying animal behavior. The teacher requested that she look over the students' research studies and raise questions relating to the research designs rather than simply describing her own research. Information about her studies was brought into the ensuing discussion as it related to the issues she raised about the students' work. The expertise of the speaker was critically important, but was delivered in a manner requiring students to interact in a challenging way.

Interviews provide still another example of how a commonly used teaching strategy can be reshaped to provide a more intense learning experience. Typically, an individual with an interesting point of view is invited to class for students to question. In such a setting, the content of the interview may be reviewed and discussed in a follow-up lesson. In an inquiry class, however, how the questions are asked, how students follow up one with another, and the way in which they handle information and reframe an unanswered question receives as much attention as the answers themselves. Additionally, a replay of the interview would be prepared (either based on a teacher's transcript or a tape or video recording) so that students could focus on specific questions and their context. In this way, students learn the importance of how the questions are framed, as well as the difference between those questions which yield interesting responses and those which are dead-ended.

Finally, finding ways that permit students to explore the subjective choices inherent in the evaluation of any body of knowledge can be approached through a strategy known as a "sort." In this activity, students are asked to make a spontaneous commitment to a question which then forms the basis of further study and discussion. Information reflecting a range of opinions on a given topic is presented on separate cards or slips of paper. Typically, each student would be given some 50 or 60 separate items from which to choose. Initially, students would be asked to rank order the five or ten statements or pieces of information they believe relate most significantly to the question posed. Sometimes, students are also asked to rank order the least important items. Following this, small groups of three or four students can be asked to negotiate individuals' choices to arrive at a group selection.

One would be hard-pressed to find an area in which this technique could not be applied. Thus, a sort can be used to determine which facts are most or least important in deciding the long-term impact of Columbus and the age of exploration, the relative dangers of different household chemicals, the ten most important figures in American history, or the most essential features of a school that works. The key to the sort is that it forces students to consider a range of possibilities, presents them with conflicting ideas, and encourages them to find rational reasons for justifying what they believe.

Inquiry Teaching emphasizes engagement around authentic questions. Its use of strategies which encourage divergent ways of thinking about these questions are intended to foster engagement and make the learning experience meaningful.

14

BLACKS IN WHITE SCHOOLS
FRANCES MOORE-BOND

Efforts to keep up with a changing society by including more students of color in predominantly white institutions is not a new idea. David Mallery (1963), in his monograph "Negro Students in Independent Schools," speaks of a young black student who attended Mt. Hermon School in 1886. The student, considered a token, was the only black student enrolled at the institution, a situation repeated many times over in other boarding schools. It took almost a hundred years before predominantly white, independent schools began to admit more black students. By the 1950s, a small number of independent schools had begun the process of desegregation, but the number of black students enrolled was small. If not the only student of color in the school, the child was often the only student of color in the classroom. This is still true in many independent schools today. Between 1955 and 1980, these schools campaigned and recruited significant numbers of African–Americans and other students of color. By 1987, according to a National Association of Independent Schools survey, 11.2 percent of students were children of color. Much of this recruitment was based on (1) a moral obligation on the part of the charitable privileged class to help eliminate poverty among the disadvantaged classes, (2) the Supreme Court decision *Brown vs. Board of Education of Topeka, Kansas* which ruled racial segregation in public schools unconstitutional, and (3) recruitment of students of color when traditional populations of white students were not available (Speede-Franklin, 1988).

The words "recruitment" and "campaign" are misnomers. Can we say, with a clear conscience, that semicollective guilt on the part of whites, or sympathy for those who are less fortunate constitutes an active form of recruitment? Is not enacting a law to enforce desegregation or exploiting students of color as substitutes until more white children apply a despicable commentary on recruitment practices?

Subsequently, these schools attempted to educate and socialize their students. But in the 1990s, as I think of people of color in our predominantly white educational institutions, old feelings of injustice and inequality resurface. I continue to be outraged by the need to speak about blacks in white schools. Major restructuring of the school environment to meet multicultural goals must be a joint effort between white educators and people of color. There is no other way to communicate the issues that matter to us.

In a multiethnic, multifaceted society which is experiencing rapid change, the inclusion of more people of color in white institutions is imperative if students are to learn how to come to terms with differences and how to deal with the effects of race on all of our lives. It is imperative that white educators become more aware of students of color in predominantly white institutions. As educators, we want to feel that the efforts of our daily hard work will provide students with quality educational opportunities. We want our schools to provide the mechanisms for students of color to become independent thinkers and full participating citizens of our democratic society. Therefore, as a black educator in a predominantly white school, I intend to enlist your support in understanding the plight of students of color.

We know that a major responsibility of schools is to insure students a relevant and adequate academic life. However, socializing students of color is equal to or perhaps more important than academic life. I emphasize the social integration because youngsters who are socialized into the school's life rather than being isolated should do well academically. This relationship needs to be examined more carefully, but according to several researchers (for example, Slaughter and Johnson [1988]), *if black students are to assume leadership positions in their communities and in the larger society, their socialization in school during these critical high school years cannot be marginal.* Several studies indicate that for black students to become a significant part of school life, 20–25 percent of the total school needs to be black (Pettigrew, 1974). Rist (1978) points out that "black students who serve as tokens in a white milieu tend to suffer" (p. 265). To quote Geraldine Brookins (1988), professor of psychology at Jackson State University, "We do know that academic competence at the expense of social and emotional health is unlikely to accrue quality to the life of the individual or the community in which he or she resides" (p. 17).

In order to achieve social integration, the school's climate must support equal educational opportunities for all students. Diversity should be prized, cultures respected, and teachers and administrators committed to develop greater understanding of the cultural patterns and behaviors of students. White teachers need to speak less, and listen and observe students of color more. In any given school, when the number of white faculty and administrators is disproportionate to the student population of color, curricular plans and teaching techniques and approaches become one-sided. Also, communication becomes confused and the understanding of cultural differences limited. No pat solutions exist to achieve an acceptable school climate, but based on my experiences, here are some important areas to consider.

It is clear to me that in many independent white schools, "traditional" clubs and other organizations that appear to be accessible to all students are, in reality, exclusive rather than inclusive. If students of color are not invited or encouraged to join the Latin club, the French club, or the Chess club, for example, these clubs will remain predominantly white. Faculty sponsors, regardless of their color, must take an aggressive stance to include students of color. Further, faculty must relinquish the fear that if more than two or three students of color join a traditional club, the eventual result will be a black Latin Club or a black French Club. I am continually amazed at this narrow attitude and at sponsors who promote the French, Latin, or Spanish clubs without including the contributions of nonwhite peoples.

Sports is another sensitive area. Too often, stereotypes about black males, which emphasize brawn over brain, are perpetuated . Frequently, black males are encouraged to entertain the student body by demonstrating their prowess in football and basketball. Another aspect of this unfortunate expectation is that the attrition rate of black males sometimes soars in schools without a football team. If we are concerned about retaining middle school youngsters in high school for reasons other than to entertain in these traditional high school sports, faculty and coaches must take time to introduce students to other "white" sports. For many youngsters of color in the United States, soccer is considered a "white" sport to which blacks have historically had no access. Coaches who recognize the importance of the contributions of people of color to these sports will highlight black soccer heroes and emphasize the parallels between football and soccer. I think coaches often acknowledge the relevance of this idea, but are often reluctant to change their familiar ways. Coaches need to be aware of their role in helping retain students of color in white schools.

Social life issues must be taken more seriously. The casual, passive, matter-of-fact attitude of whites to issues affecting the lives of students of color is an abomination. During elementary school years, black children of both sexes are invited regularly to sleep-overs and parties given by whites. The children interact, as children do, by having fun. Black and white parents speak to each other cautiously as they drop off and pick up their children, though they rarely socialize. But as students of color become middle-school aged, they are invited to fewer parties given by whites, and parties given by black students are not well-attended by white "friends." Black families often find their children become more and more isolated in school as well as out of school, especially as adolescents begin to date. I have heard the hurt in parents' voices when their daughters find no suitable young men in the school community to accompany them to school events or when no white student would accept their son or daughter as a prom date. But the greatest feelings of isolation emerge when the students' "friends" are no longer there as buddies.

Too often the harvest of parentally influenced racial bigotry surfaces in young people during these preteen and teen years. As adults socialize and interact more with culturally different individuals at work and social situations, young people will more readily follow their lead. Indeed, if enrollments are increased, students of color will have more choices, yet racist attitudes on the part of many whites, particularly during the dating period in junior and senior high, hinder the development of healthy social situations.

My experience has been that stereotypes related to integrated dating come up again and again, and many issues I have addressed here relate to the ultimate concern about race-mixing. My point is not that black or white students be forced to feel that they must date out of their cultural groups. Although blacks may dream of being accepted by whites, we know that for the most part this is not possible. Black parents have handled this awkward situation by continually reminding their youngsters to develop and retain friendships with students at other schools and with students in the black community who share the same racial and cultural experiences.

Clearly, students of color need more choices, and schools must make concerted efforts to increase the enrollment of students of color and to provide them with role models and adequate support systems. Also, more racial cooperation is needed among all groups in predominantly white schools since cooperative efforts remain the one-sided province of people of color. But there must be other, more active solutions. First, each school must do a complete internal inventory of what currently exists. One helpful tool to identify needs, problems, and solutions is the *Multicultural Assessment Plan for Independent Schools* (1988). At the same time, faculty must interact with each other and with external consultants to remove the issues related to students of color in white schools from the backburners of denial to the forefront of reality.

Without a genuine effort to achieve a truly multicultural community, slights and insensitivities can become negative yardsticks by which schools are measured. Here are several incidents I have noticed which could and should have been explosive. Some have obvious solutions and need no comment.

1. I have noticed that the viola section of the orchestra is primarily black. It turns out that the music teacher, perhaps unconsciously, has indicated to black parents that their children's arms are too long to play the violin. Even though the children's first choice is the violin, they are encouraged to select the viola. This is a covert racist remark. If the teacher is attempting to provide some balance in the orchestra, why use race as a guideline? My understanding of string instruments is that instruments come in a variety of sizes. Teachers should examine their reasons for making such decisions.

2. Why are there only a few black faculty members and administrators in predominantly white schools? An answer that I heard recently, and have heard many times, is that black educators can't be found to be hired. One principal even had the audacity to say that blacks are no longer interested in careers in education because they become doctors and lawyers now. This demonstrates

a total disregard for the black community. If energy were spent involving the black community in all aspects of the school, there would be no reason to sound so ignorant; administrators would know that various black social and fraternal groups, and ministerial councils welcome the idea of providing black candidates for positions of authority in schools. The school would also learn that because of a lingering distrust of some whites in authority positions, a more indirect approach to families of color would be appropriate. For example, receiving information from another black faculty member, friend, or alumnus could help restore trust in the search process.

3. A school disseminates a calendar to faculty, administrators, and parents with pictures of children in the school environment. Of the twelve pictures featured, there is one child of black and white parentage; another is very light-skinned, probably a black child, in a group with other children. A third picture features two athletes, one white and one black, and a coach. The caption below the picture names the two athletes. However, upon close examination of the picture, one finds something very odd. Only the legs of the black athlete are shown; his body is missing because it was cut off at the top of the picture. The unimportance of the black athlete is communicated. Several African–American students and adults who saw this picture were very angry. Students and faculty as well as administrators must take note of visual forms of communication. If calendars, school brochures, or other forms of media are disseminated, time and care must be taken to assure that all students are represented fairly.

4. Black students are reprimanded for being too emotional, too animated, and too demonstrative. Teachers and administrators in this instance lack an understanding of nonverbal and verbal cultural differences. All students deserve the right to express themselves in ways that allow diversity of learning and response styles. Teachers should not feel that students of color are disrespectful or threatening when their responses are of a different style from white students. For example, students of color are reprimanded or "graded down" when their class participation utilizes more nonverbal body and facial gestures than the white teacher's or student's. These students are thought of as being too loud or explicit when the white teacher's mannerisms are indirect and implicit and the forms of authority are presented in a soft-spoken voice. The role of a teacher is to educate and part of the process is to recognize and understand the diversity of responses appropriate to specific cultures in the classroom.

5. The Black Student Association is responsible for recognizing Black History Month. Most teachers do not write their lesson plans and units to reflect the contributions of blacks and other students of color. The message here is that if something is to be done for Black History Month, the blacks will have to do it themselves. After all, the reason for a month of recognition is generally due to the fact that black contributions go virtually unrecognized for the other eight or nine months of the school year. In many instances, faculty do not

make black contributions an integral part of the curriculum. Is the history department so ignorant that American History continues to be viewed solely as transfer of European values and traditions to America? For all students, teachers need to look toward interdisciplinary approaches to subject matter and develop versions of history that do not ignore the contributions of diverse groups. One solution has been to establish separate courses such as African–American History. These courses serve a valuable purpose but are frequently not viewed as a real part of American history or as serious curriculum. Therefore, the attendance of white students is usually very low in African–American History or courses that are taught from the Native American's point of view, even though white students might profit the most. Also, during class registration, white students are frequently told by faculty registrars to avoid taking African–American History because it is not worth the time and would not be looked upon favorably on a transcript. I was appalled to learn this from a white student not long ago who indicated that she and her friends had been interested in the course.

If schools tolerate situations like these, we should not be surprised that conflicts increase between ethnically different groups as the enrollment of students of color increases. Typically, students of color become victims of institutions that have not respected or revered them. True multiculturalism fosters cooperation. Without it, incidents such as the ones just mentioned become explosive when young people and parents begin to communicate to the general community that students of color are victims of injustice in predominantly white schools.

These incidents raise serious questions about the educational intentions of many white institutions with regard to individuals of color. We cannot continue to assume that all teachers and administrators know how to handle these instances in a way that supports the emotional health of students of color. Before administrators, faculty, and staff can be expected to act with reasonable judgment in academic and social milieus with students of color, they should be offered consciousness-raising workshops and classes to address their own biases as well as students' prejudices. One outcome of such sessions should be to understand and design different teaching strategies to meet the diverse learning styles of all students.

Too frequently, though, white faculty are insensitive to issues related to diversity, especially when the term "racism" is used. Some faculty members would rather engage in a watered-down discussion of racial interactions and multicultural education by equating the plight of people of color with prejudices against white women and white ethnic groups. In such instances, some people of color prefer to turn off their concern and anger in an effort to maintain their sanity. Therefore, I am not speaking here of seminars that allow us to engage in a series of academic excursions that perpetuate an attitude of indifference. I am speaking of sessions conducted by facilitators who help connect participants' feelings with their prejudices and stereotypes. Only then will we find viable solutions to racism.

Schools that are serious about bridging the gaps between culturally diverse groups will do well to hire a community liaison to open communication. Young people of color need these role models to find vehicles to express their feelings and desires. But a community liaison can also ease the concerns of white teachers who might ask, "Why do the black students segregate themselves in the lunchroom?" and assist teachers in understanding the behavior of some especially outspoken (or, conversely, very quiet) black boys who have often been perceived by white female teachers as aggressive or emotionally immature.

In addition, outside liaisons can help schools recruit faculty and administrators of color. Placing ads for available positions in local and city newspapers is an ineffective approach to active recruitment. A school-community liaison, for example, could establish a trust level with African-American churches and fraternal groups to aid recruitment. And recruitment must be an immediate concern if the community is going to be diverse. White faculty and administrators cannot continue to do the planning, teaching, and administrating, while paraprofessionals, frequently people of color, carry out secretarial and clerical chores. Nor can schools continue to have a few people of color in faculty support positions to help place a "stamp of approval" on curricular approaches and teaching methods.

In many predominantly white schools, the retention rate for faculty of color is very low. But to retain faculty of color, we must first be hired—and viewed as equals. Existing faculty and administration must become comfortable knowing that blacks and other people of color can teach youngsters, direct programs, and oversee educational goals. Faculty of color must be welcomed; just as with students, isolation is the greatest problem they face. A few years ago I taught at a university in the Midwest. As one of two black professors in the college of education, I was not made aware of many social events, research projects, or other professional opportunities, even though I always asked. A favorite reply was, "Gee, I don't know about anything." I was required not only to perform my teaching and supervision duties, but also to participate on committees, especially those needing minority representation. In many circumstances, I was invisible to my white colleagues and was not a voice to be heard and respected. In these situations, how can white administrators expect faculty of color to grin and bear it when the working environment is foreign, callous, and unrewarding? Faculty of color must be hired, but methods for retaining us will need to be established. We have a unique voice and valuable experiences to contribute to the life of a predominantly white school. We often live in two worlds—one predominantly white, one predominantly nonwhite. Since this is the case, it is logical that we understand the white world to a much greater extent than whites understand peoples of color.

One wise move is to stop assuming the answers are known about what is best for all students. The quality of life in schools would improve if people listened to suggestions by faculty of color regarding curriculum changes and methods for teaching racially diverse populations. It would behoove those in power to listen and to *hear what is being said!*

Further complicating the retention issue is that to my knowledge predominantly white schools do not recognize the extra duties that fall to faculty of color, particularly in relation to students of color and to those committees where representation is needed. A recent example is most appropriate. At the beginning of the school year, several black students asked me to be the faculty sponsor for the Black Student Association (BSA). This was an honor. However, the students' choices were extremely limited. There was no one else to ask if they wanted to have an African-American sponsor, because among the five black faculty members out of a faculty of 40, I was the only one who had not yet served. Schools that do not have a set salary schedule do have more opportunities to compensate faculty who have additional responsibilities. However, a salary scale is no excuse for not recognizing the extra time spent, especially when it is related to making students of color feel part of the school environment. School administrators need to look for ways to show they value these contributions by *all* faculty members.

If schools are to succeed, students and faculty must address racial issues directly and change the attitudes of whites who perpetuate the color-blind theory. Unless the adults in schools take the initiative and genuinely seek change, the school environment will remain dysfunctional for people of color, and, ironically, for whites also. For many white educators, the word change conjures up negative feelings and fears. To remedy this guilt and lack of frankness about what diversity brings, faculty and administrators must stop patronizing people of color. I am not talking about nurturing and caring behaviors. I am specifically speaking about the attitude of "I am doing you a favor," or "I am showing you an act of good will." Students of color will not respond favorably to condescension and trickery.

African–Americans must become a significant part of school life or the message becomes, "We don't want you here!" The school's climate should be designed to make students of color feel they are essential to the life of the school. Until this is done, black students and other students of color will continue to feel much more than isolation in white schools—they will be left out of the so-called democratic process.

REFERENCES

Brookins, G. K. (1988). "Making the Honor Roll: A Black Parent's Perception on Private Education." From *Visible Now: Blacks in Private Schools.* Westport: Greenwood Press.

Mallery, D. (1963). *Negro Students in Independent Schools*. Boston: National Association of Independent Schools.

National Association of Independent Schools (1988). *Multicultural Assessment Plan for Independent Schools* (A Project of the Office of Minority Affairs). Boston: Author.

Pettigrew, T. (1974). *A Sociological View of the Post-Milliken Era*. Paper presented to the U. S. Commission on Civil Rights in Hearings, Washington, DC.

Rist, R. (1978). *The Invisible Children: School Integration in American Society*. Cambridge, MA: Harvard University Press.

Slaughter, D., and Johnson, D. J. (1988). *Visible Now: Blacks in Private Schools*. Westport: Greenwood Press.

Speede-Franklin, W. A. (1988). "Ethnic Diversity: Patterns and Implications of Minorities in Independent Schools." From *Visible Now: Blacks in Private Schools*. Westport: Greenwood Press.

15

A HERO FOR FIFTEEN-YEAR-OLDS: RAOUL WALLENBERG

CHARLES MEYERS

Tears cascaded down Lisa's face as she watched what seemed to be another interminable sorrow: more corpses, more suffering, more degradation. After years of teaching about the Holocaust, I had reached an impasse. I firmly believed that my students had to be immersed in the subject to learn, but was the enormity of the catastrophe too traumatizing for young minds? I needed rays of hope, some light amidst the darkness. I found those rays in the righteous acts of the rescuers. And I found Raoul Wallenberg, a neutral Swede whose heroic acts of rescue in Budapest, Hungary in late 1944 resulted in 100,000 saved lives and gave hope to the condemned.

In an era when "hero" is a euphemism for the local sports star, we have to raise the discussion of moral stakes to a higher ground. Understanding and applying the implications of courageous acts is the fabric of our history. We teach about individuals who made a difference in the lives of others to inspire and give notice that learning from others is transferable to our own generation. Anne Hutchinson's argument for conscience in Puritan New England, Edmund Ross's vote to save Andrew Johnson from impeachment, Oscar Underwood's actions against the Klan in the 1920s in the South, and the single act by Rosa Parks are memorable. They remind us that individuals have made a difference in their time and that we can make a difference in ours. Each took risks, saw the alternatives before them, acted upon their beliefs, and made a personal statement that is a beacon for moral behavior. The actions of Raoul Wallenberg stand squarely in the corner with these paragons of virtue.

But while Wallenberg filled the need for my generation, can young people in the 1990s understand and empathize with his issue? Will they be able to seek out a cause in which to involve themselves deeply and sustain their caring beyond the classroom and the academic year into their adult lives? To me, the goal of teaching this period in our history is to convey to young people living in this country today that they are needed, that unless they care about issues and people who have been deprived of opportunities, their own lives will be impoverished. It is in the caring about our fellow human beings that we realize a better world.

One need read no further than the second page of any American newspaper to know that pessimism about our future abounds. The deficit, homelessness, the rise of a clearly discernable underclass, and contention about the future of American education disturb us. Individuals and interest groups conflict over gun control, abortion rights, and abuse of the environment. At times, the depth of these crises almost impedes our ability to alleviate them. We flounder, often aimlessly, looking for direction and perhaps for a person with the initiative to lead and the charisma to attract those who can risk to achieve. Raoul Wallenberg is such a person, a hero for these 15-year-olds.

This then, is the story I tell my class: Premonitions preoccupied Raoul Wallenberg as he prepared for his departure from Budapest on the morning of January 17, 1945. "I do not know if I am going as a prisoner or a guest," thought the Swedish diplomat as he pondered the short voyage to Russian military headquarters to discuss the status of postwar Hungary. During the months in which he had served as Secretary in charge of Section C (Rescue) in the Swedish Embassy, Wallenberg had performed miracles—standing on box cars en route to the death camp at Auschwitz, confronting Nazi officials face to face, pulling Jews from a death march. But now a shroud of mystery was about to descend on the 33-year-old Wallenberg. Later that morning, with his driver Vilmos Langfelder at his side, Wallenberg left for General Malinovsky's headquarters at Debrecen. He was never seen again outside of the Soviet Union.

Forty-four years have elapsed since Wallenberg's disappearance. Despite denials by the Soviets and an "official" announcement in 1957 that Wallenberg had succumbed to a heart attack in his cell ten years earlier, numerous sightings indicate that Wallenberg survived an entangled odyssey of constant movement and solitary confinement in the Gulag. Abandoned by powerful officials in his own nation, Wallenberg became a victim of the Cold War: the skillful humanitarian who outwitted his Nazi adversaries was transformed into a nearly forgotten figure in the postwar frenzy. How could a single man save so many? How could the most powerful nations in the world fail to act on his behalf? Where was Raoul Wallenberg?

Questions persisted long after Wallenberg's name faded from the headlines. A few people clung to his memory, including his family and a coterie of admirers and friends who wrote letters, pressured diplomats, and organized Wallenberg committees around the world. They kept the faith in the 1950s when scattered sightings continued and into the 1960s when hard information reached a number of well-placed informants and Wallenberg-watchers who monitored emigré testimony. And it continued into the 1970s when Swedish physician Nanna Swartz described an encounter with a Soviet doctor (later denied by Soviet officials) who claimed that he was treating Wallenberg.

Today, the memory of Raoul Wallenberg lives for those who admire his remarkable brand of humanitarianism and wait for new information. But how can he be of value in these times, two generations after his exploits in Budapest?

The Raoul Wallenberg Committee of Chicago was organized in 1987 to perpetuate Wallenberg's work, to learn his fate, and to propagate the kind of activity that he so clearly demonstrated could be achieved when people were willing to act when they cared. In his absence, Wallenberg could still inspire. The question raised by the Committee concerned appropriate vehicles for educating the public about his achievements and the implications of his work. Wallenberg carried a light in a dark moment of history. How could that light reach people today?

In the fall of 1988, I began to collect documents, read extant literature, and piece together the elements of what was to be a unit of study about Raoul Wallenberg. Six seminal biographies had emerged by the early 1980s when hopes were high for Wallenberg's release. Several collections of documents existed in government archives—in the War Refugee Board Collection at the Franklin Delano Roosevelt Library at Hyde Park, New York and in the records of the State Department. Recently declassified material from the Office of Strategic Services/Central Intelligence Agency (OSS/CIA) added substance to these existing records. With the aid of the Freedom of Information Act and an enlightened archivist in the National Archives, I procured many of these documents. Seen together, they give an expansive picture of U.S. participation in the selection and support of Wallenberg for the Budapest mission.

Yet there were still pieces missing. I needed the testimony of persons who knew and worked with Wallenberg. These individuals were forthcoming. Agnes Adachi, an aide to Wallenberg in Budapest in late 1944, lives in the New York area, while Lars Berg, a high official in the Swedish Embassy in Hungary, lives in Rio de Janeiro. They revealed the kind of memories that added substance to what had previously been a rather sterile portrait of Wallenberg. Lars Berg described the little-documented but well-known encounter between Wallenberg and Adolf Eichmann, whose orders resulted in the destruction of many thousands of Hungarian Jews. Berg shared the details of this memorable encounter which had occurred at his house, describing Wallenberg's irreverence towards time. Wallenberg had forgotten his appointment with Eichmann and called Berg in panic. Finally, after an amicable evening of formal exchanges, Eichmann parted with a veiled threat. "As for you, Mr. Diplomat, don't think that immunity can protect you forever. Even diplomats have accidents." As was his tendency to act under pressure, Wallenberg smiled, bid Eichmann farewell, and continued to do his work as if the threat had made no difference. A few days later his car was demolished. He was not in it.

These recollections made Wallenberg's acts so vivid they seemed almost tangible. Here was a man whose efforts were incomprehensible in light of the disaster that was occurring in Hungary in 1944, yet his innocence, simplicity, and compassion were so universally human. Here was a model of behavior that we could emulate because he cherished life.

The next step was to challenge my students to think about Wallenberg's heroism. What was the most important thing that happened in the story? Was it the numbers he saved? Or was it in his commitment to something about which he cared so deeply that he was willing to risk everything for it? These students are still too young to take the kind of risk Wallenberg did. But they are not too young to show their caring in some way—involvement with local shelters, food pantries, inner city children, the elderly. These projects, organized within the school setting, will become internalized and more powerful for them as they enter young adulthood.

If we believe that children can learn from the wisdom and actions of their elders, then Raoul Wallenberg has something to offer to the current generation. He was a paragon of action when so many were silent. His activities represented a concerned conscience amidst destruction and immorality. If this individual could make a difference, could children comprehend the degree to which they, too, might control their destinies and pull the world out of darkness?

For the Wallenberg Committees and the Adachis and the Bergs of the world, for those who continue to keep his memory alive for America (which made Wallenberg an honorary citizen in 1981), and for the 15-year-olds of today who need a special hero, the spirit of Raoul Wallenberg is very much present. Now it is their turn to continue that heroic tradition.

16

TEACHING SCIENCE AS A LIBERAL ART
ANDREW KAPLAN

For three years, I had the great good fortune to participate in an experimental program that attempted to integrate the study of science with the study of the humanities in a required course for ninth graders at Francis Parker School in Chicago. From its inception, the course, called here GALILEO, presented an unusual opportunity for teachers, students, and the community to expand horizons and discover new ways of approaching content, methods, and the circumstances of learning. While the course no longer exists at Francis Parker, it remains an important influence and inspiration, a paradigm for the study of both intellectual possibilities and institutionalized change, one that stimulates and develops the very best energies that sustain and refresh the life of a teacher. I want to use this course as an instance of interdisciplinary education, although I will save a more precise definition of that currently fashionable phrase until the end of the article.

PLANNING

The cooperative development of GALILEO began with a need, in this case the need to alter a required course for ninth graders that had been the source of bitter and fractious controversy for years; the idea was to turn the course away from the struggle for control and toward the faculty's collective responsibility. One of my colleagues, John Leary, had taught the incumbent version of the ninth grade required course with the express purpose of learning enough of its dynamics to change it. John not only thought up a new focus for the ninth grade course, but he wisely recruited the staff individually. The self-conscious

Portions of this essay were published in *Curriculum Inquiry* 18:3 (Fall, 1988), pp. 255–87. Grateful acknowledgement is made to the publishers © John Wiley and Son, for permission to use parts of this article here.

use of faculty and course as both means and end in educational development made the program an enormously successful experiment in cooperative planning. A required course that had begun eight years before as a response to a change of schedule at last achieved integrity within the structure of the academic program, as well as intellectual integrity on its own. To make sense of these claims, I need to give you a brief history.

The course began as a response to contention among faculty and administration about responsibility for a number of curricular objectives. Francis Parker is an urban private school with a long-standing position as one of the leading progressive schools in the United States. Formed at the turn of the century by a colleague of John Dewey, Parker is a 14-year school committed to social, economic, and intellectual diversity. Since the school has long been committed to the social motive in school work, we have chosen to group our students heterogeneously in all subject areas. Knowing that students have different abilities, we have sought to teach them together in order to accommodate diversity as a curricular element.

A new schedule adopted in 1974 meant that students had more choices about the placement of their courses within each trimester of the academic year. Recognizing that one of the great strengths of an elective program could be a weakness if students did not have continuous or sufficient training in certain areas, the school looked for basic courses to require in order to assure minimal competencies. The answer as the new schedule came into existence was a course for ninth graders which would insure the acquisition of "basic skills" in reading and writing. The History and English departments staffed this course and designed a number of course projects to impart skills that students would need in subsequent classes. But from such apparently modest beginnings, contention arose over whose responsibility the imparting of reading and writing skills really ought to be, and over the pedagogical issue of "basic skills" themselves.

The school's answer in the mid-1970s was that all teachers who use the written word should be teachers of reading and writing. The Skills Course now became the province of Foreign Language, Science, and presumably every other department besides. There was only limited participation from the high school departments, however, since departments set a lower priority for the shared responsibility than they did for their own subject. But the seeds of conflict which had been sown along departmental lines now blossomed inside the course itself. The staff of the course recommended that it be discontinued. Why, they asked, was it necessary to isolate these skills? Was it in fact possible to teach skills as a subject matter? Could the course have any integrity if it principally served as an introduction to skills that the student would only be able to employ concretely at a later date?

Instead of answering these questions, the school responded by inaugurating a new required course for ninth graders: Language Arts was a team taught course that all students took together in the fall trimester. The content of the course, borrowed in large part from an inspirational sophomore history course, was the problematical villainy of Richard III. Shakespeare, Josephine Tey, Sir Thomas Moore and others became the focus of study. Although the class now met as a whole rather than in sections, and despite the presence of a group of faculty, the course continued with the same disciplinary model as the previous Skills course. That is, the teachers were present to provide expert knowledge in their respective areas and to prepare students for the rigors of study in history· and literature by showing them the nature of truth and the method of inquiry in each field. While the course now had a subject matter, only the student was required to know all of the subject, and what he or she had to know came from each teacher in the team acting as an expert. The authoritarian nature of the course, enhanced by the lecture format in the school's auditorium, isolated Language Arts from student and faculty support. Politically, the course had no home base because it belonged to no department. Like the Skills course before it, Language Arts was a nondepartmental course under the general direction of the Curriculum Coordinator for the Upper School. But in a school otherwise arranged according to departments, this nonalignment created conflicts without clear responsibilities. No teacher beyond those involved with the course felt that the design, support, and future of the course devolved upon him or her.

GALILEO at once avoided the political contention and provided a new intellectual basis for cooperative planning. Instead of designing another course which would be outside of the departmental structure, the GALILEO course was, from its inception, interdepartmental. More than semantics was involved here: the course became the responsibility of the entire faculty and was an experiment in cooperative planning and evaluation. Rather than asking department heads to appoint staff members based on department representation in the course during preceding years, we sought individual volunteers. Instead of isolating the staff, the plan for the course was to involve a number of teachers as evaluators who would sit in on the planning and execution of the course and report back to the faculty as a whole at the end of the first year. Instead of approaching selected aspects of course material as an expert with a specifically assigned role, each teacher resolved to prepare and present all aspects of course material. Instead of lecturing, the staff broke the large group of students into smaller sections and tried to plan classes that would move students back and forth between small and large group settings.

The curricular significance of the change derived from its method. By removing the course from the friction of departmental staffing and the vagaries of nondepartmental control, GALILEO became at once a cooperative venture. The staff of the course presumed that it acted on behalf of the entire faculty, which would evaluate and supervise this experiment that created a required, common course for ninth graders. In all previous attempts, the curricular method had been prescriptive: a course and its teachers were appointed to accomplish the training of certain skills deemed necessary for student mastery. GALILEO proceeded from neither a prescriptive nor an administrative model. That is, the content and the ends of the course were not dictated by the prescription of certain traits that all students ought to have at this grade level; nor was the course dictated by administrative designation of certain faculty or departments as the teachers. GALILEO was instead the product of deliberation within the faculty about the ways and means of accomplishing a commitment to interdisciplinary education. The faculty thought that a common course might still be worth an effort, and GALILEO was, therefore, not only an end but a means, a deliberated attempt to discover whether the broadening of responsibility could engage the faculty in a continuing commitment to experiment in curriculum. If GALILEO were successful from this point of view, it would lead to other collaborative courses.

If the institutional structure of the course substituted collegial responsibility for administrative decree, the content and method demanded that teachers share all aspects of the course rather than simply provide the expert knowledge in one area or aspect. Instead of divorcing skills from content and presuming to teach what all students will need "later on," GALILEO considered the problems generated by the career, personality, and influence of Galileo. The objectives and the pedagogy of the course proceeded, not from an abstract prescription of skills, but from a consideration of the life and achievement of a certain human being. The course was liberal education in at least three different senses of "liberal." It freed the faculty and administration from narrow conflicts by encouraging curricular experimentation; it freed students to engage fundamental, lifelong issues by developing arts of inquiry they might apply in any subject matter; it developed skills as disciplines of mind and habits of character rather than the narrower conception of skills as stepping stones toward predictable or desirable competencies.

As an exercise in the humanities or liberal arts, GALILEO developed the writings, activities, character, and reputation of Galileo as a series of interrelated themes. The course developed each theme from a variety of materials, each student and teacher endeavoring to appreciate, understand, and at times criticize the achievements or frustrations of Galileo as scientist, writer, historical personage, and dramatic character. Of course, we engaged in a good deal of skill development in this course; but now the skills were treated as means, not ends. The difficulty and breadth of course material demanded that we aid students in developing techniques and attitudes that would assist them in the wide-ranging experiences that the course provided. The faculty had to share the responsibility to create study guides for each reading, experiment, lecture, and demonstration. Galileo's writings were especially difficult for students unused to the attention needed to follow closely observed facts and highly structured argument. Part or all of many class periods were devoted to oral reading of Galileo's writings, using the study guide as a source of questions and organization. The faculty took special care to write these guides not only for the student but also for fellow faculty who were frequently in need of assistance in understanding the meaning of the text. The times that we were able to meet as a faculty to share the results of the several class discussions about some work of Galileo rank among the very best moments of my career. The conversation that began in the classroom now had a fitting completion in communication among colleagues. We were learning to master texts at the same time that we were teaching them to our students: that kind of freshness and vitality is inspiring to share. The skills of close reading and passage analysis which we tried to develop in our small groups served, we hoped, to stretch student attention and tolerance for difficult tasks.

Although we taught many of the same skills which earlier versions of the common course stressed, these skills received very different emphasis. We introduced or applied skills because the students needed to do certain things. The skills enabled them to draw a map, read an argument, define a key term, and see more clearly the elements of an experiment. We proceeded from no theoretical sanction of which skills are important; rather, we employed skills which were practically necessary to accomplish certain tasks.

TEACHING

Since the teachers were learners in all areas of the course rather than expert authorities in one or another aspect, we were all engaged in the same activities and toward the same end. We read widely in the works of Galileo, from "The Starry Messenger" to parts of *The Dialogue Concerning the Two Chief World Systems*; we read and saw the Brecht play as well as two very different biographical accounts of Galileo; we carried out laboratory exercises on lenses and the combination of lenses, including the combination Galileo used to draw the moon in "The Starry Messenger"; we had students assemble a low power telescope and then do observations and drawings of the moon. We took great risks in the kinds of material and the kinds of activities we attempted. Some of each class we spent together as a large group, listening to a presentation from a teacher or a group of students. One day, as a teacher was lecturing about the power of the Church and the challenge of the Reformation, a fellow teacher, dressed as a monk, burst into the auditorium and began to sell indulgences. Only her colleagues knew that the speech was from John Osborne's *Luther*, but the students were quite struck with her offer to pardon not only past but future sins (she had a number of customers each year). We examined garden planning, fashions in painting and poetry, the choral music of Monteverdi and Palestrina, the evolving architecture of the Vatican: all of these elements helped us understand the world in which

Galileo lived and the forces with which he was contending. Students acquired a host of new skills as they encountered the interconnectedness of problems. One excellent example is the class field trip to observe the night sky.

The overnight trip came early in the trimester, before the students had read "The Starry Messenger" and before we had worked with telescopes or lenses. The trip was a way to bring students together socially, to introduce observational astronomy, and to practically experience the course's primary concern with the distinction between observation and inference. The observations were done in four parts.

First, we let the students loose in a field and asked them to lie down and look at the stars. After 10 minutes, we asked them to return indoors and gave each of them a blank sheet of paper on which we asked them to draw what they had seen. As they drew, there was much conversation about how impossible it was or what did the teachers want anyway. We discussed their problems and determined that there would be a number of ways to assist the process. The drawing should show direction, it should indicate what time of night the observation took place, and the stars should be drawn relative to important constellations. For these purposes, we then handed out a chart of the evening skies for 40 degrees latitude.

The second part of the activity was to return to the field with the chart and a flashlight covered in red gel, so as not to disturb night vision. This was a small group activity, with students clustered to help each other identify constellations and the teachers roaming from group to group in order to orient and assist. Standing up and moving from group to group during those 20 minutes each year, I saw my favorite image of the course: a field covered with so many witches' covens cackling to each other with the magic of the evening. Most of our students were thrilled to discover their way around the night sky, and the more they knew, the deeper became their appreciation of its fullness and beauty. When we returned indoors this time, the students were excited about all they had observed. The conversation was just as loud, but it was more cheerful. We now handed out another paper for observation, this time with concentric circles divided into quadrants. After giving them some rules of thumb (and fist) about measuring degrees from the horizon, we sent them back out to observe and to draw. The third part of the night's activity was an observation of the night sky that was more accurate and detailed than the first rough set of dots and lines with which many had begun the evening. For many students, the activities of an hour or so brought them from confusion to some measure of clarity. We called all the students in after another 20 minutes and proceeded to the fourth and final part. This was a writing assignment which would be due at the next regular class meeting the following week. We introduced the assignment with a series of mimeographed pictures showing the constellations now turned into drawings such as The Great Bear, Lyra, or Cassiopeia. We then told a story based on these drawings, from Greek or

Plains Indian mythology. The assignment for each student was then to write a story or myth about the group of stars he or she selected from his or her own drawing. Some students then proceeded to continue observations, some used the high power telescope which we set up, some went to bed, and many (usually all too many for a weary faculty) made a point of staying up all night.

The problematic relationship between observation and inference, which the students encountered during our overnight trip, became the principal theme of the course. Above all, GALILEO attempted to make students more attentive and thoughtful to discriminating experience from interpretation. For each reading in Galileo, no matter how difficult some of the particulars might be, our principal question was the relationship between the facts that Galileo adduced and the conclusions that he drew from them. For each laboratory, demonstration, or discussion, our principal question was the relationship between what students had done or seen and what statement they thought they could make about that experience.

In "The Starry Messenger" we noted that Galileo is extremely reserved about drawing inferences from the observations he records. Indeed, far from announcing a new system of the universe, he largely contents himself with the discoveries he has made with the aid of the telescope and the manner in which those discoveries overturn long-held doctrines about the nature and composition of the heavens. In-class reading, the study guides, and discussion all focused on the crucial separation of what Galileo sees from what he infers. This was a difficult distinction for ninth graders, not just in terms of reading accurately but in terms of how they think about their experience of the world. The more we taught the course, the more we realized that our students found Galileo difficult to understand for many of the same reasons that Galileo's contemporaries found him difficult: trusting as they did in the self-verification of sense experience, our students resisted Galileo because he doesn't make sense. We had no idea when we began the course just how entrenched the Aristotelian[1] sense of the world really is in the mind of a 14-year-old. We tried to work with this predisposition much more carefully in the last two years of the course. Our students' watchword was, as I once stated it for them, "What you see is what you get." Inelegant as the formulation was, we were able to use the adage throughout the course as a refrain and reminder of what we were doing.

Since we had presented a careful synopsis of Aristotelian physical theory before beginning "The Starry Messenger," students were able to recognize the "great number of philosophers" whom Galileo refers to as holding that the moon, as a heavenly body, must be "smooth, uniform, and precisely spherical" (Drake, 1957, pp. 38–39). Since our students "knew" that there are mountains on the moon (hadn't they seen them on television?) we asked them to pay particular attention to Galileo's explanations why the moon *appears* spherical even though it is not. One of the curious results of our discussion of this passage occurred as students would ask, "What's the *real* reason it looks round?" The students tended to meet the challenge of proof in two basic ways. Either they appealed to what everybody knows because that's what we all see, or they appealed to authority. Thus when we would greet their desire for the real reason with stern admonitions not to trust authority blindly, we in many ways frustrated them. They simply wanted to know the answer, while we were more concerned that they notice the manner in which Galileo presented his explanation. We wanted them to understand that the answer is not a fact or an observation; rather, it's a daring analogy between the earth and the moon. They knew enough of the scientific background to be able to recognize the heresy; they also knew, from a videotape on Galileo in Bronowski's *Ascent of Man*, that, as far as the Church was concerned, a refutation of one part of the Aristotelian system endangered the whole (Bronowski, 1973, p. 205). But for many of our students, Galileo's achievement remained tepid because they already "knew" that he was right. It became our challenge as teachers to foster appreciation for the tremendous' restraint which accompanied Galileo's communication: fundamental as he knew his work to be, Galileo yet maintained a discreet and articulate poise about his findings. When we came to the first of the sunspot letters, we underscored Galileo's contention that he could be more certain about the negative inferences from his observations than he could about the positive ones (Drake, 1957, p. 90). Here we felt that we were touching not only on Galileo's unique historical situation but on the role of method and proof in all scientific inquiry.

But the problems were not confined to questions of science or history: the relation between observation and inference is a problem of liberal education because it forces us to consider the role of the learning self in the quest for truth. As the course evolved, the staff became more concerned to develop the social issues of authority out of the scientific problem of ordering the proper relation between observation, hypothesis, experiment, and proof.

Jacob Bronowski had attempted something like this in *The Ascent of Man* (1973), in his chapter on "The Starry Messenger." We showed a videotape of that chapter to the class, in which Bronowski insisted that Galileo's great tactical error lay in believing that the Church would listen to reason. Bronowski showed us the interrogation room and fingered the instruments of torture tentatively, but his discussion of the problem of authority is simplistic and anachronistic, insisting on a dichotomy of science and religion that doesn't pertain to the culture of early seventeenth century Italy. The "facts" of history and biography became themselves subjects of dispute as we read two very different accounts of Galileo's struggles with the Church. Stillman Drake (1967) claims that Galileo was always a faithful member of the Church, whose mission in science was to bring the new truths of observational astronomy to the service of theology. Arthur Koestler (1959) indicts Galileo as a short-sighted blowhard whose great need to be famous and fawned upon made him blow the lid off a steady and responsible revolution in cosmology that many others had been engineering. Although there was still some concern to know which commentary was the "right" one, and still the sense that one *had* to be right, students were in a better position to see the complexity of making judgments rather than accepting facts passively.

Consistent attention to habits of careful observation was a second way of insisting on the difference between what you see and what you explain. We did a number of exercises with lenses, for example, asking students to account for what happens with different lenses and combinations of lenses; only after a series of activities would we ask for their inferences. Similarly, we presented pictures of the sun moving through the ecliptic, or Mars retrogressing; then we could distinguish the time lapse photographs from the explanations which Ptolemy or Copernicus would give. Although such photographs were obvious anachronisms, we used them as well as modern views of sunspots and Jupiter to enhance the value of seeing things carefully as opposed to drawing conclusions.

Perhaps the most difficult approach to the conceptual problems of observation and inference developed from the distinction of absolute and relative motion. In our reading of the *Dialogue* at the end of the course, we always began with a brief excerpt from the Second Day, which explores the distinction through the analogy of various activities on board a ship (Galileo, 1967, pp. 124–128, 186–188). We prepared for the "fact" that motion shared with a containing vessel is not perceived as motion at all with various "thought experiments" of our own. Asking our students to picture what they would see if someone moving inside a moving bus was to toss an apple up and down, or to determine where a stone dropped from the top of the mast of a moving sailboat would land, we provoked the most satisfactory controversy of the course. The students added further examples such as where someone who jumps up on a moving skateboard would land. We were able to convince most of our students of the importance of proof instead of assertion: they might not all understand the relativity of motion, but they did appreciate the necessity to keep an open mind if you are going to be persuaded by argument. Paul Feyerabend's (1978) anarchist theory of science, which focuses for many chapters on the rhetorical and scientific significance of Galileo's new paradigm of relative motion, provided useful scholarly support for our enterprise.[2] We did not make our students scientific anarchists, nor did we even "tie down" the understanding of relative motion, but we did shake the foundations of trust in authority, if just a little bit. We measured our success here by the students' selection of relative motion as one of the skits performed in their assembly presentation to the whole school.

A third device for improving the student's capacity to distinguish observation from inference was the increasingly ingenious study guides we created for the readings. Not only did we supply the standard kinds of guides, with questions about each important paragraph or idea, but we also tried to present students with strategies for coping with information and argument in a summary form. At the end of the readings on sunspots, we presented a flow chart to recall and analyze the main arguments we had covered so painstakingly in class reading and discussion. Since Galileo's letters on sunspots treat, above all, the relationship between what the observer can see with a telescope and what such an observer might infer, the flow chart organized the similar questions Galileo and a rival astronomer ask, the observations Galileo has made, and finally his conclusions. We organized the material into a series of labeled boxes with arrows indicating Galileo's process. Having filled in some of the material in class, we left the chart completion for homework. For the most difficult readings of the course, the passages from the *Dialogue* (Galileo, 1967), we asked students not only to read and respond to questions, but to draw as well. Thus the passage from the Third Day that first introduces the heliocentric theory is a paradigm not only to conceptualize but to see (pp. 319–327). We felt that if students could now produce a drawing, they would enact the new relationship between observation and inference which we were trying to suggest. The idea for this assignment is Galileo's, and we were basically asking our students to play the part of Simplicio, who draws according to his responses to Salviati. For the later passage on planetary motion (pp. 341–345), we also asked students to prepare a drawing that would picture one example each of forward, stationary, and retrograde motion. These assignments were relatively easy and straightforward once the ideas were clear. But the conceptual basis of the assignment was very difficult indeed. We presented the basic lore of planetary observation in pictures and transparencies, but no explanation worked so well as having a group of people perform on the auditorium stage the relative positions of the planets from month to month. As students were able to perceive the connection between position and motion, they finally began to appreciate that in many cases, "What you see is *not* what you get."

LEARNING

From the first year of the course, it became clear that the teachers' relationship to students in this course challenged many presuppositions about discipline. Since the subject matter of the course constantly provided reminders that independent inquiry and the free range of questions are not only the ends of education but the means, teachers and students frequently found themselves exploring self-consciously the relationship they had to each other, to the material of the course, and to the purposes of our collective enterprise. Galileo's own struggles with religious and secular authority set the tone for the course's abiding concern with the personal, intellectual, and institutional responses our students might anticipate to such matters in their own development. One of our concerns as teachers was the hegemony of passive acceptance and self-interested competition which so narrows the community of our school.

During the first year of the course, I was absent the day that a colleague presented his lecture on the Ptolemaic system as the true order of the universe. I rued my absence because I was certain that the students would jump all over my colleague, and I relished the singular wit and cleverness he would certainly display in response. No group of Parker students would long sit still for such authoritarian presentations, I was certain. When I returned the following day, I asked for a review or report from several students and then the colleague. The students were rather uncertain as to just what my colleague had been up to, but they thought there was something a bit strained about his lecturing them on the geocentric system, which of course they knew wasn't true. When I asked them if they had openly defied or even questioned Mr. Barrett, they looked at me quizzically and replied, of course not. It was just a lecture.

Barrett confirmed the dull results. He had finished with a defiant flourish about truth, and then asked for any questions. There was a long silence, and he was afraid that this was going to be all. Then there was a question about the technical terms he had used, and another about the relationship between size and distance. But still no one questioned the overall conception. Finally, one brave soul ventured that the earth was not in fact the center, and Barrett defied him to prove it. The student, frankly abashed at such contentiousness, gave up the chase. No one else spoke on the subject. When I arrived at class the next day, I reviewed these reports with the class as a whole and asked how it could be that they had permitted Barrett to get away with such nonsense. First of all, they pointed out that it was his prerogative to say whatever he wanted. When I asked whether that permitted him to instruct them erroneously with their compliance, they replied that they had trusted him for years as their math teacher and even if he seemed to be stretching things a bit, they still would listen respectfully. Next, I asked how many students had believed that what Barrett had told them was indeed the truth: four hands. I now asked how many students would have assented to supporting Barrett's Ptolemaic position if he had so requested after the lecture: about a third of the class. By now, I was really intrigued, so I pushed a step further. How many, I asked, would have signed a statement endorsing the Ptolemaic system if Barrett had demanded it before they were permitted to leave for the day? Nearly half the class assented, explaining afterward that signing it wouldn't actually mean anything since they all knew that it was nonsense: they were merely appeasing, not capitulating. Was this, I wondered, the equivalent of crossing your fingers behind your back? My last question was even more extreme: what would you have done if the staff had made signing an endorsement of the Ptolemaic system a requirement for passing the course? Nearly every student would have signed. The episode was an unlooked for but powerful example of the social and political environment, and it made our examination of the historical Galileo, as well as Brecht's version, that much more urgent and provocative.

We had thought of the issue of authority as an important theme which the course would have to labor to present in its historical context. We had anticipated some difficulty with the Brecht play because the oblique reference to the role of the scientist in serving the state involved the history of World War II. But what we had to contend with in addition were the social and personal roles which our students conceived as possible. Galileo's struggles with temporal and spiritual authority were not merely historically recondite, they predicted the outline of struggles and decisions which we wanted our students to know about and to participate in. If the persuasion of a new cosmology required the course to ask the student to be able to prove what he or she knew by relating observation to inference, the moral suasion of a new authority required the course to ask each student for a measure of self-examination. Galileo labored mightily to produce a new attitude toward the validity of scripture, arguing that while the Bible can never say untruth, it was written for the common folk and thus says many things which are on the face of it heretical, contradictory, and foolish.

Whenever the Bible has occasion to speak of any physical conclusion (especially those which are very abstruse and hard to understand), the rule has been observed of avoiding confusion in the minds of the common people which would render them contumacious toward the higher mysteries (Drake, 1957, pp. 181–182).

Since fidelity to the actual phenomena is not the primary purpose of scripture, to take the Bible as final authority on the physical world mistakes altogether the higher purpose. Galileo's eloquence made the urgency of the problem and the nobility of his solution much clearer to our students than their own problems with unexamined obedience to authority. Not only was Galileo so lucid, but we could articulate the dimensions and elements of the problem with much greater clarity in historical and religious terms than we could in present and emergent conditions that our students might face. The experience of trying to locate objects in the night sky, for example, was a sufficiently difficult and memorable one that we did not have to entreat our students to marvel at Galileo's observational powers. They had difficulty locating the planet Jupiter despite having accurate sky maps. Galileo had not only found the planet but had somehow noted the position of nearby "stars" such that he could eventually trace their movements. Here was clear confirmation that no prejudice should permit the refusal to "see things as they are." In scene four of his play, Brecht further dramatized the stupidity of refusing even to look. When we tried to insist that responses to authority might be an ongoing problem which we all face as citizens, however, we found ourselves facing a more subtle and difficult problem.

Part of our difficulty, of course, is the fact that as teachers we represent a fundamental authority for our students. For us to suggest that perhaps they should not take everything we say and tell them as "gospel" (we did find our-selves using such terms sardonically if not loosely, I admit) met with some consternation. But the greatest measure of the difficulty is the form in which our students conceive authority. As Richard Sennett (1980) details the forms of authority in our society, he notes that one prevailing image is paternal.[3] Now it is not surprising that our students would conceive authority in such a way; but what makes our job as educators so difficult is that the paternal form is so socially pervasive that we really have to help our students and ourselves imag-ine forms of authority beyond the common mode. I can by no means report any successes on this score during the brief life of GALILEO, but I am certain that we need to invent more curricular situations which will test the meanings and limits of authority for our students, our institutions, and our world. In this regard, we found that our students were still too young to be ready for the kinds of questions we wanted them to consider. Since at 14 or 15 they were growing into their first full-scale confrontation with paternal authority, opposi-tion and defiance were their principal offensive weapons and the sullen silence of the group opposition their principal defense.

It is another story to unfold the ways in which the theme of authority became the predominant educational problem of the course, but I can say briefly that the historical, dramatic, and scientific senses of the conflict enriched our collective awareness of responsibility on the one hand and limi-tations of individual action on the other. We all learned from our study of Brecht about the problem of experts, of too narrowly conceiving our roles and our goals. In Brecht's ideology, Galileo was weak because he was selfish: had he aligned himself with the people more firmly, he would have triumphed. When Galileo's pupil Andrea takes his final leave of the master, Andrea remarks: "Unhappy is the land which breeds no hero." In good Marxist pro-fundity, Galileo corrects his pupil one last time: "No, Andrea. Unhappy is the land that needs a hero" (Brecht, 1966, p. 115).

THE IMPORTANCE OF AN INTERDISCIPLINARY CURRICULUM

Ever since the Renaissance, our culture has had to struggle with the separation of knowledge into sciences and the humanities. It was during the fifteenth and sixteenth centuries that European thought responded to the abstract verbalisms of the late Middle Ages by inaugurating a view of the liberal arts as subject matters, each with its own claim to accuracy. Since that time, we have accepted the notion that a field is a subject to be mastered, without consider-ing at all what arts, skills, or methods are necessary to learn that material. The hindrance of our view is all the more poignant in a culture that increasingly considers experts its primary educational products: I call it a hindrance because experts don't create the problems, they merely offer solutions. If we are going to produce educated citizens for the complex roles they must play in late twentieth century society and culture, then it is not enough for us to fill students up with so many bits of isolated and random information. We need, as Dewey said 50 years ago, to give our young people the skills to prosper in a technological culture, and the human values and background to make their lives worth living. A new sense of the disciplines would ask us to consider not only the ways that subjects can be combined, but the arts or methods common to many fields of inquiry. Courses such as GALILEO attempt to do a job that I would call interdisciplinary in the most fundamental sense of articulating and clarifying the implications for learning in general. GALILEO's concern to investigate the human import of a major scientist's life and times addresses fundamental issues of responsibility and political process.

There is a certain poignancy to any review of the literature concerning the milieu of teaching and learning over the last twenty years. Two of the most articulate analyses written at the end of the 1960s concentrate on an aroused student population, an America crying out in protest. Schwab (1969) diagnosed a neurotic personality type which could be treated with curricular resources because many of the disorders had been caused by the curriculum of schools in the first place. Silberman (1970), starting out to write a report for the Carnegie Commission on the education of teachers, discovered that he had first of all to explore the critical situation of the schools which could no longer supply an appropriate education. He concluded that most, if not all, of the problem was due to mindlessness.

The poignancy of these comments is in the measure of how docile our students and our society at large have grown; not that the ills of the 1970s have been addressed and overcome, simply that America and especially its young appear to have lost the capacity for outrage and the heart to disagree. We have returned to a situation that Goodman (1964) described only a few years earlier than Schwab and Silberman: students too respectful of their teachers, inclined to work too hard at educational tasks for which they may be ill-suited, and all for the sake of goals that have too little to do with education. If mindlessness was the problem then, it continues to be so now. But rather than the mindless rejection of all values except those consecrated by the sincerity of opposition and rejection, we now have to contend with the vapidity of consumerism. If 15 years ago we had to be concerned about moderating the strident shrieks of confrontation so that reason and truth might at least have a hearing, now we have to tease the silent torpor of passive acceptance and encourage our students to be passionate, discriminating, and skeptical. Because GALILEO focused on the conflicts and ambiguities of facts and values, it provided a forum for the personal and institutional questions which young people ought to be asking.

If students and teachers have returned to docility after a brief flirtation with activism, we need more than ever to encourage and develop critical mindedness. Beyond the imminent dangers and needs of adolescence, there are issues and problems which education must lead toward. The planning task must anticipate the needs of the coming generation by engaging in serious moral, cultural, and intellectual criticism as a first step. The secondary school curriculum should not be allowed to stagnate in its various departments, sanctioned as the junior versions of higher education. Before we can know what courses we need to teach, we need to inquire into our ends—what we think education is for. Courses like GALILEO are instrumental in stimulating such thoughts because they shake up our preconceptions and make us lose the safety of our expertise. The peculiar virtues of GALILEO come from the quality of reflection which the elements of the course provoke. Not only the questions of authority, method, and argument which I have already touched on briefly: beyond these, GALILEO opens up questions about the human uses of science and technology which ought to be at the center of education. The Brecht play in particular raises questions of social responsibility in the most contemporary manner. I am not arguing a peculiar "relevance" here so much as a set of texts, problems, and relations which present a useful matrix of concerns for teachers and students alike. GALILEO is relevant, not merely to our contemporary scene but to our abiding humanity. It points to the need for other courses and other combinations of materials which explore the history, artifacts, and ideas of the humanities.

NOTES

[1]While we presented a synopsis of Aristotle's physical theories each year, we also made it clear that Galileo's main argument was with the latter day followers rather than with the philosopher himself. We stressed the systematic approach, the interconnectedness of Aristotle's physical theories with other parts of his philosophy. Galileo himself distinguishes Aristotle as a great empiricist from the hidebound dogmatism of his followers, who refused to alter their views of the "celestial substance" when presented with new data that confirmed the opinion of several ancient but unheeded philosophers. Aristotle "himself would not have departed so far from their view if his knowledge had included our present sensory evidence, since he not only admitted manifest experience among the ways of forming conclusions about physical problems, but even gave it first place" (Drake, 1957, p. 118).

[2]Feyerabend points out that Aristotle is the consummate empiricist, while Galileo has to go to great lengths to present to his readers a radical reordering of every day experience in order to gain conviction. Feyerabend details the ingenuity of this subtle, sly, subversive activity. "The whole rich reservoir of the everyday experience and of the intuition of his readers is utilized in the argument, but the facts which they are invited to recall are arranged in a new way. Approximations are made, known effects are omitted, different conceptual lines are drawn, so that *a new kind of experience* arises, *manufactured* almost out of thin air. This new expe-

rience is then *solidified* by insinuating that the reader has been familiar with it all along" (p. 160, emphasis in original).

[3]"Paternalism stands at one extreme of the images of authority in modern society. It is power exercised for the good of others. No hereditary obligation binds a person to do so, nor do religious injunctions. The care for others is the authority's gift, and he will bestow it only so long as it serves his interests" (Sennett, 1980, p. 84).

REFERENCES

Brecht, B. (1966). *Galileo.* Translated by Charles Laughton. New York: Grove Press.

Bronowski, J. (1973). *The Ascent of Man.* Boston: Little, Brown and Company.

Drake, S. (1957). *Discoveries and Opinions of Galileo.* New York: Anchor Books.

Drake, S. (1967). "A Biographical Sketch." From *Galileo: Man of Science.* Edited by E. McMullin. New York: Basic Books.

Feyerabend, P. A. (1978). *Against Method: Outline of an Anarchist Theory of Knowledge.* London: Verso Editions.

Galileo (1967). *Dialogue Concerning the Two Chief World Systems—Ptolemaic and Copernican.* Translated by S. Drake; foreword by A. Einstein. Berkeley, CA: University of California Press.

Goodman, P. (1964). *Compulsory Mis-education.* New York: Horizon.

Koestler, A. (1959). *The Sleepwalkers: A History of Man's Changing Vision of the Universe.* New York: The Macmillan Company.

Schwab, J. J. (1969). *College Curriculum and Student Protest.* Chicago: University of Chicago Press.

Sennett, R. (1980). *Authority.* New York: Alfred A. Knopf.

Silberman, C. E. (1970). *Crisis in the Classroom: The Remaking of American Education.* New York: Random House.

17

EDUCATING AGAINST ALL ODDS

MARY MATHIAS

In February, 1984, I walked up the steps of a crumbling building in Winnipeg's North End and entered Argyle Alternative High School for the first time. The new principal had invited me to "get a feel" for the place and consider the possibility of working there. She was looking for someone with an elementary school background. I certainly qualified, having spent 10 years with first graders; but I couldn't imagine how my experience with young children would translate to high school, and frankly, I was terrified of adolescents! The long-haired young men in black leather lounging on the steps didn't reassure me; however, I breezed past them into an extremely stimulating and progressive educational setting. The school had small classes with an emphasis on working together. It was clearly a people-oriented place where the staff supported one another. After classroom visits and several long discussions with the principal, I made a three-year commitment to Argyle High School. Now, six years later, I am still deeply involved with this unique place.

When I began at Argyle, the staff was in the midst of transforming the school's structure and curriculum to meet the needs of a changing student population. Argyle was established in 1970 as a small program for adolescents from middle and upper income families who were disenchanted with conventional high school approaches. By 1980, however, Argyle was attracting mainly inner-city kids from low income families.

At present the school enrolls students who are 15 to 21 years old. Approximately 85 percent of these young people are Native—that is, descendants of Canada's Aboriginal peoples. Like Native Americans in the United States, many have rejected the term "Indian" for Aboriginal or First People. Argyle's Aboriginal students are diverse. They represent several cultural and linguistic groups. Some of their families have lived in the city for years. Others reside in remote reservations and travel hundreds of miles to attend high school in Winnipeg because the reserve schools end at ninth grade. Some of the students have virtually lost their Aboriginal identity, while others have maintained or seek to establish close ties with their heritage.

What unites Argyle's Aboriginal students is their history of economic poverty and oppression. Most have experienced considerable discontinuity and lack of success in previous school settings. Many have been involved with the child welfare system and the criminal justice system. Many struggle with chemical dependency and the effects of abuse. A large number live on their own and lack a supportive family network. Approximately one fourth of the female students are parents caring for their children. All of these factors make it difficult for our students to get to school daily and stay in school for any length of time. Argyle's challenge has been to develop an environment which addresses the personal, social, and educational needs of these young people.

The environment which has evolved looks and feels much more like a progressive elementary school than a conventional high school. Students rather than subjects are placed at the center of the educational process. Relationships are valued as the foundation of learning and growth for students and staff alike. Several structural factors support this person-centered approach. Argyle is a small school, with a maximum of 250 students registered at any one time and a staff of 25. The school is now housed in a new building designed to enhance the informal and interactive atmosphere which has always characterized Argyle. Curved hallways, benches near sunny windows, classrooms with tables rather than desks, and an attractive student lounge are important features of the new facility. The day is divided into three blocks of 80 to 90 minutes each. These long periods allow for the development of close relationships within class groups and also promote flexible, innovative programming. Classes end at 2:30, and the remainder of the teacher's day is set aside for meetings, planning, and preparation.

Argyle has several program options. Approximately half of the students are enrolled in an academic program which follows the provincial curriculum guidelines for grades ten, eleven, and twelve. Generally students take only two academic subjects per semester. The courses operate on a continuous progress basis, and individuals who do not complete a course during one school year begin wherever they left off upon returning to school. For their third subject, students choose electives which meet daily for a six-week period. Argyle's other programs offer students who have not completed their junior high grades the opportunity to prepare for the academic program, develop independent living skills, or get preemployment training and work experience. Movement between programs is encouraged and supported. Staff and students jointly determine program placement, based on the individual's school history, skill level, commitment, and goals.

In each of Argyle's programs, much of the curriculum is developed at the school level and referenced to the students. As a first grade teacher, I had always started my planning by studying the children, not the curriculum guides;

and a great deal of what happened in those classrooms emerged from the experiences and interests of the kids. At Argyle we recognize that the basic philosophy of building on what the students bring is as important for 16-year-olds as it is for six-year-olds. Our students' cultural heritage is reflected in the curriculum. Credit courses in Aboriginal crafts, languages, and traditions are offered regularly. Social Studies classes emphasize the history of Aboriginal peoples, language arts programs incorporate traditional legends and literature by contemporary Native authors, and current events discussions focus on issues facing the Aboriginal community. In response to the needs of Argyle's many teenage parents, the family studies curriculum has expanded to include a major unit on child development and parenting. This unit, as well as electives on the same topic, take place in the school's child development room, which is set up as a stimulating environment for young children. As part of these classes, teenage parents are invited to bring their children to school at specified times in order to observe and interact with them under the guidance of staff members.

Sharing of classroom activities and materials, and of thoughts and feelings with colleagues was one of the things I valued most as a teacher of young children. This collaboration and mutual support has been an important part of my Argyle experience, too. The school features several levels of teaming. Most class groups are taught by a team of two teachers. Support staff members, including an art teacher, two counselors, a drug and alcohol worker, and a family studies specialist, team with classroom teachers for specific projects or units of study. Larger teams meet regularly to do program planning, share ideas and concerns, and review individual students.

Working at Argyle is challenging, demanding, and often exhausting—yet staff morale is high. The team structures provide a great deal of support. Teachers have ownership over their daily lives and are encouraged to make decisions, to experiment, and to innovate. Staff members tackle a variety of roles and responsibilities. In my six years I have been a classroom teacher, a curriculum development coordinator, a team leader, and a support teacher collaborating in several classrooms. This varied experience has expanded my vision of myself as an educator.

At Argyle, we are educating against all odds. Each day is an unpredictable mixture of frustration and satisfaction. Students withdraw from school or simply disappear, and new students enroll regularly. On top of this high turnover, daily attendance is erratic for many. One morning I discovered a teacher sitting in a deserted classroom at 9:30. He began pouring out the stories: two girls from the same group home had slept in and would be late, one pregnant class member was home with morning sickness, two young men were in jail, another had gone back to his reserve due to an illness in the family, someone else was babysitting, and so on.

Fortunately, there are other mornings: a quiet student contributes to a small group task for the first time; a spontaneous class discussion takes off; several pieces of writing are polished and submitted to a community newspaper; a guest speaker comments on the students' interest and involvement; a young woman who had disappeared weeks ago comes back, ready to try again.

A former staff member once said of Argyle, "This school shouldn't work." After six years, I've sorted out some of the reasons why it does work. It works because within the school community we treat each other with caring and respect, relating openly and honestly as persons, not as members of a hierarchic institution. It works because we focus on strengths rather than deficiencies, recognizing and validating what each of us brings to the situation. It works because, for students and staff alike, we combine high expectations with high support.

When I began at Argyle, I frequently wondered whether I would last until June. Now I find it difficult to contemplate leaving. I have often been stretched to my limit, but within a strong circle of caring and support. On that first February day, I was faced with what seemed to be an impossible challenge, but I know that I have translated my experience with young children into the language of adolescents and young adults. Education is not so different for six-year-olds or 16-year-olds or 40-year-olds. We all need to engage important issues, ask significant questions, learn with others, give and receive support, and construct our own path in life.

FTERWORD

BOOKS TO NOURISH DEMOCRATIC EDUCATORS
LILLIAN WEBER

I hope for change for the better in life and in schools and I learn about possibilities as I read. Obviously, I read books about educational philosophy, organization, and classrooms. But I read books that are not about education, and since I am an educator, I relate them to education. What I call progressive and what I note as I read is anything that supports the psychological and physical space needed for developing the human capacities of *all* the children, the parents, the teachers, and the strengths of the communities where they all live. I remember books that base themselves on confidence in capacity and access to resources and that speak of diversity as adding interest and richness to life, qualities that enrich us all. I mention authors who, telling of themselves or telling a story, add to my knowledge of children because I identify with this bit or that as true, true as if it were part of my own personal development. Of course, I choose from Dickens, from Tolstoy, from Louisa May Alcott, from the Brontës. I include also Louis Sullivan's 1924 description of his childhood, *Autobiography of an Idea;* Booker T. Washington's *Up from Slavery;* Colette's descriptions from *My Mother's House;* John Stuart Mill's 19th Century description of his childhood; Willa Cather's many fictional descriptions of childhood and prairie life. My list draws from a wide base; the medley includes John-Paul Sartre's *Les Paroles,* Gordon Parks' *The Learning Tree,* and Henry Roth's painful descriptions in *Call It Sleep.*

The books that I call to mind to bolster my thoughts about education speak of confidence in life, even in bad times, of growing up, of survival, of resilience. Wole Soyinka's *Aké: The Years of Childhood,* describing such survival is only one example in a whole series of books by modern African authors. Then there are the books about the American South, about slavery, about sharecroppers. There are books about immigrants, about labor struggles that describe resilience in the face of enormous difficulties and describe personal grappling to actualize possibility. These include the professional studies that are extremely personal like Claudia Lewis' *Children of the Cumberland*. Eliot Wiggington's *Foxfire Books* contribute oral histories revealing warm and deep relationships between young and old which detail the dignity of craft in a changing world. Anton Makarenko's *Road to Life* suggests a blueprint for survival of the orphaned children lost to family life after the 1917 Revolution. Martin Andersen Nexø, in *Pellé, the Conqueror* describes his own pre-World War I childhood. An account that is both personal and professional is Mike Rose's *Lives on the Boundary*. Edward Rivera writes of his own growing up in *Family Installments: Memories of Growing Up Hispanic,* as does Mark Mathabane in *Kaffir Boy*. All these give us additional accounts of childhood within a specific culture and are yet universal. Bringing texture and depth to descriptions, and certainly adding to what I consider my store of almost personally experienced children's lives, I think of George Moore's *Esther Waters,* Samuel Butler's *The Way of All Flesh,* Richard Hughes' *High Wind in Jamaica,* and Harriette Arnow's *Dollmaker*.

In addition, my list includes James Baldwin's *Go Tell It on the Mountain* and Paule Marshall's *Brown Girl, Brownstones,* both written in the 1950s. Add more recent works: Sandra Cisneros' *House on Mango Street;* Sally Morgan's *My Place,* an account of finding one's place in the mixed world of Aborigines and Europeans; and Lily Patience Moya's *Not Either an Experimental Doll,* a similar account in South Africa. Finally, add *The Autobiography of Malcolm X,* a statement using autobiography as a weapon in a democratic liberation struggle.

Of course, I could add more. All I have to do is remember in this vein and the remembrances go on and on. We all have our own bank of such memories to add. I hope teachers allow these memories to spill over in talk with each other. I particularly hope teachers share these memories as relevant to teaching, to knowledge of people and place. What they share may be a different sense of books important to their development of person or teacher–person, and by sharing, enrich us all.

At the root of continued confidence in possibilities is the constant grappling of a wide variety of peoples and communities for space for their development. This is much broader than the good arrangements in any progressive school. Teachers who seek to contribute to this development must themselves constantly grapple with constrictions on their work, impediments to their supportive role. They must constantly try to see human development broadly, and read books that support this development in contexts other than schools.

BIBLIOGRAPHY

Alcott, Louisa May (1989). *The Works of Louisa May Alcott 1832–1888. Irvine, CA: Reprint Services Corp.*
Arnow, Harriette (1954). *Dollmaker*. New York: Macmillan.
Baldwin, James (1953). *Go Tell It on the Mountain*. New York: A. A. Knopf.

Brontë, Charlotte (1903). *The Life and Works of the Sisters Brontë (Vols. 1–7)*. New York: AMS Press, Inc. Originally published 1846–1883.

Butler, Samuel (1916). *The Way of All Flesh*. New York: E.P. Dutton. Originally published in 1903.

Cather, Willa (1970). *Collected Short Fiction 1892–1912*. Edited by Virginia Faulkner. Lincoln: University of Nebraska Press.

Cisneros, Sandra (1988). *The House on Mango Street*. Houston: Arte Publico Press.

Colette (1922). *My Mother's House and Sido*. Paris: Ferenczi et Fils.

Dickens, Charles (1986). *The Works of Charles Dickens*. Library Edition. London: Chapman and Hall. Originally published 1837–1871.

Hughes, Richard Arthur Warren (1929). *A High Wind in Jamaica*. London: Chatto and Windus.

Lewis, Claudia (1946). *Children of the Cumberland*. New York: Columbia University Press.

Makarenko, Anton Semenovich (1951). *The Road to Life: An Epic of Education*. Translated from the Russian by Ivy and Tatiana Litvinov. Moscow: Foreign Languages Publishing House. Originally published in English in 1936.

Marshall, Paule (1959). *Brown Girl, Brownstones*. New York: Random House.

Mathabane, Mark (1989). *Kaffir Boy in America: An Encounter with Apartheid*. New York: Scribner's.

Mill, John Stuart (1823). *Autobiography*. London: Longmans, Green, Reader and Dyer.

Moore, George (1983). *Esther Waters*. Oxford: Oxford University Press. Originally published in 1894.

Morgan, Sally (1987). *My Place*. New York: Seaver Books.

Moya, Lily Patience (1988). *Not Either an Experimental Doll: The Separate Worlds of Three South African Women*. Edited by Shula Marks. Bloomington, IN: Indiana University Press.

Nexø, Martin Andersen (1915). *Pellé, the Conqueror: The Great Struggle*. Translated by Bernard Miall. New York: H. Holt and Company.

Parks, Gordon (1987). *The Learning Tree*. New York: Fawcett.

Rivera, Edward (1982). *Family Installments: Memories of Growing Up Hispanic*. New York: Viking Penguin, Inc.

Rose, Mike (1989). *Lives on the Boundary: The Struggles and Achievements of America's Underprivileged*. New York: Free Press.

Roth, Henry (1960). *Call It Sleep: A Novel*. Paterson, NJ: Pageant Books. Originally published in 1934.

Sartre, Jean-Paul (1964). *The Words*. Translated from the French by Bernard Brechtman. New York: G. Braziller.

Soyinka, Wole (1983). *Aké: The Years of Childhood*. New York: Random House.

Sullivan, Louis (1924). *Autobiography of an Idea*. New York: Dover Press.

Washington, Booker T. (1907). *Up From Slavery: An Autobiography*. New York: Doubleday.

Wiggington, Eliot (1972). *The Foxfire Books*. New York: Doubleday.

X, Malcolm (1966). *The Autobiography of Malcolm X*. With the assistance of Alex Haley. New York: Grove Press.

B IBLIOGRAPHY

PROGRESSIVE EDUCATION (1880–1990)
MARIE KIRCHNER STONE

Originally this bibliography was created in two parts, "Progressive Education: Selected Works" and "To Understand the Larger Progressive Ideas," for the 1983 Miquon Conference on Progressive Education. The rationale for the present bibliography is changed from the original. Selections are classified in three categories: Part I identifies the major works from 1880 to 1949 listed in chronological order to show how progressive education evolved; Part II names, this time in alphabetical order, the general titles influential as history or criticism of progressive education after World War II; and Part III annotates the books written about schools. The bibliography focuses mainly on books, but some key articles are included.

PART I: THE EARLY ROOTS (1880–WORLD WAR II)

Adams, Charles F. (1879). *The New Departure in the Common Schools of Quincy*. Boston: Estes and Lauriat.
  The text is a discussion of the work done at the Quincy School. Francis W. Parker talks for the first time about central subjects, a topic which later becomes the basis for his theory of concentration, defined in his 1894 text *Talks on Pedagogics*.

Parker, Francis W. (1883). *Talks on Teaching*. New York: A.S. Barnes.
  A small volume of Parker's lectures on his teaching theories delivered in 1879 at Martha's Vineyard.

Parker, Francis W. (1894). *Report of the School Committee of Town of Quincy (1878–1879)*. New York: E.L. Kellogg.
  Reports on work at Quincy School.

Parker, Francis W. (1894). *Talks on Pedagogics, An Outline of the Theory of Concentration*. New York: A.S. Barnes.
  A discussion of the nature of the child being educated, and a definition of the central subjects and the theory of concentration.

Chicago Normal School Envelope (1894–1899). Chicago: University of Chicago Library.
Leaflets and records of work written by Francis Parker and most of the fifty members of the faculty at the Chicago Normal School.

Dewey, John (1900). *The School and Society*. Chicago: University of Chicago Press.
A discussion of "the new education" in terms of social progress and in relation to the life of the child in the elementary school.

Dewey, John (1902). *The Child and Curriculum*. Chicago: University of Chicago Press.
The early discussion of the nature of the child and the curriculum requirements needed.

Dewey, John (1916). *Democracy and Education*. New York: The Free Press of Macmillan Publishing.
The statement of the ideas implied in a democratic society and the application of those ideas to the problems of the enterprise of education, including a chapter on the differences between conservative and progressive education.

The Twenty-Sixth Yearbook of the National Society for the Study of Education: The Foundations and Techniques of Curriculum Making (1926). Bloomington, IL: Public School Publishing Company.
Divided into two parts, the text describes curriculum description and criticism in "Curriculum Making: Past and Present" and provides a statement of foundational principles for curriculum reconstruction by some of the outstanding leaders of modern educational thought in "The Foundations of Curriculum Making."

Kilpatrick, William H. (1926). *Education for a Changing Civilization*. New York: The Macmillan Company.
An analysis of the status of education and the need for change.

Dewey, John (1929). *The Sources of a Science of Education*. New York: Horace Liveright Kappa Delta Pi Lecture Series.
This influential and valuable essay defines education and science, and poses two questions: (1) What are the ways by which the function of education in all its branches and phases can be conducted with systematic increase of intelligent controls and understanding? (2) What are the materials upon which we may and should draw?

Counts, George S. (1932). *Dare the School Build a New Social Order?* Carbondale, IL: Southern Illinois University Press.
Published in 1932, 1956, and 1978, this text analyzes three themes of past and contemporary importance: the criticism of child-centered progressive schools, the role of the teacher in social reform, and an explanation of the author's view of the interrelationship between the American economy and the public interest. Counts argues that child-centered progressives were naive in their belief in an education free of social content.

Reisner, Edward H. (1933–34). "What Is Progressive Education?" *Teachers College Record*, 35, pp. 192–201.
One answer that provides a description of progressive education.

Pedro, Orata T. (1936). "Fifty-Seven Varieties of Progressive Education." *Educational Administration and Supervision*, 12, pp. 361–374.
An introduction to many of the approaches to education that are called progressive.

Tyler, Ralph W. (1936). "Defining and Measuring Objectives of Progressive Education." *Educational Record*, 17, pp. 78–85.
A description of Tyler's approach to evaluating curriculum in the Eight Year Study.

Bode, Boyd H. (1938). *Progressive Education at the Crossroads*. New York: Newson and Company.
The purpose of the book is to contribute to a better understanding of the philosophy in which the progressive movement finds its justification and in which it must be tested. The roads of progressive education cross between student-centered and society-centered schools. Bode states that instead of turning to democracy for guidance, progressive education has too often turned to the individual.

Tyler, Ralph W. (1949). *Basic Principles of Curriculum and Instruction*. Chicago and London: University of Chicago Press.
This short text defines the four questions of the Tyler rationale to evaluate curriculum. Tyler created this rationale during the Eight Year Study, applied it during the Cooperative Study in General Education at the University of Chicago, and refined it in 1958, 1966, and 1976.

PART II: HISTORY AND CRITICISM (WORLD WAR II–PRESENT)

Bowers, C.A. (1969). *The Progressive Educator and the Depression: The Radical Years*. New York: Random House.
The thesis posits that by politicizing educational theory, Counts, Kilpatrick, Rugg, and other educators diverted the thrust of progressive education away from the humanistic experimentation of its earlier phase and influenced education politically from World War II onward.

Caswell, Hollis L. (1950). *Curriculum Improvement in Public School Systems*. New York: Teachers College Press.
The examination of curriculum changes in public schools.

Cremin, Lawrence A. (1964). *Transformation of the School*. New York: Random House.
This well-documented and highly readable history of progressive education is divided into two periods. Part I (1876–1917) provides an intellectual history of the beginning of progressive education until the end of World War I. The founding of the Progressive Education Association, in the year 1919, is cited as a turning point. Part II (1917–1957) presents the history of progressive education during the period when it became a movement.

Curti, Merle E. (1966). *The Social Ideas of American Educators*. New York: Charles Scribner's Sons.
A critical presentation of progressivism and other social ideas influencing American education.

Filler, Louis (1957). "Main Current in Progressivist American Education." *History of Education Journal*, 8, pp. 33–57.
The major thoughts that influenced American education are analyzed.

Gonzalez, Gilbert G. (1982). *Progressive Education: A Marxist Interpretation.* Minneapolis: Marxist Educational Press.
The opening assertion is that the critiques of progressivism have been unexamined in their relationship with capitalism. The book analyzes the ideological nexus between the growth of monopoly capitalism and the development of progressive educational theory and practice. Gonzalez outlines the principles of Marxist analysis, writes an exposition of the bourgeois educational theory of Locke and Rousseau, and describes the central role of Dewey in articulating an educational theory adapted to the needs of capitalism.

Graham, Patricia Albjerg (1967). *Progressive Education: From Arcady to Academe.* New York: Teachers College Press.
The first comprehensive history of the Progressive Education Association traces the historical roots of the Association established in 1919. World War I interrupted the reforms—scientific education, child study, and learning by doing—that were beginning to permeate the American educational system. After World War I, progressive education became more prevalent in private and wealthier public schools. Until the 1930s, the Progressive Education Association acted as a "clearinghouse" for information concerning progressive education.

Gutek, Gerald (1970). *The Educational Theory of George S. Counts.* Columbus: Ohio State University Press.
The central focus of this critical and scholarly work is upon Counts's achievements. His social philosophy is compared with Thomas Jefferson and John Dewey, and his writing with Thomas Paine and Voltaire. Counts is also criticized for his idealization of the labor class. Counts's cultural approach to education and his relation to Marxism are two significant chapters.

Gutek, Gerald (1974). *Philosophical Alternatives in Education.* Columbus: Charles E. Merrill Publishing Company.
In chapters on Progressivism and Cultural Reconstructionism, the concepts are differentiated briefly and well. Progressivism is seen as a rallying point for those opposed to traditionalism. The chapter traces the inspiration of Rousseau, Pestalozzi, Freud, and Dewey. While progressives identify with Dewey's pragmatic instrumentalism, reconstructionists claim to be successors of Dewey's experimentalism. Reconstructionists assert that schools and educators should bring about reform.

Kilpatrick, William H. (1951). "A Modern Theory of Learning." From *Philosophy of Education*, pp. 237–247. New York: The Macmillan Company.
The presentation and analysis of a learning theory.

Kliebard, Herbert M. (1986). *The Struggle for the American Curriculum 1893–1958.* Boston: Routledge and Kegan Paul.
Kliebard traces four competing interest groups and their fight for ownership of the curriculum, which he concludes is an amalgam of all four groups. He traces Dewey's efforts to transform the American curriculum from his work at the University of Chicago Laboratory School between 1896 and 1904.

Lagemann, Ellen Condliffe (1985). *Jane Addams on Education*. New York: Teachers College Press.
This excellent educational biography traces the significant relationships of Addams to isolate the reasons that impelled Addams to choose education as her instrument of social reform. Viewing education broadly, the author shows the extent to which Addams saw the school, the club, the workplace, the settlement houses as agencies in which people can learn to lead democratic lives.

Macdonald, James B. (1970). *Open Education: The Legacy of the Progressive Movement*. Washington, DC: National Association for the Education of Young Children.
An analysis of the relationship between progressive and open education.

Nash, Paul (1964). "The Strange Death of Progressive Education." *Educational Theory*, 14 (2), pp. 65–75.
A discussion and interpretation of the reasons for the status of progressive education in the mid–1960s.

"Progressive Education and American Progressivism." (1958–59). *Teachers College Record*, Volume 60.
A presentation of personal experiences by leaders in the movement and criticism of progressive education.

Reese, William J. (1986). *Power and the Promise of School Reform: Grass-Roots Movements During the Progressive Era*. Boston: Routledge and Kegan Paul.
The author asserts that too much radical scholarship in education and the history of education suffer from a cultural pessimism or a preoccupation of structures of domination. The book identifies the major social and ideological factors that lead to the institutionalization of changes. The book begins with the origins of mass education and concludes with the dawn of progressivism. Of particular interest is the chapter on "The School Health Movement." The concept of a healthy mind and body became related to the education of the whole child theory. Some progressive schools were in the vanguard in this area.

Rugg, Harold, and Shumaker, Ann (1969). *The Child-Centered School*. New York: Arno Press.
An appraisal of the child-centered schools in an historical perspective. With a thorough belief in these schools, the authors provide descriptive and sympathetic criticism based upon nine years of residence in one child-centered school, and a decade of active participation in the scientific study of education. Rugg identifies the two goals, "tolerant understanding and creative self-expression," of child-centered schools.

Sarap, Madan (1982). *Education, State, and Crisis: A Marxist Perspective*. London: Routledge and Kegan Paul.
A critical survey of current educational debates focuses on developments occurring in the sociology of education, which is being transformed by the contributions of history, economics, Marxism, feminism, and black studies. Themes which the author believes have taken on a new urgency include: the problematic nature of progressive education and discipline, the changes in the labor process and youth unemployment, the nature of the state and its relationship with schooling, the growth of state intervention, and specific discrimination in a society undergoing an

economic crisis. Chapter 1, "The Attack on Progressive Education," is of particular interest because it explains that progressivism can be theorized on three levels: the rhetoric, the practice, and the ideal, which the author suggests is reason for attacks on it from both the left and the right.

Smith, Philip (1980). *Sources of Progressive Thought in American Education.* Washington, DC: University Press of America.
This excellent text examines the history of ideas surrounding progressive education. The author places progressive thought in the perspective of the contributions of Chauncey Wright, C.S. Pierce, William James, George Herbert Mead, and John Dewey, focusing especially upon Dewey's instrumentalism, a concept of special interest to the child-centered progressives.

Squire, James R. (1972). *A New Look at Progressive Education.* Washington, DC: Association for Supervision and Curriculum Development.
This yearbook interprets progressivism broadly by viewing it as a major social and educational reform movement from the turn of the century through World War II. The book reviews major ideas and efforts of progressive education and relates them to today's efforts to reform American education. Two major questions are answered through the examination of both research and practice: (1) What has happened to the powerful concepts that once welded together progressive thoughts? (2) Have subsequent research, experience, and professional thinking proved or disproved the basic assumption of progressive education?

Stone, Marie Kirchner (1985). *Ralph Tyler's Principles of Curriculum, Instruction, and Evaluation: Past Influences and Present Effects.* Ann Arbor, MI: University Microfilms International.
A doctoral dissertation traces an intellectual legacy from John Dewey to Ralph Tyler and Tyler's colleagues, Charles Judd and George S. Counts, to present-day curricularists such as John Goodlad.

Van Til, William (1962). "Is Progressive Education Obsolete?" *Saturday Review* 45, pp. 56–57 and 82–84.
An analysis of the status of progressive education.

Washburne, Carleton (1952). *What Is Progressive Education?* New York: The John Day Company.
A slim volume describing progressive education in a general way for the lay audience.

PART III: PROGRESSIVE ELEMENTARY AND SECONDARY SCHOOLS

Bensman, David (1987). *The Story of the Central Park East School.* New York: Desktop.
A thoroughly documented discussion of this progressive school.

Bourne, Randolph (1970). *The Gary Schools.* Cambridge, MA: Massachusetts Institute of Technology Press.
A description of the Gary Schools.

Clapp, Elise R. (1939). *Schools in Action*. New York: Viking Press.
    The description of the life and program in two community-centered schools in
    Kentucky and West Virginia in which learning and living converged for students,
    teachers, and the community.

Dewey, Evelyn (1919). *New Schools for Old*. New York: Dutton.
    Included in the text is a description of a rural Missouri school's transformation from
    traditional to community-centered curriculum.

Dewey, John, and Dewey, Evelyn (1915). *Schools of Tomorrow*. New York: Dutton.
    A discussion of the challenges facing the schools in regard to a child's personal
    development and in relation to the community.

Feldman, Marilyn Moss, ed. (1979). *Dalton School 1919–1979: 60 Years, A Book of
    Memories*. New York: Dalton School.
    Reflections on the Dalton School. *See also* Parkhurst, H. (1922).

Geer, Amanda K. (1982). *The Progressive Origins of the Putney School Examined
    Through the Life of Carmelita Hinton*. Putney: Putney School.
    The story of the Putney School (1935). *See also* Lloyd, S. (1987).

Johnson, Marietta (1974). *Thirty Years With an Idea*. Alabama: University of Alabama
    Press.
    A recount of the development and organization of the Organic School at Fairhope,
    Alabama.

Lane, Robert Hill (1938). *The Progressive Elementary School*. Cambridge, MA: Riverside
    Press.
    A description of the early progressive school.

Lauderdale, William B. (1981). *Progressive Education: Lessons From Three Schools*.
    Bloomington: Phi Delta Kappa Educational Foundation.
    The story of three progressive schools: Caroline Pratt's City Country School (1915);
    Elmore County, Alabama's Holtville School (1929); and John Dewey's Laboratory
    School at the University of Chicago (1896).

Lloyd, Susan (1987). *The Putney School: A Progressive Experiment*. New Haven, CT:
    Yale University Press.
    The story of the Putney School (1935) as a direct outgrowth of Carmelita Hinton's
    educational philosophy, concentrating on the child's undiminished interest and
    delight in knowledge. *See Also* Geer, A. K. (1982).

Mayhew, Katherine C., and Edwards, Anna C. (1936). *The Dewey School*. New York:
    Appleton-Century Company.
    The description of the Dewey School.

Mitchell, Lucy Sprague (1951). *Our Children and Our Schools*. New York: Simon and
    Schuster.
    A description of how schools are carrying out their responsibilities.

Parkhurst, Helen (1922). *Education on the Dalton Plan*. New York: Dutton.
    The story of the Children's University School, founded in 1919 by Parkhurst, con-

centrates on the Dalton Plan, which is to tailor each student's program to student needs, interest, and abilities in order to promote independence and dependability, and to enhance social skills and responsibility. *See Also* Feldman, M. M. (1979).

St. John, George (1986). *Individuals and Community: The Cambridge School.* Cambridge, MA: Windflower Press.
The story of the Cambridge School.

Stone, Marie Kirchner, ed. (1976). *Between Home and Community: Chronicle of the Francis W. Parker School 1901–1976.* Chicago: Francis W. Parker School.
Framing the text in the John Dewey and Francis Parker philosophy of education, the book contrasts 75 years of progressive tradition with original documents and current updates or criticism. Beginning with the origins and aims of the school, the work traces the school's philosophy, community involvement, educational process, and students to the present.

Washburne, Carleton, and Yeomans, Edward (1930). "The Inception of the Winnetka Technique." *Journal of the American Association of University Women* 23, pp. 129–136.
This article tells the story of the famous Winnetka Plan of education from Winnetka, Illinois.

Winsor, Charlotte, ed. (1973). *Experimental Schools Revisited.* New York: Agathon Press.
Selected bulletins from the Bureau of Educational Experiments about early childhood education in New York's progressive schools from 1917 to 1924 are republished.

Yeomans, Edward (1979). *The Shady Hill School: The First Fifty Years.* Cambridge, MA: Windflower Press.
This history of the Shady Hill School from 1915 to 1965 is divided into three parts: the beginning years of the Hockings School, the Shady Hill School under the leadership of Katharine Taylor, and the school directed by Edward Yeomans. Each section focuses on the faculty's views of teaching and learning.

About the Contributors

WILLIAM AYERS is an assistant professor of education at the University of Illinois at Chicago. He is the author of *The Good Pre-School Teacher: Six Teachers Reflect on Their Lives*, Teachers College Press, New York, 1989.

PATRICIA CARINI is the co-founder of The Prospect Center in North Bennington, VT. She is presently completing a follow-up to the 1975–80 in-depth study of the New York State PreKindergarten Program.

ANN COOK is the co-director of The Inquiry Demonstration Project and The Urban Academy, an alternative high school in New York City.

ELEANOR DUCKWORTH is professor of education in the Graduate School of Education, Harvard University, and director of The Harvard Teachers' Network. She is the author of *The Having of Wonderful Ideas*, Teachers College Press, New York, 1987.

HUBERT DYASI is a professor of science education and the director of The Workshop Center at City College in New York, NY.

JOSEPH FEATHERSTONE is professor of education at Michigan State University, East Lansing, MI. He has had a long-standing interest in progressive education.

MARIANA GASTÓN is a parent founder and teacher at The Brooklyn New School, Community School District #15, in Brooklyn, New York.

KAY HIBL is a bilingual teacher at University Hills Elementary School in Boulder, CO.

KATHY IRWIN is director of the Aspen Community School in Woody Creek, CO.

KATHE JERVIS is a teacher and the founding editor of *PATHWAYS: A Forum for Progressive Educators*. She is currently Co-coordinator of the Urban Sites Classroom Documentation Project at the Institute for Literacy Studies, Lehman College, Bronx, NY.

BRUCE KANZE teaches at Central Park East School, Community School District #4, in New York City.

ANDREW KAPLAN is the Chairman of the English Department at the Francis W. Parker School in Chicago, IL.

JERALD KATCH has recently received a Ph.D. in education from The University of Chicago. His dissertation examines John Dewey's school.

MARVIN LAZERSON is Dean, and George and Diana Weiss Professor of Education at the Graduate School of Education, University of Pennsylvania, Philadelphia, PA.

MARY MATHIAS teaches at Argyle High School in Winnipeg, Manitoba, Canada.

DEBORAH MEIER is principal of Central Park East Secondary School, Community School District #4, in New York City.

CHARLES MEYERS teaches social studies at The Carleton Washburne School in Winnetka, IL. He is a coordinator for the *Facing History* project, Boston, MA.

CAROL MONTAG is a classroom teacher at The Laboratory Schools of the University of Chicago. She is the founding editor of *Nota Bene*, the faculty journal, and also designs professional development projects. In 1989 she coordinated the Conference on Progressive Education, co-sponsored by The Laboratory Schools and the Winnetka Public Schools.

FRANCES MOORE-BOND is the high school learning consultant and the middle school/high school testing coordinator at The Laboratory Schools of The University of Chicago.

DONALD MURPHY is a teacher at P.S. 27, Community School District #15, in Brooklyn, NY, and an education activist.

VITO PERRONE is Senior Lecturer and Director of Teacher Education at the Harvard Graduate School of Education, and Senior Fellow at the Carnegie Foundation for the Advancement of Teaching in Princeton, NJ.

MARIE KIRCHNER STONE is a teacher and former head of curriculum at Francis W. Parker School in Chicago, IL.

LILLIAN WEBER, now retired, was the founder and director of The Workshop Center at City College in New York, NY, as well as director of the Advisory Service to Open Corridors, also in New York.

ANN WIENER is director of Crossroads School, Community School District #3, in New York City.

INDEX